Secular Lyric

Secular Lyric

The Modernization of the Poem
in Poe, Whitman, and Dickinson

John Michael

FORDHAM UNIVERSITY PRESS

New York 2018

Fordham University Press has no responsibility for the
persistence or accuracy of URLs for external or third-party
Internet websites referred to in this publication and does not
guarantee that any content on such websites is, or will
remain, accurate or appropriate.

Fordham University Press also publishes its books in a
variety of electronic formats. Some content that appears in
print may not be available in electronic books.

Visit us online at www.fordhampress.com.

Library of Congress Cataloging-in-Publication Data
available online at https://catalog.loc.gov.

Printed in the United States of America
20 19 18   5 4 3 2 1
First edition

CONTENTS

SECULAR LYRIC

The Secularization of the Lyric: The End of Art, a Revolution in Poetic Language, and the Meaning of the Modern Crowd

Secularization as a threat to the poetic imagination, the loss of belief as an enemy of song, becomes a familiar topic in lyric poetry by the early decades of the nineteenth century. The disenchantment of the world was already a literary commonplace when Edgar Allan Poe published his "Sonnet—To Science" in 1829, though Poe, with his characteristic taste for ornament, opts for an archaized version of the topos: "Hast thou," the poet asks Science, "not torn the Naiad from her flood, / The Elfin from the green grass, and from me / The summer dream beneath the tamarind tree?"[1] The association of secularization with disenchantment—with the replacement of animism and faith with corpse-cold rationality—remains common today. But, as Charles Taylor and others have indicated, to understand secularism simply as the subtraction of belief does not adequately capture secularism as a characteristic experience of modern life.[2] Even in Poe's lines one senses, in their stagy, pagan allusiveness, something other than a simple crisis of faith, something different from a univocal ebbing of available belief. In his return to an archaic past, Poe's poet plays at being something like a modern mythographer, the advocate for new forms of belief—even

I

if only in the imagination or poetry itself as a vivifying principle—that might take the place of beliefs that have waned.

In a secular world, the poet, whom Shelley claimed was the world's un-acknowledged legislator, can dream of becoming, like Whitman's poet, "commensurate with a people," or like Emerson's ministering spirit, a "new born bard of the holy Ghost."[3] Moreover, the poet can have this dream because secularization entails not the loss but the proliferation of beliefs and the realization that every understanding of the world, even those based in science, rationality, and the human capacity for progress, rests ultimately on belief. What becomes questionable in a secular age (to borrow the title of Taylor's book) is the naïve security with which any reflective believer might hold any conviction in a field of contending and potentially antago-nistic alternatives. The erosion of common grounds for belief tends to pro-liferate possibilities of believing rather than to create legions of atheists and agnostics. For the poets I will consider here, for Poe, Whitman, and Dickinson, this alteration in the grounds of belief had a specifiable effect on the poetry they wrote. For them, secularization became the inspiration for—or perhaps the provocation of—lyric. In exploring the potentials and incapacities of lyric in a secular age, each of these poets contributed to the transatlantic phenomenon of the modernization of poetry.

Whitman sensed that secularization could be a force for poetry, as when he announced, at the threshold of his own poetic mission, "There will soon be no more priests." But there will be, he added, "gangs of kosmos and prophets en masse" ("Preface" to *Leaves of Grass* 1855, 24). Emerson, de-spite his thwarted hopes that inwardness could discover a unifying and transcendent lawfulness governing human meaning and purpose, under-stood that in practice plurality remains the rule in the modern world. As he put it in his essay "The Poet," the "poets are thus liberating gods. . . . The religions of the world are the ejaculations of a few imaginative men" (462–463). These liberating gods and their audiences assume the imagina-tive task of inventing or selecting a system of beliefs and meanings amid an apparently endless proliferation of contending and conflicting options and opinions. Secularism, in this light, is not the loss of belief but the name of a condition in which beliefs proliferate and contend, in which every-thing, even science and progress, become both articles of faith and subject to doubt. As Taylor argues, the welter of beliefs in the modern world makes secularization not so much a loss of belief as a change in the conditions of believing. The end of naïve belief, secularization in a word, forms an impor-tant aspect of the stresses and strains that we now call modernity. The context of this modernity marks the content and, most important, the form of the lyric poetry that Poe, Whitman, and Dickinson wrote, and it does so in surprisingly material and aesthetically compelling ways.

Taylor describes secularization as follows: "this new context . . . puts an end to the naïve acknowledgment of the transcendent, or of goals or claims which go beyond human flourishing. . . . This is the global context in a society which contains different milieux, within each of which the default option [of belief or value] may be different from others, although the dwellers within each are very aware of the options favored by the others and cannot just dismiss them as inexplicable exotic error."[4] Thus a new level of uncertainty about the ultimate meanings of human life and death that we associate with modernity is the hallmark not of an emptying out of categories of culture or belief but of a plethora of competing beliefs and cultures. Most interesting, this does not occur in the abstract realm of pure ideas or ideology but is rather embodied in a multiplicity of specific milieus, of heterogeneous subcultures and belief communities, each with its adherents and all constituting a variety in social and cultural life that in the Western world, at least since the Middle Ages, had no precedent in degree or in kind.

This aspect of modernity possesses a special immediacy for those, like poets and other literary writers, who confront the crowd, its expectations and beliefs, in and through their work. In that sense, one might say that the lyric—with its formal insistence on the subjective perspective and its disjunctive relationship to public discourse—is as much a symptom of the heteroglossic babble of modern society as is the novel, the genre that comes to dominate the nineteenth century.[5] Matthew Rawlinson has argued that lyric "remains one of the two genres in which Victorian print culture claimed to mediate a social totality incorporating all classes and a history from which nothing needed to be erased" and that the "other such genre" is "the novel." I would add, that unlike the novel, the lyric tends not to do this by direct mimesis but by an enactment, often through its own fragmentariness of form and peculiarity of perspective, of the heterogeneity and fragmentation of the social totality from which it emerges and upon which it reflects. As Rowlinson notes, this is one reason that Matthew Arnold, interested as he is in the amelioration of fragmentation in a unifying literary and artistic culture, abandons the form after 1850.[6] The insistent and conflicted subjectivism of modern lyrics constitutes a paradoxical heteroglossia of the single voice. The foregrounded "I" of the lyric always suggests the presence of a "you," an other who hears or overhears the poem, the audience who reads it. This "you" in the modern lyric increasingly becomes a locus of possible conflict, the problematic and heterogeneous presence of the reader and the reader's putative discourse in the poem.

This engagement with a second person in lyric poetry is not merely an ideological or thematic issue. It registers the altered material conditions of modern literary production. For artists, especially for the nineteenth-century U.S. writers and poets we will consider here, this modern difference becomes manifest in the newly intensified pressures that the crowd as a mass audience for literature entailed. This is one aspect of what Benedict Anderson called "print capitalism."[7] Matthew Rowlinson has identified the presumptions of print as one of the nineteenth-century lyric's "most distinctive characteristics." This is poetry, as Rowlinson explains, writing of similar and related developments in Great Britain, "that understands itself variously as preserving, succeeding, incorporating or remaking earlier lyric forms with other modes of circulation and reception." Moreover, this is what is most strikingly new in the modern lyric, "only in the nineteenth century does print become for lyric the hegemonic medium, with the result, on the one hand, that all lyric production takes place with a view to print, and on the other, that lyrics which had previously been circulated and received in other media are now remediated through print."[8] The pressure of a medium addressed to an anonymous and heterogeneous literary marketplace, the materialization of the secular crowd as a provocation of and a challenge to lyric, can be felt in Poe, in Whitman, and even, as I hope to show in the final chapters of this book, in Dickinson.

The Nineteenth-Century Lyric and the Secularization of Address

Of late, lyric itself—especially in the nineteenth century—has become a questionable category. Recent studies of nineteenth-century poetry tend to pit historical contextualization against close reading, the recovery of social and communicative immediacies against an assumed anachronistic formalism that Virginia Jackson has called "lyric reading."[9] The term refers to the practices of close reading that characterize academic criticism, especially of lyric poetry, since the middle of the last century and that critics, like Jackson, have recently called into question. We have, Jackson charges, particularly in Emily Dickinson's work but in our reading of nineteenth-century lyric generally, suppressed that poetry's "figures of address," the invocations of "you" in the poem, that, were we to attend to them, would "insist that we not make about [Dickinson's] writing [and about lyric generally] the very generic decisions we have made."[10] Those generic decisions, the decisions that these poems are lyrics at all, leads to the "disregard . . . [of their] circulation, [and the] understanding [of lyric poetry itself] as an image of ultimate privacy," as Michael Warner has argued.[11] Recovering the significance of the "you," Jackson argues—developing Warner's point—permits the recovery of lyrical poetry's public dimension, a sociability of engagement and face-to-face communicativeness that she sees as characteristic of nineteenth-century verse and that calls into question the assumption that "to be read as lyric is to be printed and framed as lyric," for example, as the "the personal subjective utterances of historical subjects" removed from social contexts.[12] Instead, she and Yopie Prins have argued, considered in context, the nineteenth-century poetry that has come to be known as lyric seems less subjective and more public, more a "vehicle for transporting, and potentially displacing, representative identities" and communicating with specific and knowable publics.[13]

Whether or not lyric reading has ever conformed to the rigid limits and temporal dysplasia that Jackson, Prins, and others describe, this critique has reinvigorated debates about nineteenth-century poetry and its publics and has renewed interest in approaches to literature through genre studies. It has inspired controversy as well. Jonathan Culler, for example, has been moved to offer a qualified polemical response to the project Jackson and Prins outline. He is "happy to endorse" their call for a "critical history of the process of lyricization," but he balks when the critique of lyric reading threatens "to dissolve the category of lyric" itself and the particular poems gathered under its rubric into a set of generalized generic attributes. Their aim, as Culler puts it, is "to return us to a variety of particular historical practices," by refocusing our attention on the generic conventions in play at the moment. The danger he sees is that the particularity of specific poems and the peculiarity of specific artists will be lost as historical reconstruction rather than close analysis comes to the fore. How pervasive this tendency actually is in the work of those pursuing the new lyrical studies, he adds, "is not entirely clear."[14]

Culler recognizes that the tendency he fears in this theoretical position is not often actualized in the readings its adherents produce. Indeed, at their strongest moments, Prins and Jackson seem to embrace the practice of lyric reading that they began by critiquing. This can be confusing, and at the conclusion of their provocative essay "Lyrical Studies," Prins and Jackson themselves make this confusion invigoratingly clear: "While contemporary critics debate about whether to read nineteenth-century women's poetry for aesthetic value or historical interest—a question that tends to reveal any given reader's 'formalist' or 'cultural studies' bent—it seems to us that such oppositions dissolve at the touch of the poems themselves."[15] This call to "read lyrically" may in practice be difficult to distinguish from modes of lyric reading, like the one that Culler himself champions at the end of his own consideration of the lyric "you":

> Often that you is expressed—the you of the beloved, or the wind, a
> flower, a yearning. But the lyric "you" is also a bit of language, a trope,
> and [Archibald] Ammons [in "Aubade"] concludes that this "nearly
> reachable presence" is also "something/we can push aside as we get up
> to rustle up a/little breakfast." It is through preserving the notion of
> lyric as genre, an open process of generic negotiation, that such historical
> variations in function and effect can be registered and analyzed.[16]

In what follows, I will elaborate close readings of Poe, Whitman, and Dickinson that emphasize their engagement with and renegotiations of the lyric—and of both the subjective identity and the "you" of address that the lyric traditionally presupposes or contains. For in these nineteenth-century poets, the representative identity of the poet and the nature of lyric address change.

In Poe, Whitman, and Dickinson, attention to the figures of address within their texts indicates an intense engagement between the lyric personae they project and the culture of print and the pressures of a mass audience for print that redefine literary culture in the nineteenth century. Here it is also true, as Prins and Jackson suggest, that the consideration of a specific poem often collapses the distinction between formal and cultural studies. For example, Whitman insists, especially in the 1855 and 1860 editions of *Leaves of Grass*, on evoking the immediacy of lyric's oral origins by conjuring the singer's physical presence before his audience. At the same time, however, he characteristically mediates the poet's presence by reminding the reader that he exists only in and through his book. He literalizes the trope of self-presence by identifying himself with the medium of print. This is a recurrent topos in the "Calamus" poems first published in 1860, such as "Whoever You are Holding Me Now in Your Hand," where Whitman writes,

> And in libraries I lie as one dumb, a gawk, or unborn, or dead,
> But just possibly with you on a high hill, first watching lest any person
>   for miles around approach unawares,
> Or possibly with you sailing at sea, or on the beach of the sea or some
>   dead island,
> Here to put your lips upon mine I permit you . . . (271)

The distance between the intimacy of an erotic embrace and the impersonality of print collapses in this evocation of the book. The figuration of reading as a kiss is enabled and mediated by the existence of print. The reader's lips touch the poet's mouth by mouthing the words on the printed page. It is as a book that the poet imagines living the intimacy of companionship with the anonymous you he addresses: "Or if you will, thrusting me beneath your clothing, Where I may feel the throbs of your heart or rest upon your hip" (271). But Whitman's poet never forgets that such contact remains imperfect. He also figures such mediation as frustration. As often as he evokes reading he nearly as often refuses to deliver—or enacts an inability to deliver—himself or his meaning to his reader, to consummate the union he imagines. He says here: "For all is useless without that which you may guess at many times and not hit, that which I hinted at; / Therefore release me and depart on your way" (271). What Whitman hints at remains a hint, can only be a hint, and becomes the sign of the limits of communion and communication that his poetry, at moments like this, so powerfully evokes.

This tension between intimacy and mediation in Whitman has much to do with the commodification of print and the emergence of a mass audience that begins to alter the character of lyric poetry, and of literature more generally, in the nineteenth century. Whitman, like Poe, knows that an appeal to the critical and popular taste means life and death for the poet confronted not with an individual interlocutor but with that most modern phenomenon, the anonymous and heterogeneous literary marketplace.[17] Moreover, marketplace and audience become, for these poets, indistinguishable—the audience for poetry is available to these poets most readily through the mechanism of the modern marketplace, and I will use the terms "audience" and "marketplace" as if they were synonymous. I will argue in this book that the heterogeneity of the audience, the heterogeneity of the crowd and the literary market, near the beginning of what Charles Taylor calls a secular age, is decisive for these poets. Poe's self-described intention in writing "The Raven," "the intention of composing a poem that should suit at once the popular and the critical taste," might describe Whitman's intention and with some modification Dickinson's as well. There is a difference between critical and popular taste, and there are differences as well within each of those categories. As the literary market expands in size and importance, it fragments and becomes more unpredictably contentious as well. In a way that has no precedent in literary history, the question of the audience as literary market becomes a problem in lyric poetry.

This is not merely a context for Whitman's or Poe's poetry; it is also a condition each reflects upon in the texture of his poems. Even Dickinson, who, as Jackson, Jerome McGann, and other historicizing critics have shown, seems to resist the pressures of print culture, often wrestles with figurations of print and a larger audience in her poems:

> This is my letter to the World
> That never wrote to Me—
> The simple News that Nature told—
> With tender Majesty
>
> Her Message is committed
> To Hands I cannot see—
> For love of her—Sweet—countrymen—
> Judge tenderly—of Me. (F519)

It is not cultural capital or hard cash won on the open marketplace for books that Dickinson here imagines, but the approbation of a large anonymous readership to which she forwards nature's unspecified message. This readership, present in the imagination of this poem, is different from those immediate family, friends, and companions with whom she shared her verses as letters and gifts. It is very often present in her poems as well, I will argue, not only as an imagined addressee but also in the very texture of her art. She had a remarkable ear for the dissonances and conflicts of the public discourses around her—including the conventional language and tropes of nineteenth-century poetry. For her, the presence of a mass audience of "Sweet—countrymen," whose tastes and expectations were shaped by those conventional discourses, posed a complex and engaging challenge and a point of departure for many of her most suggestive poems. Her family and friends were, as her letters indicate, also participants in these conventionalities, also representatives of a troublesome wider audience. She sometimes mocks them, for example in her well-known second letter to Thomas Wentworth Higginson, for their prudishness and their piety, "[They] are religious—except me—and address an Eclipse, every morning—whom they call 'Father.'"[18] At moments like this, her most intimate associates and interlocutors blend with the audience of anonymous countrymen and she has little hope they will understand her or judge her kindly.

Dickinson often resists her audience's expectations—local or national— and frequently resists not only the demands of generic conventionality but also the very possibility of comprehensible discursive statement. She often creates instead a suggestive fragmentation:

I would not paint—a picture—
I'd rather be the One
It's bright impossibility
To dwell—delicious—on—
And wonder how the fingers feel
Whose rare—celestial—stir—
Evokes so sweet a torment—
Such sumptuous—Despair—(F348)

Dickinson elects to dwell not on the accomplishment of the picture or the filling in of meaning but on the bright inadequacy of art to fulfill the desire for presence or significance, the sweet torments and sumptuous despair of the poet. Whose fingers create a celestial stir and why they, rather than their unnamed owner, possess feelings is suggestive but must remain open to conjecture. Even Dickinson, who took extraordinary measures to insulate herself against exposure to the welter of opinions and the friction of received ideas in the print-dominated public sphere for art, withdrawing to her circle of familiars and resisting publication, registers the pressure of the heterogeneous crowd and literary marketplace around her. She resists the commonalities of sense that are sedimented into the common language, and she sometimes resists making sense altogether.

The Modern Crowd and the End of Art

The rise of print culture and the advent of the mass audience constitute a special case in the contextualization of poetry, especially for Poe, Whitman, and Dickinson. The conditions of art alter in the nineteenth century in ways that these artists were early to sense and quick to register in the texture of their work. The alteration in the place and function of art in the nineteenth century was a transatlantic phenomenon, and it complicated the nature of lyric address and lyric reading both. As Walter Benjamin observed, in "On Some Motifs in Baudelaire," "The crowd—no subject was more entitled to the attention of nineteenth-century writers. It was getting ready to take shape as a public in broad strata who had acquired facility in reading. It became a customer."[19] The crowd, figured as a reader and a customer with the power to express a judgment by buying or refusing to buy, by reading or ignoring, unsettles the place of art not just because of its mercantile pressures but also because this marketplace functions largely without unifying ideas or transcendental hopes that might elevate or ennoble the transaction—which is not merely a business transaction—between artist and audience, author and reader.

Art seems, to some of the nineteenth-century's most ambitious artists, newly unsuitable to express the truths of religion or the wisdom of the world or the comforts of consolation. As Hegel noted, in the modern era, art, as an important vehicle for spirit's evolution, ended. In his comments on the crowd and in his better-known analysis of the lost aura in modern art, Benjamin gives a materialist twist to Hegel's idea.[20] Art ends when, as a commodity addressed to a heterogeneous audience, its relationship to that audience becomes at once essential and questionable. It becomes more difficult to imagine art, in such a situation, as a purveyor of truths or a vehicle for transcendence. According to Hegel,

> it is certainly the case that art no longer affords that satisfaction of spiritual wants which earlier epochs and people have sought therein, and have found therein only; a satisfaction which, at all events on the religious side, was most intimately and profoundly connected with art. . . . Therefore our present in its universal condition is not favourable to art. . . . In all these respects art is and remains for us, on the side of its highest destiny, a thing of the past.[21]

Yet, Hegel and his numerous commentators also make clear that the passing of art's highest destiny does not mean that art ceases to be made. Art continues after its assumed intimacy with the unfolding self-consciousness of the human spirit, its determining relationship to meaning in the world, its coincidence, as Arthur Danto puts it, with History itself, no longer functions as it was once imagined to do.[22] As Danto says, "the energies of history" and "the energies of art" no longer coincide, but after art as a vehicle of transcendence ends and it comes more fully into its form as a modern commodity, its ends proliferate.[23]

Poe was one artist who early sensed the implications of this shift in the place and meaning of art. He steadfastly denied that art and truth had anything in common. This is one lesson Baudelaire learns from Poe and passes on to generations of European poets.[24] Poe models one way that art can continue after it becomes a commodity on the open market. For Poe, poetry must "suit at once the popular and critical taste" (1375) and be dedicated only to the sensation of beauty understood as an affective response rather than a cognitive content. He is content to leave the pursuit of truth to philosophy and to prose (1376).

This alteration of art, and especially poetry, from an avatar of spirit to a sensational commodity, might seem to contradict the bold claims made on poetry's behalf by poets like Whitman and Emerson. But these claims that the artist might, as the divine afflatus, replace the priest and reunite a disparate and conflicted populace are themselves symptoms of the secularization of society that entails the secularization of art as well. Secularization entails not the end of available belief but the proliferation of contending beliefs—the implication of the stratified and heterogeneous modern crowd to which Benjamin referred and that Charles Taylor and others have recently described.[25] It is not the end of belief but the end of what Taylor calls naïve belief to which Emerson referred as a "new disease . . . fallen on the life of man" in his 1841 "Lecture on the Times":

> Every Age, like every human body, has its own distemper. Other times have had war, or famine, or a barbarism, domestic or bordering, as their antagonism. Our forefathers walked in the world and went to their graves tormented with the fear of Sin and terror of the Day of Judgment. These terrors have lost their force, and our torment in Unbelief, the Uncertainty as to what we ought to do; the distrust of the value of what we do, and the distrust that the Necessity (which we will at last believe in) is fair and beneficent.[26]

It is not the absence of belief that Emerson notes here; the root of this uncertainty lies in the welter of contending beliefs, reforms, positions and projects that define public discourse and artistic life in the middle decades of the nineteenth century on both sides of the Atlantic. As he notes, "the subject of the Times is not an abstract question" (154). It takes material form in the modern crowd, the myriad selves that, as Emerson imagines them in this essay, "walk and speak, and look with eyes at me" (154). For Emerson, the distemper of the time is embodied in the crowd and its incalculable regard. If a proliferation of contending beliefs makes naïve belief impossible, as Taylor suggests, then art becomes, for those artists attuned to their times, just one more possible form of belief among all the other religious or scientific, pietistic or rationalistic, conservative or progressive beliefs, practices, modes of thought and life contending for space in the modern public sphere.

Hegel believed that enlightened religion and the philosophy of *Geist* could take the place of art as spirit's world historical vehicle. For most readers, history would seem to have proven his optimism misplaced. In the modern, secular world, a naïve belief in *Geist* is no easier to maintain than any other belief. Poets like Emerson and Whitman can make overreaching claims for their art because they live at a moment in which virtually any claim can be and is valid for someone, at least sometime, and therefore, no one meaning can unquestionably hold sway or be relied upon to hold good. In the realm of literature, at least, the adventure of spirit has gone astray.

While Emerson remains ambivalent about the errancy of art (his essays seem more attuned to the times than his poetry does), Poe, Whitman, and Dickinson reflect and even embrace it. They differ from more conventional poets like Longfellow, Bryant, and Whittier (or Emerson himself in most of his poems), and from the sentimental elegists like Lydia Signorney and the many Sapphic poetesses with whom Poe frequently collaborated. These all, in their various ways, continue to regard poetry as a conveyance for hopeful truths, useful wisdom, or soothing sentiments meant to conform and appeal to their audience's expectations. Poe, Whitman, and Dickinson manifest more mindfulness in their poetry of the ways in which their art engages the conflicted heterogeneity of the modern crowd, and becomes distant (though not wholly separate) from transcendental meaning, universal truth, or conventional consolation. When Poe, in "The Philosophy of Composition," distances poetry from the provinces of truth, when Whitman, near the beginning of *Leaves of Grass*, sets himself apart from the "fog" in which "linguists and contenders" contend, when Dickinson, in her famous letter to Thomas Wentworth Higgenson, mocks her family's conventional piety and the "eclipse" to which they pray, each reflects the temper or distemper—as Emerson would have it—of the times. Their poetry registers the secularization that repositions art in the modern age. It is the altered relationship of art to its audience and to meaning that leaves its mark in different forms in poetry written by Poe, Whitman, and Dickinson, which in turn affects the poetry that comes after them. Each of these poets creates tensions between their individual art and the literary and social practices that determine their contexts and audiences. This tension between these poets and their audiences, which they both address and resist, is what makes them modern.[27]

After the End of Art, or the Lyricization of Truth

Perhaps it seems paradoxical that secular tensions between these poets and common expectations that poetry convey truth or wisdom or comfort should emerge at a moment when the audience becomes so crucially important. These poets tend to fix upon the bright impossibility of art, as Dickinson puts it, even as they refocus art's attention on subjectivity. Modernity alters the relationship of subjectivity to meaning. It tends to make subjectivity not merely the place on which the world leaves its mark but, importantly, the site through which the world receives whatever sense of meaning or purpose might be, however tentatively, assigned to it. Subjectivity becomes an important locus of belief and the self, a crucial judge of meaning. One thinks immediately of Emerson's difficult essay "Self-Reliance" and Thoreau's equally challenging "Life without Principle." Modernity in this sense seems less a specific historical moment, less what Emerson called a distemper of the age, and more a recurrent, perhaps a persistent, state of mind over the long duration of history. Moments, or writers at moments, seem modern when, in their work, subjectivity becomes the site of meaning and meaning itself becomes questionable, becomes heterogeneous and contentious. In this sense, Sappho, Catullus, Petrarch, Montaigne, and Shakespeare can all seem uncannily modern. Lyric poetry—for Poe, Whitman, and Dickinson as for the others I have named—enacts and negotiates the openness of the poet's subjectivity to the countersubjectivities the imagined readers of the poem possess and their resistance to those countersubjectivities as well. These poets may be said to renew an old tradition of the modern. This is not poetry that offers answers to life's mysteries or solace for suffering. This art is not simply embedded in history, nor does it necessarily aspire to alter history's course. Instead, this poetry remains open to experience and existence, without precisely trying to define either, while remaining resistant to commonly received wisdom or ideas. This poetry dedicates itself to what Whitman called "the puzzle of puzzles,/And that we call Being." Whitman asked in 1855 and continued to ask until his death, "To be in any form, what is that?" (55); but, he never really tries to formulate an answer. An answer to the questions of existence would depend upon a reliable (or naïve) common belief in transcendent or spiritual realities, and such a belief in such heteronomous references no longer seems reliably available except for the credulous or naive.

Whitman, Poe, and Dickinson were neither credulous nor naïve. Their poetry invests less in consolation and more in provocation. They resist their readers even as they solicit their attention. Whitman writes, again, early and late in his career, "to die is different from what any one supposed, and luckier" (32), or "I keep as delicate around the bowels as around the head and heart,/Copulation is not more rank to me than death is" (51). But he never tells the reader why death is lucky or whether the rankness linking sex and death is desirable, nor even whether copulation and death are finally rank at all. This refusal to answer the questions his work poses in a poet who sometimes posed himself as "the answerer" is a remarkable aspect of Whitman's work.[28] This solicitation and provocation of an audience, brought into the poem and distanced from it with the same gesture, reflects the poet's engagement with the secular and material conditions that are poetry's modern context.

Poe, Whitman, and Dickinson, in their different ways, dedicate their poetry to thinking through existence. Each employs language as the vehicle of thinking that seeks to disrupt what is commonly thought. Each takes a distance from meaning and truth as commonly understood. Each is very good at provoking thought but increasingly uninterested in delivering the results of thinking as meaning or truth. Reason can lead to meaning, and usually meaning's determination appears to be reasoning's end. These poets tend to resist the arrival at that end, the end of conclusion or certainty. "This world is not conclusion," Dickinson will say, and though she also says "A Species stands beyond," her poem moves steadily away from the certainty another world might offer and ends with the gnawing doubts that characterize modern life, "Narcotics cannot still the Tooth/That nibbles at the soul" (F373). Poe, Whitman, and Dickinson find ways to exploit the resources of language to keep certainty at bay and to reject any narcotic belief that would dull the experience of existence. They take Keats's idea of negative capability, the artist's imaginative capacity to tolerate the suspension of meaning, to an artful extreme. They represent one way that lyric subjectivity becomes a crucial reflection of a secular age. They make lyric's ancient art seem modern.

Lyric Modernity and the Revolution in Poetic Language

M. H. Abrams observed over sixty years ago that, in the nineteenth century, the lyric, which had been one poetic mode among many, came to dominate the field of verse. By the nineteenth century's end, lyric had become the "poetic norm," making subjectivity or individual experience the primary poetic topic. "The lyric form," Abrams wrote in *The Mirror and the Lamp*, including "elegy, song, sonnet, and ode . . . had long been particularly connected by critics to the state of mind of its author."[29] By the time that John Stuart Mill defined poetry as "feeling itself," Abrams continued, "the 'imitative' elements, hitherto held to be a defining attribute of poetry or art, become inferior, if not downright unpoetic; in their place those elements in a poem that express feeling became at once its identifying characteristic and cardinal poetic value."[30] The lyric, the poetic figuration of a single speaking subject, becomes synonymous with poetry itself.[31]

In response to this position, Virginia Jackson, Jerome McGann, Cristanne Miller, Dana Luciano, Yopie Prins, and others have argued that the assumption that lyric is or has become the poetic norm has itself become an exclusive frame of reference that leaves out too much poetic culture and too many forms of poetic expression. It also distorts contemporary visions of those poets, like Poe and Dickinson, that it includes. Today's readers forget most of the verse produced in the nineteenth century and tend to ignore the complex ways that the nineteenth-century poets they do read engage social and political contexts and conflicts.[32] This argument has many virtues. Versions of it figure in important work by, for example, Jackson and McGann, who have added richness to our readings of Dickinson by recovering poetic fashions and verse practices that ground her verses in their era. Similarly, Terence Whalen and Eliza Richardson have reengaged Poe with the marketplace and with the other poets, especially those "poetesses" he collaborated with and competed against, borrowing and twisting their figurations of endless yearnings and ceaseless melancholy, editing their work and presenting his own together for poetry's growing popular audience.[33]

There is in each of these readings a tendency to normalize the poets discussed by demonstrating how they exemplify generic features and publishing practices typical of their time. Virginia Jackson has argued that this recontextualization of poetry reveals that the current fashion of close explication, which she calls "lyric reading," is an anachronism when applied to nineteenth-century verse. The significance of this poetry lies in its contexts and engagements and material embodiments as social praxis and not in the densities or ironies of the poems as printed objects.[34] Their tendency, or at least their programmatic desire, is to dissolve the lyric into the context of the historically specific practices that surround it, as Jonathan Culler says. But focusing on the anachronisms of lyric reading and the ways it can vitiate a contemporary reader's appreciation of the occasional, sentimental, elegiac, and political aspects of nineteenth-century poetry, can, in turn, obscure the abiding strangeness of the poetry that Poe, Whitman, and Dickinson wrote, and that only a close consideration of their idiosyncratic lyric language can capture. "We may ask," as Kerry Larson does, noting that "recognizably modern" definitions of lyric already flourish in the early decades of the nineteenth century, "whether reading practices associated with modern versions of formalism are always and necessarily anachronistic when applied to nineteenth-century verse."[35] One need only recall the criticism of Coleridge and of Poe himself, to take the best-known Anglo-American examples of a close critical attention to questions of expressive form over public sentiment, to realize that in certain circles, poetry was quickly modernizing in the sense that it was becoming particularly lyric in the modern sense that Jackson and others criticize. The poetry that Poe,

Whitman, and Dickinson wrote was, in fact, often purposively at odds with traditional genres and the expectations they represented, including the lyric traditions that they took as their points of departure. This angle of vision on their work brings into focus a slightly different set of problems, for it may be that lyric reading is not always the anachronism it has sometimes appeared to be.

To assess the distinctiveness of the poetry Poe, Whitman, and Dickinson wrote requires turning the historical question of lyrical reading on its axis. If it is not simply an anachronism to read them as lyric poets, however peculiarly modern our sense of the lyric as a mode of personal expression may be, the questions become these: How does the United States, in the nineteenth century, furnish a context that enables the production of poetry that anticipates and, in part, inspires the ascendency of the modern lyric as a particular and perhaps a privileged site of articulation for the individual subject? How does their work shape that ascendency by reshaping their audience's assumptions about lyricism as a form of self-expression, and also about the nature of the self that the lyric might express? How does their poetry reflect the altered relationship of the poet to the world? To put these questions in a broader context: How does lyric, a form as old as some of the oldest poetic fragments we have—as old as Sappho—alter in the hands of these poets to become a privileged modern mode of self-expression and self-interrogation? Along with the definitively modern genre of the novel, lyric poetry becomes a site for the codification of a secular mood, one that emphasizes peculiarities of experience over commonalities of belief.[36]

It may be that, as Julia Kristeva has argued, this codification of secular experience in the lyric entails an actual revolution in poetic language. But if so, that revolution has some of its roots in the United States, especially in Poe. Her description remains instructive. In Lautréaumont and Mallarmé, she claims, poetic language becomes an investigation of signification itself. That the first is best known for *Les chants de Maldoror,* a long narrative in poetic prose, indicates that for Kristeva the revolution in poetic language is not limited to the lyric. The texts these writers, both readers of Poe, reveal a "heterogeneous functioning in the position of the signifier." She continues, "This functioning is the instinctual semiotic, preceding meaning and signification, mobile, amorphous, but already regulated."[37] This revolutionary poetic language, in Kristeva's view, does not so much carry meanings as it exposes the linguistic and ideological machinery that makes meaning possible. It manifests both erotic and aggressive drives that constitute the desire to signify and to approach the other, and the desire to disrupt signification and to refuse the other's embrace. The revolutionary language she describes has the capacity to trouble the smooth functioning of everyday language and to give expression to conflicted fantasies that undercut while they enable an approach to the other in and through language. Poetic language, as Kristeva describes it, constitutes the poet's self in and as utterance, simultaneously projecting subjectivity as real and exposing it as a linguistic effect. This is, as she makes clear, not merely a matter of personal desire or pleasure (*jouissance*). It involves aggressively confusing the codes of society and confronting what she calls "social censorship." This poetry transgresses against propriety and proper usage:

> All poetic "distortions" of the signifying chain and the structure of signification may be considered in this light. . . . As a consequence, any disturbance of the "social censorship"—that of the signifier/signified break—attests perhaps first and foremost, to an influx of the death drive, which no signifier, no mirror, no other, and no mother could ever contain. In "artistic" practices the semiotic—the precondition of the symbolic—is revealed as that which also destroys the symbolic, and this revelation allows us to presume something about its functioning.[38]

Thus, the literature Kristeva describes as revolutionary is not primarily concerned to convey meanings or to reproduce ideologies, progressive or otherwise. It exposes (and thereby evacuates) the linguistic mechanisms that make meaning and ideology seem natural.

Kristeva identifies this revolution in language with a particular, moment and with the work of a few authors, with the middle and later years of the nineteenth century and especially with work by Mallarmé and Lautréaumont. But this reflective move of poetic language toward language itself and away from significance seems difficult to delimit to one historical moment or one particular place (and for Kristeva that moment was short-lived and had already passed by the time Apollinaire took up the poetic vanguard during the first decades of the twentieth century). Before Lautréaumont and Mallarmé, something very like this revolution in poetic language had already occurred in the United States, largely in the first half of the nineteenth century, particularly in the poetry of Edgar Allan Poe, Walt Whitman, and Emily Dickinson, and especially in the ways in which their work negotiated the ever present pressure of the modern crowd of potential readers.

Mallarmé himself frequently acknowledged his debts to Poe, about whom he wrote the following lines:

Tel qu'en Lui-même enfin l'éternité le change,
Le Poëte suscite avec un glaive nu
Son siècle épouvanté de n'avoir pas connu
Que la mort triomphait dans cette voix étrange!

Eux, comme un vil sursaut d'hydre oyant jadis l'ange
Donner un sense plus pur aux mots de la tribu
Proclammèrent très haut le sortilege bu
Dans le flot sans honneur de quelque noir mélange.[39]

In as much as in Himself at last eternity changes it,
The Poet arouses with a naked sword
His century frightened by having ignored
The death triumphant in this peculiar voice!

Like the vile recoil of a hydra that once heard the angel
Give a purer sense to the language of the tribe
They loudly proclaim the bewitchment they imbibe
In the undistinguished stream of some foul mélange.[40]

To give a purer sense to the language of the tribe might be considered the text that Kristeva's *Revolution in Poetic Language* seeks to gloss. Long ago, angels and revolutionary poets might purify the befouled stream of common language. For all Poe's well-known political conservatism, Mallarmé recognizes a revolutionary strain in his work. This straining against a common language that she nonetheless deploys is strongly marked in Dickinson's most challenging poetry as well, though her lyrics usually seem as distant as possible from political engagement. And a similar challenge to the spell of received meanings occurs at crucial moments in Whitman's antebellum poetry as well, whatever his explicit political commitments on issues like emancipation and union might have been.[41] If this is revolutionary poetry, it is not political in any commonsense sense of the term. Kristeva and Mallarmé find in poetry a potentially more fundamental and more fundamentally critical and subversive engagement with language than explicit advocacy would allow. This poetry may reveal the reliance of any politics (like any meaning and like poetry itself) on the necessarily tensed and conflicted relationship to—a dependence on and subversion of—the common language and discourse of society, but it has little positive by way of remedy to recommend. Such poetry, almost by definition, creates the lyric as a space of significant insignificance, a space where the mélange of the commonplace languages of the crowd and the commonplace meanings of society's orders become, for a moment at least, uncommon and strange. That is the power and the limits of poetic language's revolutionary implication.

As important as it is to note, it is easy to overstate the case for the historical specificity of such a revolution in poetic language. Lyric indeterminacy, the poetic exploration of signification and the limits of meaning, is not simply a creation of a modern avant-garde. Poetic language, because of its close affinity to music and to the materiality of language (the percussion of consonants and the singing of vowels and the repetitiveness of rhythm and rhyme), often draws the reader's attention away from meaning, which is the province of the signified, and toward beats and echoes, which are characteristics of the signifier's morphology. If, as Roman Jakobson would have it, poetry moves from the axis of combination (the delimiting force of metonymic enchainment in sentences that enables the emergence of univocal meanings against an indeterminate range of possibilities) toward the axis of substitution (the associative force of language's metaphoric structure that disseminates meaning along a range of associated possibilities), then poetry seems inherently prone to open up spaces of indeterminacy within its signifying structures.[42] There is a simpler way to say this. Poetic language often sets itself athwart normal circuits of communication and, at least momentarily, disrupts them. The language of lyric poetry often surprises its audience. What I have just said may be a dominant feature of only a small part of the poetry or literature produced in any historical period. It may well be, as Kristeva suggests, an aspect of literary language whose dominance in a specific historical moment becomes a revolution, or it may be, as Virginia Jackson argues, a modern way of reading poetry anachronistically imposed on early forms of verse better understood in terms of their communicative contents rather than their disruptions of significance. It is, however, to aspects of this disruption of communication—the ways rhythm, rhyme, and trope draw the reader's attention away from the conveyance of meaning and focus it on the means by which meaning might be conveyed—that modern readers most often refer when they identify something as poetic.

No reader who values a poetic work would want to reduce it to a condensed expression of its meaning or a statement of its idea. Paraphrase remains a heresy among poetry's readers, and it is difficult to think of a moment when this is not the case for a significant number of poets. Milton's seventeenth-century readers, who awaited the promised explanation of God's ways, would not have asked to have the matter simplified by a clearer communication or a less seductive portrayal of Satan. Poetry, qua poetry, in any period, does not so much convey an idea as it provokes an experience of hesitancy in the face of language or, if one prefers, of wonder in the presence of a world. As Kristeva suggests, in so far as such poetic language exists, it is not well designed to convey dogma or reproduce ideological positions, but it can be good at disrupting a sensitive reader's habitual expectations and perceptions, the sense of certainty that, like a bewitchment, dulls the senses and removes the subject from contact with the world. It is seldom the poem's message that holds the reader's attention or focuses the reader's desire. A poem often demands that the reader accept the frustration of the common passion for conclusive significance to enjoy the masochistic pleasures of doubt and the terrors of being awakened to possibility.

No doubt, as Jackson and others contend, modern readers find this pleasure sometimes where the poet might not have intended it. Poe, the most programmatically modern though formally traditional of these poets, mobilizes the machinery of prosody, the temporal displacements of rhythm and rhyme and the cognitive conflations of simile and metaphor, to elicit only to disappoint the reader's desire for meaning and transport. Whitman, on the other hand, was a poet who sometimes manifested the desire to convey a unifying patriotic message to his fractious countrymen—and therefore one might well question whether much of his poetry is lyrical or literary at all. *Leaves of Grass* nonetheless most often holds the modern reader's interest in those moments when he foregrounds the massed objects of the world, including the manifold aspects of the mortal body, and brackets any question of deeper or transcendent meaning. This is evident in the poems he wrote between 1855 and 1860, when he writes of death and amativeness, sex and love, with a vigor and frankness that, for the most part, distanced him from his intended audience's sensibilities for all his populist posturing as one of the roughs. His work remains, at times, startling even today. What does a couplet like "Something I cannot see puts upward libidinous prongs / Seas of bright juice suffuse heaven" mean? The cosmic orgasm it describes asks the reader to receive the ache of desire rather than find a meaning in the poet's words drawn from or added to the common store of wisdom. To be a poet in a secular world, as Dickinson knew as well as Mallarmé, is to distance oneself from the language of one's tribe, to work with and against it, to remove oneself from the current of human communication's normal flow and, in small but significant ways, to create catachrestic eddies in an audience's benumbed linguistic complacency, to make of utterance something other and purer than a communicative act. The poet's distance from the commonplace can make the poet feel, as it apparently made Dickinson sometimes feel, like a stranger in the land, like "The only Kangaroo among the Beauty." This fanciful image of the poet as animal resonates when we recall how much a revolutionary poet like Poe or Whitman or Dickinson deviates from the everyday usages around them.[43] Their poetry exists within the common language but, as it were, in a space apart as well.

Kristeva's characterization of a revolutionary modernism in poetic language can seem to describe Poe, Whitman, and Dickinson not because of the anachronism of lyric reading but because their works belong to the long history of literary modernity, where they occupy a special place. That nineteenth-century American literature is precociously modern is an old idea but it is no longer as familiar as it once was.[44] These nineteenth-century American poets significantly influenced those European poets, like Mallarmé, associated with modernity's self-conscious emergence.[45] The ascendant modernity within which literary modernism took shape and against which it often reacted brought with it a prevalent secularization of society. The interaction of these poets with the secular society around them was not merely a matter of registering the waning of traditional modes of belief and the triumph of a disenchanting and utilitarian instrumental reason in all aspects of human life. Each of these poets in their differing ways removes poetry from the circuits of meaning and foregrounds the mechanisms of prosody (Poe), the materiality of language (Whitman), and the breaking of tropes (Dickinson). These become, in a real sense, what an important strain of modern poetry is about. This focus on the material substrata of their linguistic art rather than on the usefulness of poetry in the service of truth or nation constitutes a modern response to a secular age. In these differing ways, Poe, Whitman, and Dickinson register the pressures of the shifting contexts of belief, the massification and heterogeneity of the audience for literature, and the alteration of the place of poetry in the modern world. This aspect of their poetry can only emerge in the close lyric readings of their texts that each requires. The following chapters aim to unfold the implications of these statements in the lyric reading of these poets, and to show how each of them made secularization not an enemy of but an occasion for their art.

PART I

Edgar Allan Poe

Poe's Posthumanism: Melancholy and the Music of Modernity

In his poems, Poe stages the modern poet's predicament, the necessity, as he put it in "The Philosophy of Composition," to compose poems "that should suit at once the popular and the critical taste."[1] In this chapter I will consider how Poe's revision of a lyrical tradition that includes Sappho and Petrarch forms the basis of his engagement with modernity and its crowds of readers, the embodiment of that bifurcated and frequently conflicted critical and popular taste, an audience that may or may not purchase an author's work and may or may not recognize the writer as an artist at all. Poe recognizes that the place of poetry has changed in modern society, that its ability to serve higher truths or offer spiritual affirmation had been serious compromised by its existence as a commodity for mass consumption in a secular marketplace of heterogeneous tastes and beliefs. He adapts and alters familiar prosodic mechanisms of meter and rhyme and the tropes and conventional postures of loss and grief to produce that tone of melancholy that he defines as beauty's highest form and identifies as the "most legitimate of all the poetic tones" (1377). In the final analysis, it is the loss of the self, especially the lyric self, and its privileges that he mourns and exploits in his poems. He transvalues this loss as poetic beauty and makes its melancholy tone the poem's only true topic, the truth, such as it is, that the poem conveys.[2]

In his emphasis on "tone," Poe famously distanced poetry from truth, from the conveying of meanings or messages. In "Marginalia," the frequently enticing, usually elusive jottings and epigrams that Poe offered his readers in *The Democratic Review* for December 1844, he expressed his long held conviction "that the *indefinite* is an element in the true ποιησις" or true poem.[3] The true poem thus must be ill suited to communicate truth or convey consolation based on Christian certainties. Poe's insistence on poetry's indefiniteness looks forward to his most notorious formulation of these ideas in "The Philosophy of Composition," which he published two years later, and in which he specified poetry's incapacity not only to serve truth but also to evoke passion: "Truth, in fact, demands a precision, and Passion, a *homeliness* (the truly passionate will comprehend me) which are absolutely antagonistic to that Beauty which, I maintain, is the excitement, or pleasurable elevation, of the soul" (1376). "Beauty," as "the sole legitimate province of the poem," for Poe, has nothing to do with truth.

In its "highest manifestation," it is a matter, again, of "tone" (1376–1377). In fact, beauty, as Poe defines it, remains appropriately indefinite and accords with the true nature of the true poem, which, as Poe specified in *Marginalia*, is indefiniteness. Beauty is not a "quality, as is supposed, but an effect" (1376), not discernible in the object contemplated but felt in the response of the audience or reader who experiences that "intense and pure elevation of *soul—not* of intellect, or of heart" that Poe calls "the beautiful" (1376). "Beauty," Poe famously continues, "of whatever kind, in its supreme development, invariably excites the sensitive soul to tears" (1377). Poetry's proper intensity of pure melancholy stands for a moment diametrically opposed to the antagonistic elements of precision and homeliness, necessities for the expression of truth and passion for which prose is the appropriate vehicle. While beauty may remain, in itself, indefinite, Poe's sense of poetry's power and limitations seems clear, but only for a moment. For as he continues, it becomes apparent that passion, and even truth, may yet play their part in creating a poem's beauty: "It by no means follows from anything here said, that passion, or even truth, may not be introduced, and even profitably introduced, into a poem—for they may serve in elucidation, or aid the general effect, as do discords in music, by contrast" (1376–1377). The "true artist," Poe says, "will always contrive . . . to tone them into proper subservience . . . and to enveil them, as far as possible, in that Beauty which is the atmosphere and the essence of the poem" (1377). Poe is careful to elucidate nothing.

In light of what Poe has just said about poetry's true nature, "to enveil" (a well-chosen anti-apocalyptic term that signals the attentive reader that nothing here will at last be revealed) the prosaic certainties of truth and passion in beauty renders both indefinite, makes both serve the intensification of melancholy that Poe calls beauty. Any reader looking to verse for edification or enlightenment will be disappointed. For Poe, the poem seems best described as a musical effect, a melancholy tone that strikes the audience's ear but has no definite cognitive content to speak of. He does not imagine truth and beauty as harmonious consorts, as Keats did in "Ode on a Grecian Urn"; neither does he define the lyric as strong emotion recollected in tranquility, as Wordsworth did in his preface to *Lyrical Ballads*. Truth and passion in Poe become musical effects, and the lyric self the poem figures finds itself reduced to an effect of its sonorous tonality. In this way, Poe's poetry begins the knell of humanism's end.

Consider that Poe inherits a tradition of lyric poetry as self-figuration from classical and renaissance humanism, but he also transforms and modernizes poetry and the humanist tradition on which it relies in response to the pressures of a secularized age. Humanism rested on the belief that human presence or potentiality could center the universe on the self. It is this idea of a centered self that Poe's secularity most profoundly challenges.[4] Nonetheless, his poetry remains recognizably traditional in form. He borrows liberally from the stock of romantic and sentimental conventions and clichés. Poe's poet's melancholia, his poetry's otherworldly settings, his appeals to transcendent desires, even his diction and allusions, would all be familiar, conventional attributes of poetry for his readers.[5] Nonetheless, Poe often seems determined to confuse his readers and to confound their expectations. He adamantly refuses, as we have been seeing, any utilitarian purpose for poetry, however lofty such a purpose might be imagined to be. His poems and tales often appeal to an otherworldly ideal, a "Dreamland" "out of space, out of time" (79), but they characteristically dwell on death as physical decay, as inevitable and irredeemable loss. Dreamland in Poe tends to become a nightmare. Most important, the self that Poe presents seems committed to a perverse and destructive melancholy, a perpetual mournfulness or self-mortification that appears not as a vehicle to higher understanding or renewed commitment but an end in itself, the only possibility of poetic enchantment that the modern world affords. His musical effects are all committed to the conveyance of melancholy. Even this aspect of Poe's poetry engages the expectations of his audience. He capitalizes on the poetics of suffering, the popularity of which was helping to make lyric the dominant nineteenth-century verse form.[6]

The most fascinating recent work on Poe has focused on his relationship to the new phenomenon of mass culture and its networks of media and markets. The strongest claims made by these critics of nineteenth-century print culture reintroduce Foucault's disappearance of the author in a more concretely historical and institutional register. Poe becomes a test case for a new approach to literary history that emphasizes patterns of dissemination, practices of reprinting, and the fluidity of texts over more traditional author-centered approaches that have characterized both scholarly and critical work for over a century.[7] Such an approach would seem to afford little place for individual psychology. As Jerome McGann puts it, "That kind of field [of print culture] is much less a psychological space of personal expression than a social space of dialogue and dispute. Poe's individual work is exemplary because more than anyone else in the period, his writings regularly and deliberately make a spectacle of their social relations."[8] It is perfectly appropriate that Poe should become a test case for the new literary history of nineteenth-century print culture. But it is also true that Poe's deep ambivalence about the marketplace and the audience that he both courted and resisted is everywhere evident in his work.[9] For McGann, the spectacle of Poe's professional and social relations is best seen in his showy pieces like "Marginalia," in his printed attacks on Longfellow and Emerson, or in his transparent attempts to capitalize on the success of "The Raven" or "The Murders in the Rue Morgue" by following them, respectively, with "The Philosophy of Composition" and "The Mystery of Marie Roget." In texts like these, McGann says, we observe Poe's "demonstrative explanation and interpretation of the social dynamics of his world and the people who live in it."[10] To this, I would add that this socially dynamic field does not supersede the psychology of Poe's texts; it constitutes the author's psychology as social and conflicted and as fundamentally linked to the figure of his reader. In Poe's works, the poet's subjectivity is linked inexorably to the opportunities and mischances that the reader represents. The shaping pressure of the modern marketplace is everywhere present within the form and texture of the lyrics and the tales. This pressure shapes formal elements and structures the persona that these works spectacularize for Poe's readers. Ultimately, it is the nineteenth-century print marketplace that drives Poe's decentering of himself, his delivery of the self to and resistance of the other his readers come to represent, and it is this decentering of the self that constitutes his psychology and his challenge to humanistic optimism.

Eliza Richards has noted something similar in her reading of "The Raven" and "The Philosophy of Composition." Each, she shows, "underscores the reader's instrumental role in the poem's operations," hence the author's reliance on the reader to prove his genius.[11] Other critics, as different as John Irwin and Terence Whalen, have traced the audience's aspect in Poe's tales, especially in those that dramatize the inner split of subjectivity or that externalize self-conflict as fantasies of revenge like "The Cask of Amontillado" and the tales of ratiocination.[12] This melancholy split of subjectivity, this incorporation of the alterity of the reader into the composition of the poet's self, becomes the hallmark of modernity in Poe's poetry.

In the literary marketplace, the music of melancholy was Poe's stock in trade. For him, the pleasure of poetry and the agony of loss famously intertwine. "Romance (Introduction)," with all its stagy poetizing, is Poe's truest self-description:

> . . . being young and dipt in folly
> I fell in love with melancholy,
> And used to throw my earthly rest
> And quiet all away in jest—
> I could not love except where Death
> Was mingling his with Beauty's breath—
> Or Hymen, Time, and Destiny
> Were stalking between her and me. (54–55)

Poe's poetic mood differs from mourning processes commonly figured in popular elegiac and sentimental traditions. He does not seek or proffer consolation; neither does he appear to believe that love conquers all. He falls in love with loss itself and it is the pain of loss that he seeks. Mourning for Poe's poet does not work through grief to reengage life. Grief is an end in itself and the highest pleasure life, or at least poetry, affords. There is no easeful death in Poe's imagination. There is no balm in the unction of his gorgeous phrases and exaggerated sonorousness. Unlike Keats, who declared himself half in love with death and the hope that he might "cease upon the midnight with no pain," Poe imagines death as the inspiration for an agony that mixes self-torment and delight, pleasure and pain, beauty and the grotesque.[13]

Poe makes melancholy sonorous and oddly beautiful in the overwrought, incantatory music of his verse and in the poetics of his best tales as well. A sympathetic reader (Poe requires considerable patience) can be strangely moved and even "elevated" or "excited" by his work, in just the ways that Poe suggested in "The Philosophy of Composition." He may not move the sensitive soul to tears (that seems a sop to the popular culture of sentiment with which he is in continuous negotiation), but he can create "that intense and pure elevation" (1376) of something other than intellect or passion, something Poe calls soul, that responds to the music of his verses. The beauty of Poe's best poems fixes attention not on the mournful commemoration of the beloved's memory, but on the never-ending, rhythmic reiteration of the lover's loss and the melancholy self-torture to which Poe imagines abandoning the self. This is the tone—and the plot—of his most suggestive poems, like "The Raven" and "Ulalume." These poems may be best understood in terms of their musical effects rather than their representational contents. Poe tunes the musical devices of his prosody to a single melancholy tone. It is loss itself, ultimately the loss of self, rather than any particular, representable absent other, around which Poe's poetics turn.

Poe's Petrarchism, or the Beginning of Humanism's End

Poe's modernity emerges against the backdrop of the poetic and humanist traditions of love and lyrical grief that shaped his audience's expectations. He belongs to and transforms this tradition. The association of lyric poetry with love and melancholy recalls the origins of the modern lyric in Petrarch's humanism, though Poe, as will become clear, was himself no humanist. Poe pays homage to, continues, and distances himself from the poetic practices that Petrarch helped to establish. In "An Enigma," Poe's poetic mouthpiece scorns the shopworn conventions of the conventional sonnet as "Trash of all trash!" He denounces "your Petrarchan stuff" as "Owl-downy nonsense that the faintest puff . . . Twirls into trunk-paper the while you con it" (92). While Poe characterizes "Petrarchan stuff" as insubstantial and as out of date as yesterday's newsprint, his ambition is not to make his own poetry weightier in terms of its significance or timeliness, nor does he seek to alter the familiar forms and prosody of post-Petrarchan verse. More fundamentally, he invents a poetics that, while more in tune with its times, presages the end of poetry's humanist project or self-recuperation and gives a more material twist to the lyric's traditional melancholy tone. One might say that Poe takes on the question of what sort of poetry one might compose on trunk paper or in newsprint for a modern audience, an ephemeral mass marketplace of heterogeneous readers, embodying both critical and popular tastes as a demand on and for the poet. This audience constitutes a situation for poetry quite different from the situation Petrarch faced in the smaller and more homogeneous audience for which he and the humanists once wrote.

The social and textual psychology, what one might call—following Mc-Gann's hints cited earlier—the print psychology of Poe's authorship and his relationship to his readers, can be brought in to focus by briefly considering this Petrarchan tradition and Poe's debts to and differences from it. Giuseppe Mazzotta, Thomas Greene, and others have found in Petrarch the humanistic origin of a modern sense of the lyric self, one that establishes subjectivity and its incoherent fragmentation as an important poetic topic, and which also finds in poetry a way toward the reunification of the subject. Around his complex articulation of himself and his desire, Petrarch creates a poetry of suffering and loss, regret and aspiration. Petrarch, even more than Sappho, may be the origin of Poe's idea that the death of a beautiful woman was "the most poetical topic in the world" (1379).[14] Petrarch's Laura—like Catullus's Lesbia before her—becomes the beloved object whose loss epitomizes all the other losses and self- sunderings that comprise the poet's life. But Laura also embodies Petrarch's consoling hope for reconciliation with himself and God. Through Laura, Petrarch can sometimes imagine overcoming loss, looking toward a consummation that might restore the self's self-possession and serve as a grounding for the subject and hence for a humanistic worldview centered in it. As Mazzotta puts it:

> Critics have long spoken of Petrarch's humanism and modernity
> precisely in terms of his discovery of the centrality of the self: this self
> appears as they have acknowledged, fragmented, wounded in his will;
> or, as the poet himself writes, alluding to his moral drama, "et veggio
> il meglio et al peggior m'appiglio." (I see the best, but still cling to the
> worst.)[15]

Thus, Petrarch's humanism, humanism itself, depends on a double movement. A recognition of the self as torn and fragmented by loss and desire and a hope that this wounded soul might be healed and that love might restore faith and provide a happy ending to the mortal drama. Such hope is, of course, programmatically absent in Poe's work and has become difficult to assume in the secular era near the beginning of which he wrote.

Poe's affinities for Petrarch may be clearer if one considers the whole of the final section of Canzione 264 from which Mazzotta takes this final line:

> Song, this is how I live and my heart is
> Colder with fear than snow that's turned to ice,
> Feeling for certain that I am perishing;
> in trying to decide I've wound the spool
> by now with a good length of my short thread;

never was there a weight
heavier than the one I carry now,
for with Death at my side
I seek new rules by which to lead my life,
And see the best, but still cling to the worst.[16]

In Petrarch, the sense of the self as internally divided against itself—seeing
the best but impulsively drawn to the worst, obsessed with death but struggling to live, looking for some sort of redemption or resolution in art or
through writing—is already clearly evident. In Poe, however, this wounded
and divided self becomes not something the poet should lament or seek to
overcome but poetry's truest topic. Loss itself becomes the poet's obsessively reiterated theme.

Poe transforms the Petrarchan tradition and undermines the humanism at its foundation. The vision of "man" at the center of a meaningful
universe requires an imagined ending to the fragmentations of the self. It
requires the capacity to believe in an end to suffering and to hope for an
ultimate transcendence. Poe imagines no such ending and manifests no
such capacity to believe or hope, and that becomes his own original contribution to Petrarch's tradition.[17] In this way, Poe signals the beginning
of humanism's end. Comparing Poe to Petrarch, despite all their similarities, quickly becomes an exercise in contrasts. Poe reflects changes in the
nature of belief and in the nature of the human self and its place in the world.
Petrarch's humanism, his centering of art on subjectivity, articulates
his profound investment in and his hopes for a Christian salvation that he
shared in common with religious authority and that he could imagine
he shared with the people for whom he wrote. Moreover, the audience to
which he addresses his poetry and letters remains relatively small and homogeneous, a community of Catholic readers and patrons for whom art
remains an important record of spiritual striving and a primary vehicle of
spiritual elevation. For Petrarch, poetry can credibly convey both aspiration and meaning, desire and fulfillment. Laura, for Petrarch, becomes,
especially after her death, the vehicle of the poet's hopes, the reader's
edification, and the occasion of a recommitment to the belief that human
suffering will be redeemed by faith in a beneficent God.

Art plays an important part in Petrarch's humanist drama of redemption.
As Gur Zak argues, for Petrarch writing becomes a discipline of self-
centering, a spiritual exercise that aims at "the care of the self." Self-inscription
becomes a tool of self-mastery.[18] Gur is particularly interested in Petrarch's
authoring of a dialogue with Saint Augustine in a text he called *My Secret*

Book. There Petrarch imagines himself challenged by Saint Augustine to defend his long obsession with a lover who threatens to distract him from his spiritual exercises. He writes that Laura is "not a body I have loved, but rather a soul, whose ways transcend what is human and teach me what life with the angels is like" (60). His love for Laura and his record of that painful and futile romance in his poems become spiritual exercises in themselves.

In Poe's work, by contrast, art cannot hope to recover or save the self and Poe never intends to try doing so. There is no esoteric message and the figures of dead women who furnish occasions for his poetry remain mere pretexts for the ecstasies of self-lacerating melancholy that the poet identifies as poetry's truest and most beautiful topic and occasions for the melancholy music that constitutes poetry's proper tone. Writing, for Poe, leaves both the poet and the audience confronting the burden of the beloved's corpse, as at the end of "Annabel Lee."

> And so, all the night-tide, I lie down by the side
> Of my darling, my darling, my life and my bride
>   In her sepulcher there by the sea—
>   In her tomb by the side of the sea. (103)

For the lover who sleeps each night in his beloved's tomb, the physicality of the beloved's corpse—there is no suggestion that she is a soul and not a body—carries no hope for a reintegrated life. Poe's poet imagines melancholy with no end and dedicates himself to it.

For Poe, writing does not heal or care for the self. Writing abandons the self to the other. The poem becomes the medium and the record of the artist's fragmentation in a secular world. In the poem, he addresses no deity, except perhaps his audience, the newly evolved mass market for literature that he simultaneously solicits and resists. Writing subjects the poet's self to the laws of commodity and the fortunes of commerce, to the "horrid laws of political economy" as Poe along with Terence Whalen would have it. These laws are antithetical to spiritual transcendence or unquestionable belief and they constitute a new situation for art and for the artist.[19] The pressure of the market, for Poe as a modern writer, becomes another impersonal law that undermines, subjects, and scatters the self that humanism had hoped to return to self-possession and set free.

This is the material dimension of Poe's redefinition of beauty. He defines beauty not as a quality in itself but as an appeal to the reader, the hopefully designated "sensitive soul" who might be moved to tears. But this reader, however sensitive a soul she or he may be, is first a potential customer with cash to spend, a "capital reader" as Whalen puts it. En masse, these readers form a roiling crowd of anonymous others, a heterogeneous and conflicted marketplace of multitudinously contending appetites, ideas and beliefs, a mass audience whose tastes and desires, however unschooled or refined, determine the artist's fate in a world where impermanence rules the field. Poe, however, cannot simply yield himself and his art to the laws of such an economy. He struggles within the confines of a secular world to make art a place of momentary elevation for sensitive souls, though it can no longer credibly be a celebration of transcendence or the absolute.

Poe's poetry often stages the impermanence of art as it affects the artist. Consider "The Enigma." The poem offers a showy display of Petrarchan wit. The poet pays homage to a woman by concealing the letters of her name in the poem and offering it as tribute to her: "But *this* is, now,— you may depend upon it—/ Stable, opaque, immortal—all by dint/ Of the dear names that lie concealed within 't'" (91–92).[20] But, even as he engages this familiar aspect of the Petrarchan tradition, he reflects the altered status of meaning in his own more modern art. He subverts the traditional association of permanence, stability and immortality that humanists associated with art and assigns these qualities to his patroness. Consider, for a contrasting example, Shakespeare's Petrarchan exercise in Sonnet 18 ("Shall I compare thee to a summer's day?/ Thou art more lovely and more temperate"). The sonnet concludes, "So long as men can breath or eyes can see,/ So long lives this, and this gives life to thee."[21] In this poem, Shakespeare's investment in art as a form that transcends time as a repository for lasting achievement and permanent meaning, however ironic, remains centered on the intentions and achievement of the poet. By contrast, Poe, in his own moment of ironic courtliness, recognizes that the place of poetry and of fame has changed and diminished. It is the hidden name that makes his poem "stable, opaque, immortal," and rescues it (and, perhaps, the artist) from the flux of impermanence that characterizes the new phenomenon of periodical publication in which the poem's medium can become yesterday's news and today's mere trunk paper in an instant. Poe pretends that Sarah Anna Lewis's name might grant his work a substantiality it otherwise lacks and not vice versa.[22] In making this preposterous assertion (Poe must have known that Sarah Anna Lewis could not count as an immortal), Poe draws attention to the fact that nothing stable remains in his world, that art itself, as a commodity among commodities, is not designed to last.

For Poe, poetry can neither express the unified sensibility of the poet nor recover or preserve the presence of meaning in the world. In the modern world, neither stylistic consistency nor rhetorical power can serve these ends, as Petrarch could still imagine they might.[23] For Poe, beauty only deepens the traces of grief and intensifies the disjunctions of desire. For Poe, "mournful and never ending remembrance" (1385)—the burden of "The Raven"—expresses poetry's highest mood, a condition defined by an agonized awareness and fevered pursuit of self-torment, without any transcendence or salvation in sight. In Poe's poetry, humans dwell among and are limited to the fleeting, the fragmented, and the contingent. Poe's speakers are defined and their consciousnesses are constituted by loss. In this way, Poe begins to constitute through poetry a guide to an aspect of modern experience that remains familiar today.

For Poe, the realities of modern existence represent a continuous challenge to the common desire to read meaning in the experience of loss and to recover thereby the equilibrium of the self. This is the work of mourning that elegy in its traditional and popular forms means to do. As Jahan Ramazani puts it, "the modern elegy offers not a guide to 'successful' mourning but a spur to rethinking the vexed experience of grief in a modern world."[24] The rethinking of the vexed experience of grief may be said to begin with Poe. For Poe, mourning never accomplishes a positive end nor does he want it to. The present in his most melancholy poems, like "The Raven," "Annabel Lee," and "Ulalume," becomes poetic only as it registers the absence and loss around which it takes shape. Any hopes for healing the fragmentation of the self in the future are attenuated, frustrated, or altogether abandoned. More accurately, loss itself is what the poet embraces. In this sense, he differs extremely from Petrarch and much of the poetry that followed him through the Renaissance and beyond.

Poe's love poetry, like Petrarch's, emphasizes the extremity of the lover's melancholia and the painful, obsessive probing of the gap in the self that loss leaves. But Petrarch dedicates himself, for all his fragmented consciousness, to the hopeful project of restoring love, belief, and self-possession through writing. Poe explores the irrational impulsions of life and the place of art in the absence of any such hope for art or life. If Petrarch's poetry initiates the long development that will become Renaissance humanism, based on ideals of rationality and perfectibility that hoped to make the centered self the measure of all things, Poe's poetry stands near the beginning of humanism's end at the beginning of late modernity and the recognition that hopes for a human-centered world in the rational control of self-possessed human subjects may in fact be forlorn.[25] Thus Poe, for all the unfashionable diction and cultivated, prosodic preciousness in his poetry, which can seem the antithesis of modernist experimentations with form, remains very much our contemporary.

Audience and Affect, Beauty and Abjection

For Poe, the loss of self-control is, in fact, what shapes his theory of beauty. In the "Philosophy of Composition," Poe makes the equation between beauty and perpetual melancholy explicit in a theory of poetry that seems to describe Petrarch's practice as well as his own. But for Poe, unlike his precursor, the primary consolation that poetry offers seems to be an intensification of grief and an abandonment of the self to tears. "Beauty," he asserts, "is the sole legitimate province of the poem," and beauty adheres not in objectively measurable external forms like symmetry or sound (though no poet more fixated on rhythm and music than Poe), nor does it reside—as it sometimes does for Petrarch—in the beloved's ability to lift the poet to thoughts of god and salvation. Beauty for Poe is merely an affective register or "tone," a way to represent and convey suffering. It is a "tone" for Poe that proves itself in the affective response of the susceptible reader. The best-known sentences of this still fascinating essay assert: "Beauty of whatever kind, in its supreme development, invariably excites the sensitive soul to tears. Melancholy is thus the most legitimate of all the poetical tones" (1377). Poe, as he often does in his tales, conflates the expression of internal states with their involuntary or compulsive external manifestation. Beauty as an inner experience manifests itself by calling forth tears or making the sensitive reader weep, not as an expression of the reader's depths of emotion but as a superficial expression of her or his mere susceptibility. Sensitivity here seems to be a nervous condition and the poem, in its highest manifestation, depends upon the contagiousness of its mood. Poe's account of beauty constructs a powerfully transferential relationship between the poem and its reader, the poet and the world, but one that has little to do with cognitive contents that might be communicated. Cognition and communication belong to the realm of prose. In the beautiful indefiniteness of poetry, the poet's masterful control and self-abjection become confused and identified. The self-consuming misery represented in the perfectly constructed poem excites a mimetic melancholy of self-torture in the reader that manifests itself in the reader's tears. The poet's originary power provokes a movement of doubling or repetition in the audience, which validates, indeed constitutes, the presence of beauty in the text and ratifies even as it challenges and decenters the poet's claim to mastery or genius. Since this version of genius depends upon a relationship that rediscovers itself in the reaction of the other, it cannot be a simple form of mastery. The reader, indeed a crowd of readers, is always in this important sense a central and complex character in Poe's poetry. The effect of the work on the audience is the object of his poetics.

The pressure of an audience registers even within the closeted setting of "The Raven." This was Poe's most commercially successful poem. Self-torture is, of course, what Poe says "The Raven" is about, but the poem does more than simply reflect the contemporary fashion for self-tormented romantic poets. It adds a novel aspect to the Sapphic agony popular with Poe's audience.[26] The poem's narrator does not suffer alone. He manipulates an audience, figured both as the bird to which he addresses himself and as the reader to whom he repeats his tale, and in whom, presumably, he hopes to provoke the "human thirst for self torture" that the he is himself seeking to satisfy and which is, as well, the burden of his poem (1378). Poe's poet makes repetition serve self-difference and uses it to heighten the pain of his grief, to intensify his awareness of loss, and to communicate his beautiful melancholy to his readers. The poem's speaker fastens upon the Raven's monotonous refrain, "Nevermore," and makes it the motif of his own carefully orchestrated misery. He frames ever more agonized inquiries around this reliably repeated answer. The narrator "experiences," as Poe explains, "a phrenzied [sic] pleasure in so modeling his questions as to receive from the *expected* 'Nevermore' the most delicious because the most intolerable sorrow" (1379). Poe imagines a poetry designed to maximize that masochism, the "luxury of sorrow" he identifies as beauty (1384). Such beauty requires an abjection of the self, a reveling in self-wounding, and opens that self to the audience's response, which the self simultaneously solicits and resists. Like the Raven's refrain, the audience at once fulfills and disrupts the poet's desire. Poe's use of grief is thus related to the work of elegy, but his substitution of the masochistic pleasures of melancholia for more traditional forms of Christian consolation or stoic self-possession alters that tradition. Above all, Poe's confusion of pleasure and pain and his incorporation of otherness into the self his poems describe calls any idea of the self's coherence in to question. Pain and beauty, self-abjection and elevation of the soul become confused in ways that foreground and project the self's interior divisions and irremediable fragmentation.

In *The Raven*, the narrator's pain amounts to a "phrenzied pleasure," an ecstasy of self-torture in which he realizes himself by expressing (or making the world around him impress upon him) the loss that constitutes and threatens his inner life. He expresses this loss only to repeat endlessly his trauma, the moment of self-sundering, through the figure of his audience. The narrator manipulates the bird whose meaninglessly sonorous utterance becomes the renewed occasion of the poet's self-abjection and grief. Finally, he makes the bird a metaphor, not for the lost lover but for loss itself:

> And the Raven, never flitting, still is sitting, still is sitting,
> On the pallid bust of Pallas, just above my chamber door;
> And his eyes have all the seeming of a demon's that is dreaming,
> And the lamplight o'er him streaming throws his shadow on the floor;
> And my soul *from out that shadow* that lies floating on the floor
>   Shall be lifted—nevermore. (374)

There is more to be said about Poe's tropes of comparison in the next chapter. For now, note that the narrator and the poem externalize the mourner's vacancy and convey it to the reader as a metaphor. They make the raven's shadow the container and expression of the speaker's soul, a soul expressed as and through an absence. The shadow or absence of light becomes the absence of the beloved, which becomes the presence of grief. This represents the achievement or undoing of metaphor itself, since the tenor or meaning that the vehicle conveys here becomes, finally, nothing. But this nothing is transvalued and given substance as an experience of beauty that the poet hopes to convey. This is different from more traditional views of the modern artist as either simply antagonistic to the interests or desires of the audience or a purveyor of popular sentiments to the marketplace. The nothingness, absence, or beauty that Poe seeks to convey is something nonetheless, a link of negation and a bond of affect that make the poet, the poem, and the audience into one conflicted unit.

Poe and Baudelaire: Melancholy in the Artist of Modern Life

Baudelaire, Poe's most influential European reader, had a good deal to say about Poe's attempt to create poetry under the pressure of the massified marketplace that defines secular modernity for the artist. As Walter Benjamin remarks, Baudelaire found the artist's experience of the modern world "set down with incomparable power in the work of Poe . . . Poe described the world in which Baudelaire's whole poetic enterprise had its prerogative."[27] For Benjamin and for Baudelaire, Poe becomes exemplary of the ways in which the world of nineteenth-century print culture had become a difficult place for the poet and ultimately required a reevaluation of poetry's place and utility.

In 1852, Baudelaire wrote an elegiac essay on Poe for the *Revue de Paris*. He dwelt upon the miseries of the American's life, the details of which he culled from Rufus Griswold's sensationalized biography in the edition of Poe's collected works upon which the French poet would base his translations of the tales. Baudelaire was far from scandalized by Griswold's accounts, instead finding Poe's miseries and excesses edifying as an illustration of a principle he first found in Alfred de Vigny's philosophical novel *Stello* (1832): "society always sacrifices its poets no matter what the political regime."[28] Baudelaire judges that in the United States, where democratic society had made popular opinion a modern tyrant more inexorable than any monarch (he seems to have taken Tocqueville's lessons to heart), the poet's plight is especially tragic. Baudelaire follows Griswold who claims that if Poe had "managed his genius and applied his creative faculties in a manner better suited to the American soil, he could perhaps have been an *auteur à argent*, a money making author."[29] According to Baudelaire, Poe did not manage his genius or apply his talents according to the market's dictates, and this put him at odds with his readers and their values. "If you are speaking with an American and if you mention Poe to him, he will admit his genius, perhaps he will even be proud of him, but he will end by telling you in a superior tone, 'But me, I am a practical man.'"[30] As Baudelaire imagines it, the American will then speak of those souls who, however great, do not know how to husband their resources and will recount Poe's exorbitant life, his alcoholism, his breath reeking so that if brought near a candle it could catch fire—just as Griswold described them. Baudelaire admires this portrait of Poe. He savors the poet's resistance to the prudent, vulgar practicalities of moneymaking and management that delimit the horizons of bourgeois aspiration and accomplishment.[31] If, as Baudelaire saw it, Poe experienced the United States as a "vast cage," then the squalor and waste of his life-long debauchery stood as perverse testimony to his noble talent, a gift too exalted and a soul too pure for mundane existence in the world's most modern nation.

Baudelaire imagines Poe as a poet largely at odds with the audience from whom he must gain his living. He, of course, ignores the extent to which Poe could and did calculate his effects to court a popular readership. For him, the American becomes the romantic type of the poet in modern times, the *poète maudit*, a soaring talent who finds himself grounded among uncomprehending fools, beset by a crowd of little people who mock him for stumbling over his magnificent but impractical wings. Readers of Baudelaire will of course recognize the figure of the poet that he describes in "L'albatros," one of the opening poems of the second edition of *Les fleurs du mal* (1861), in which he makes the pathos of the damned poet a mythical romantic and modern archetype. The last stanza reads: "The Poet is like a prince of the clouds/Who hovers in storms and mocks the hunter;/In exile on the ground amid the heckling crowd/His giant wings hobble his stride."[32] Baudelaire made Poe an expression of his own antipathy to the emergent mass society of capitalist modernity and all the challenges that this entailed for an ambitious writer constrained to woo this audience.

Terence Whalen, in his indispensable book on Poe and mass culture, continues Baudelaire's vision of Poe's struggle with his readers and his times. Whalen writes that Poe "struggled in open and subtle ways to elude the worst excesses of the 'magazine prison house,'" but found himself compelled to "please the Capital Reader first in order to survive as a commercial writer."[33] The pressure of bourgeois society took material form in this audience of "capital readers," in their expectations and tastes that constituted the marketplace for magazines and books, poems and stories. Poe's calculations regarding this marketplace are, of course, everywhere evident in his work, including in his poetry. But the influence of that audience is far from simply negative.

The romantic myth of the outcast artist misses how often the pressure of a popular marketplace was, for Poe, an energizing challenge, one more positive than Baudelaire was willing to admit in his own literary performances, which, like Poe's, were carefully calibrated to seduce and titillate, outrage and amuse his readers, and to reinvent art while doing so. Poe was unabashedly interested in courting and entertaining a mass audience. He made no secret of the fact that "The Raven," his most commercially successful poem, began not with a visit from the muse, a fever of demonic possession, or an intense emotion recollected in tranquility but with his journeyman's desire to produce a poem that might appeal to the critical and the popular taste (1375). Poe offered Baudelaire an example of a poetics that balanced seduction and resistance, a poetry that represented a complicated negotiation between the artist and the modern audience. It may be true, as Benjamin says, that "Baudelaire was perhaps the first to have had the idea of a market-oriented originality,"[34] but he found his great model for this market orientation of art in Poe, whose defiance of the market he celebrated and whose negotiation with the market's demand he learned to imitate. A market-oriented originality consists in more than just a resistance to market valuations; it requires negotiations with the market, an appeal, as Poe puts it, to the popular taste a poet, however lofty his aspirations, cannot afford simply to despise. The strains of appealing to those divergent inclinations frequently show in Poe's work, and are especially evident in his notorious rejection of truth or utility as proper ends for poetry.

In Poe, as in Baudelaire after him, the appeal to and the struggle against the mass audience are often difficult to distinguish. Discussing Poe's essay on the poetic principle, Baudelaire explains Poe's crucial vision of poetry's problematic place in the modern world:

> A utilitarian movement that wants to make poetry as useful as everything else has long held sway in the United States. One finds there humanitarian poets, suffragist poets, poets in favor of abolishing grain laws, poets who want to build workhouses. . . . In his criticism [*lectures*], Poe declared war on all these useful poets. He did not hold, like certain fanatical partisans of Goethe and other mumbling poets . . . that all beautiful things must be essentially useless; but he emphatically rejected that which he spiritually termed the *great poetic heresy of modern times*. This heresy is the idea of immediate utility. . . . We have a fundamental faculty that perceives beauty; it has its own ends and its own means. Poetry is the product of this faculty; it addresses itself to our sense of beauty and to no other end. *It is an insult to this faculty to submit it to criteria other than its own.* . . . That poetry may be subsequently and consequently useful, that is beyond doubt, but that is not its primary purpose; it comes for free, thrown in as an extra! (cela vient *par-dessus le marché!*)[35]

Baudelaire distances poetry from both the fanatical aestheticism of art for art's sake as well as from the philistine assumption that poetry can be a tool of progress and reform. Following Poe, he specifies an intimate relationship between poetry and the human mind, especially the human capacity to appreciate beauty. Like Poe, he removes beauty from the sort of practical moral engagement and pragmatic rhetorical address that immediate utility in the interests of progress and reform requires.

But beauty, Baudelaire insists, is far from useless. Like Poe, Baudelaire finds that modern life demands a tone of beauty closely allied to melancholy, a fixed disposition and determination to mourn, in order to reach and express the dark under currents of a superficially optimistic age. The rejection of positive utility, the fixation on chronic agony and endless doubt rather than on elegiac consolation or moral optimism, serves truths of its own that cannot be reduced to market values, and may in fact be opposed to them. These are the truths of experience in a secular age.

Poe's attempt to seduce a readership while altering accepted ideas of art's utility involves what Mallarmé, in his elegy for Poe, called the purification of the language of the tribe (see the Introduction). Language's utility as a servant of industry was itself receiving a revaluation in Poe's time. Terence Whalen describes antebellum America as a context in which "cultural upheaval and industrialization were accompanied by the emergence of information as an acknowledged instrument of economic development" (22). In a competitive marketplace, knowledge as the handmaiden of technology becomes power. Poe's removal of literature from the realm of knowledge, instrumentalized as techné or know-how, leads him to revise poetic language or prosody itself.[36] He does not merely resist the language of commerce (which, in fact he often uses), he subverts the role of language in literature as a conveyer of information, of truths, wisdom, or comfort. In this sense, Poe does seek to purify the language of the tribe, but only by seriously troubling its functional utility. In doing so, however, he also communicates certain truths of existence that are not always congenial to the audience he confronted or congruent with their beliefs.

Chief among those important truths is the reality of doubt and the impossibility of naïve belief in a secular age. Put more succinctly, Poe commits himself to the truth that art and truth no longer coincide. Baudelaire, at one point in his essay, analyzes Poe's skull and discovers that the poet seems to lack a capacity for belief. The head is not in harmony with itself, he notes, and the critical faculties of comparison, construction, and causality seem to dominate even its aesthetic sense. In Baudelaire's estimation, a certain melancholy withdrawal from the world emerges as the characteristic of Poe's work and the hallmark of his identity as an artist: "The despairing echoes of melancholy that traverse Poe's works have a penetrating accent, it is true, but one must also say that this is a solitary melancholy, with little sympathy for the common lot of humans."[37] Poe's art takes its distance, as we have noted, from humanism and from humanity itself. Yet, Poe emerges in Baudelaire precisely as a sort of exemplary sufferer who, as one might say of the Christian God he replaces—and as Baudelaire does say of Poe—"has greatly suffered for us."[38] The poet's suffering, however, does not save him or his reader. If Poe finally becomes a sort of secular martyr, the type of the artist as a solitary figure in an endless Gethsemane, this questions remains: How does modernity's pain register in Poe's terribly influential poetry?

The Prosody of Pain: Poe's Material Music, or How to Mark Time

If Poe celebrated extravagances of emotional abjection he also exhibited a consummate, even classical, mastery of traditional form, a virtuoso skill in manipulating poetic language. If, for Baudelaire, Poe distinguishes himself from confused and mumbling poets by speaking clearly in that beautiful tone of loss that Poe claimed as poetry's sole legitimate province, then one might well wonder what lyrical devices the poet finds to represent and convey that sadness, that beautiful absence, to the reader. What in a poem most conduces to that elevation through agony that might convey beauty to a sensitive soul? It is no secret that in his critical writings on verse, Poe focuses on poetry's musical elements: meter, rhythm, and sound. These depend not on language's signifying function but on the sign's material existence. In this way the poem's significance becomes distanced from its meaning.

Readers have often remarked on Poe's distinctive foregrounding of sound in his poetry and the ways in which it compromises the sense of his verses. Even before T. S. Eliot criticized Poe for valuing sound over sense, resistant readers had long registered similar complaints. Emerson, after all, barely noticed Poe except as "the jingle man." And Lowell mocked him in popular verse. ("Three-fifths of him genius, and two-fifths sheer fudge") by pointing out that he "talks like a book of iambs and pentameters, / In a way to make all men of common sense d—n meters."[39] Common sense dictates that the poet who tarries too long with sound is probably not sensible. Poe, of course, was not abashed by such criticism. In an anonymous review of "A Fable for Critics," Poe cites Lowell's disparagement of "Mr. Poe" and offers this dictum by way of reply: "*profound* ignorance on any particular topic is always sure to manifest itself by some allusion to 'common sense.'" He goes on to demonstrate that Lowell, a poet he sometimes admires, exhibits fatal ignorance concerning the formal requirements of satire, and especially about the science of metrical composition. He manifests this last, according to Poe, in his misguided belief that he can compose anapests by ear. Poe lists numerous instances of the botched meter of "A Fable" and finally criticizes Lowell not for what he has said but for how he has said it, for what Poe calls his "faux pas"—the false steps or faulty feet of his verse (814–822).

Poe, no doubt, intends his effrontery to amuse his readers and to cultivate interest in his own work by creating an atmosphere of controversy around it; but as he does so often, Poe uses his most outrageous performances to make a serious point. Commonsense criticism fails to consider the interesting questions Poe's poetic theory and his poetry pose: What is the relationship of poetic music to poetic meaning? Of pure prosody to that melancholy affect that Poe claims is beauty itself and poetry's only proper province?[40]

Inevitably, the consideration of music in poetry, like the consideration of music more generally, turns the reader's attention to time and to forms of repetition that, quite literally, mark time by constituting the reader's temporal experience through modalities of repetition. Rhythm, which Poe's verse often foregrounds, orders duration by patterning repeated stresses. The *Oxford English Dictionary* offers the following definition of "Rhythm": "The measured recurrence of . . . long and short, or stressed and unstressed, syllables in a foot or a line." Rhyme, another foregrounded aspect of Poe's poetry, also, again according the *OED*, depends upon repetition in the form of consonance or a "recurrence of the same or like sounds." These measured repetitions capture what people commonly mean when they speak of marking time and constitute a large part of what we call the music of poetry.

In addition to meters and rhyme, Poe's poetry depends upon other forms of repetition. For example, in "The Philosophy of Composition," Poe considers the use of the refrain, another musical element entailing regular repetition. For Poe this is crucial, for in his estimation the refrain enjoys wide spread use because it affords a "pleasure . . . adduced solely from the sense of identity—of repetition," and, in his desire to satisfy the critical and the popular taste, he counts on this pleasure to woo an audience. This sense of identity and repetition in Poe's formulation requires further consideration. For Poe turns this popular ploy to surprising ends. The pleasure of identity entails repetition, as suggested by the printer's dash with which Poe distinguishes and links his terms. Repetition inevitably links identity to difference. For each recurrence to be recognizable as a repetition, it must be identified with but also different from—if only through the displacement in time that repetition constitutes—the instance that precedes it. Poe foregrounds this structural tension between identity and difference in "The Raven" by fashioning a refrain whose single word emphasizes identity while its varying meanings in each recurrence underlines difference. "I resolved to diversify, and so vastly heighten, the effect [of pleasure in identity and repetition], by adhering, in general, to the monotone of sound, while I continually varied that of thought" (1377). The apparent stability of the signifier does not stabilize but actually intensifies the reader's awareness of alteration in and over time, and therefore, of time itself. Science, as in Poe's sonnet, may be the "true Daughter of Old Time," but the poet's melancholy depends on time's passing even as it marks it. Poe designs a refrain that reminds the reader repeatedly of temporality and of the losses time entails by foregrounding temporality through the rhythmic structure of a variably significant refrain.

Poe emphasizes prosody as music. His masterly demonstration of metrical skill in "The Philosophy of Composition" can seem like a parody meant to hoax and impress a gullible readership. Having settled upon the refrain as a device, with its "pleasure of identity—of repetition" and on a single word refrain that foregrounds differences in meaning over time and therefore foregrounds time's passage, he next considers not the meaning but the music that the single word refrain should have: "That such a close, to have force, must be sonorous and susceptible of protracted emphasis, admitted no doubt: And these considerations inevitably led me to the long *o* as the most sonorous vowel, in connection with *r* as the most producible consonant." And then, "In such a search it would have been absolutely impossible to overlook the word 'Nevermore,'" which, in fact, was "the very first" word to present itself (1378). Poe's inductive (or is it deductive?) tour de force reverses what readers might assume a poet's normal order of composition to be. The music of the poem, its rhythmic structures and sonorous phonemes come first and these generate its force, its affective effect.[41] Its meaning or content—the commonplace "subject" to which an audience might look for edification—is presented as an afterthought and mere occasion for a musical effect. The poem's length, its province, its tone, its refrain, its sonorousness are all musical elements in place before the bird and the bereaved lover enter the composition (1377–1378). Poe reduces both characters to mere devices that motivate the poem's music.[42] Meaning here assumes a subordinate place to form as the mere pretense for the music. Music is largely the province of the sign's materiality. This alone distinguishes Poe from the legions of edifying and uplifting "utilitarian" poets around him.

In Poe's analytical exposition, he instrumentalizes the bereaved lover, the black bird, and the dead woman as rationales for the poem's music. They are nearly deprived of any meaning of their own. In a specific sense, Poe's ideal for poetry is nonmimetic. Poetry's highest concerns involve neither objects to be represented nor meanings to be conveyed, but the repetition of a tone or sound suggesting melancholy. Here is the most notorious passage of "The Philosophy of Composition":

I asked myself, "Of all melancholy topics, what, according to the *universal* understanding of mankind, is the *most* melancholy?" Death—was the obvious reply. "And when," I said, "is this most melancholy of topics most poetical?" From what I have already explained at some length, the answer, here also, is obvious—"When it most closely allies itself to *Beauty*: the death, then, of a beautiful woman is, unquestionably,

the most poetical topic in the world—and equally is it beyond doubt
that the lips best suited for such topic are those of a bereaved lover."
(1378–1379)[43]

Poe must have enjoyed the abysmal circularity of this demonstration.
Beauty equals melancholy, which bespeaks loss and loss becomes most perfect and most beautiful when the loss is the loss of beauty. Loss may be
embodied in a woman but the woman represents loss itself and becomes
most beautiful when she is lost. Beauty is loss and loss beauty; that is all
you know in this world and all you need to know, or perhaps can know.
But loss, as an alteration of existence, can only be manifest in time, as a
temporal phenomenon. Loss is what the poem's music, which Poe has been
elaborating, orders and communicates in its various modalities of repetition. These constitute the poem not as a representation of the lost lover but
of time itself. "Nevermore" becomes not only the point where the poem's
musical structure and its thematic content meet in the refrain (1379), it
embodies the essentially time-bound logic of beauty as loss and of melancholia as a state of being. Unlike Petrarch's poet, Poe means to recover
neither the lost beloved nor the poet's self-possession. He dwells in the sonorous aftermath of loss.

The foregrounding of musical effects in Poe's poetry refocuses the reader's attention from both incident and meaning, from the abstract concept
of the sign's attenuated referent, onto the material form of the signifier's
sound, the sonorous vowels and resonant *r*'s of the refrain. In Poe's account
of the poem, repetition itself precedes the poem's mimetic function, and
what the poem represents serves primarily to motivate its refrain. Poe
makes the province of poetry and the material means by which poetry maps
and governs that province, unite in a single word.[44] "Nevermore," mechan-
ically repeated by an "ungainly foul," finally signifies nothing in itself. It
suggests and approximates Poe's view of art's insignificance.

In a gesture that toys with an audience's expectations that poetry will
edify, Poe concludes his tour de force explanation of "The Raven" by pointing
out that in the poem's very last line, the final repetition of "nevermore,"
the reader at last distinctly perceives the poet's intention of rendering the
Raven metaphorical, "as emblematical of Mournful and Never-ending
Remembrance." This seems familiarly sentimental and the Latinate diction seems to guarantee the poet's seriousness. But this reading of the bird
as the vehicle for even so attenuated a tenor as never-ending remembrance
may also remind the reader how inappropriate an emblem the ungainly,
comical fowl is to convey the solemnity of loss as an elevated sentiment.

As is so often the case, Poe leaves the reader in doubt concerning where the ironies lie, and what, if anything, has finally been revealed. "The Raven," for all its music, may even be a joke, a parody of popular sentimentality and bourgeois bad taste. But it is never just a joke. Poe makes a serious point about melancholy beauty and inevitable loss that no recurrence to common sense or elevated sentiment can simply reduce to or redeem through meaning. In this resistance to meaning lies one of the keys to Poe's modernity, one of his strange purifications of the common language.

Consider, as another example of sound and sense, one of Poe's most musically impressive poems, which, like "The Raven," is about melancholy loss and perpetual (if intermittent) remembrance:

> The skies they were ashen and sober;
>   The leaves they were crisped and sere—
>   The leaves they were withering and sere;
> It was night in the lonesome October
>   Of my most immemorial year;
> It was hard by the dim lake of Auber,
>   In the ghoul-haunted woodland of Weir. (89)

"Ulalume," in its oddly childish way, comes as close to pure music as any poem in English. While it is not difficult to follow, the poem seems unconcerned to communicate any clear sense. Poe constructs these verses from the darker, more sonorous English vowels that require the mouth to form itself into a resonate chamber. He deploys these *o*'s and *oo*'s in compelling anapestic trimeter, where the three feet in the line emphasize the syllabic triplet within each foot. Substituted iambs at the beginning of the first three lines set the poem's stage and a suspended or catalytic beat marks a dramatic pause, heard almost as a caesura (which would normally come in the line's middle) at the ends of lines one, four, and six, marking the appositive repetitions that constitute the three parts of each of the stanza's major clauses. Thus, repetitions within repetitions bind the stanza together. The propulsive rhythmic force generated by these lines feels nearly regressive, in a way that Julia Kristeva or Allan Grossman might make clear.[45]

Poe's affection for such effects, no doubt, lent credence to the oft-voiced critical opinion that his immaturity mars his verses and characterizes those who admire them. "Ulalume" at times seems perilously close to the sort of sound poems that rivet infants, like the clickety dactyls of "Hickory, dickory, dock." Yet for readers willing to regress with Poe, for the susceptible soul as Poe would have it, something occurs in these lines that approaches pure poetic affect, the incantatory effect that T. S. Eliot called, in his criticism of this poem, "the magic of verse," and makes this poem remarkably compelling.

Eliot frames his grudging praise for Poe's musical effects with complaints about the unscrupulous measures the poet takes to create them. In his "choice of the word that has the right *sound*," Eliot writes, "Poe is by no means careful that it should have also the right *sense*." Tennyson uses the word "immemorial" correctly, according to Eliot, but Poe does not. Poe meant "memorable" and settled for "immemorial," its opposite, attracted to the word's timbre and to its metrical fitness.[46] Of course, Eliot has a point about Poe's affection for sound over sense. Words like "Titanic," and "Yaanek," and even "boreal" in the next stanza contribute little but their sound. But had Eliot thought "Ulalume" worth more serious attention, he would have noted that "immemorial" is just the right word for Poe's composition. Forgetting, or failing to forget, remembering the immemorial, is precisely what "Ulalume" is about, regardless of what the burden of that recollection might be. For this poem does not treat melancholy as the affect of the perpetually unforgettable, but instead as the recollection of something, for a time, unremembered, something—a dread burden—"beyond memory" and, momentarily at least, "out of mind," both phrases that figure in the *OED*'s definition of "immemorial."

The unremembered or "immemorial" differs, as the poem suggests, from things that one simply forgets. Like the poem's musical structure, what "Ulalume" depicts as immemorial, the dread burden haunting the just-passed year and about to be recollected, is less a matter of forgetting or remembering than it is a question of recurrence and intermittency, the oscillation between the loss of loss through forgetting and the periodic remembering of loss through recollection. In this poem, it is not the lover but the memory of the lover's loss that marks the passage of time by returning like a dread burden or refrain.

The poet does not remember what, during this most immemorial year, he and Psyche have been doing. Though the next stanza moves beyond the hobgoblin gothic setting of the ghoul-haunted woodland—a Halloween version of Dante's wood in which the poet and psyche discover they are lost—it does so only to regress to an earlier, more libidinally charged moment. Here the election of sound over sense that irritated Eliot actually seems motivated. For Poe's nearly nonsensical language here marks both the poet's regression and the reader's sense that something remains hidden within the lush sounds and grandiose images that the poet produces.

> Here once, through an alley Titanic,
> > Of cypress, I roamed with my Soul—
> > Of cypress, with Psyche, my Soul.
> These were days when my heart was volcanic
> > As the scoriac rivers that roll—
> > As the lavas that restlessly roll
> Their sulphurous currents down Yaanek
> > In the ultimate climes of the pole—
> That groan as the role down Mount Yaanek
> > In the realms of the boreal Pole. (89)

Despite the lurid passions that these lines with their frequent recursions suggest—volcanic hearts effusing restless lava that rolls like melted rock (scoria) down mythical mountains in ultimate climes—the poet, with his soul, remain alone on the scene. The "once" in this stanza's first line unsettles the specificity of place (by the dank tarn of Auburn) and time (a night in the lonesome October of the poet's most immemorial year) that the first stanza seemed to establish. Does this refer to a past action in that specific October that the poem began to narrate or to an action further in the past that the poem's narrator begins to remember just as he repeats it? This temporal confusion between the immediate past and the pluperfect, between different modalities of repetition as retelling and temporality as re-acting, predominates as well in the next stanza, which also uses the word "once," though in a way that complicates, even as it clarifies, these temporal questions:

> Our talk had been serious and sober,
> > But our thoughts they were palsied and seer—
> > Our memories were treacherous and sere—
> For we knew not the month was October,
> > And we marked not the night of the year—
> > (Ah, night of all nights in the year!)
> We noted not the dim lake of Auber—
> > (Though once we had journeyed down here)—
> We remembered not the dank tarn of Auber,
> > Nor the ghoul-haunted woodland of Weir. (89)

Thus the poem elaborates the burden of "immemorial" in the first line. "Ulalume" makes what is unremembered into a function of memory's astringent betrayals. For what force does "once" have if neither the former time nor the previous place of the now repeated action emerges into

consciousness for the Poet or his soul or the reader until just this moment? Because the poet momentarily fails to recognize a place where he
has apparently been before, the poet and Psyche momentarily exist in an
immemorial dreamland, something or place "out of space, out of time."
But that is not where the treacheries of memory and of immemorial melancholy will leave them.

The poet's momentary forgetting of time promises to lead him toward
a desirable transport, "the path to the skies—/To the Lethean peace of
the skies" (90) that he associates with the newly risen star on his horizon,
a Petrarchan metaphor for the woman whose praises he briefly sings and
who promises both warmth and light:

> And I said—"She is warmer than Dian:
> She rolls through an ether of sighs—
> She revels in a region of sighs:
> She has seen that the tears are not dry on
> These cheeks, where the worm never dies. (90)

But Psyche's uneasiness signifies trouble, suggesting that the double horned
star—either celestial Astarte or a crescent moon—might lead them astray.
For recollection appears more treacherous than memory itself. For though
the poet's undried tears suggest his undying remembrance of loss and the
worm that never dies recalls mortality, love's promise of human intimacy,
warmth, hope, and beauty helps him forget, for the moment, what beauty
truly is, the never-ending remembrance of loss.

As the poem moves to its climax and the poet moves to comfort an increasingly distraught and mistrustful Psyche, the rhythm and repetitions
of the poem intensify, enacting—indeed perhaps creating—the end of the
immemorial in the poet's quickening recollections. The end of the immemorial actually occurs in a moment of intensified repetitive articulations
of the word with which the lost lover's name rhymes and seems to have
been created to do so. Rhyme itself reminds the poet that for sublunary
mortals no transcendence is possible, that beauty means loss and the melancholy pleasure of self-torture is the highest possible end of true art:

> Thus I pacified Psyche and kissed her,
>   And tempted her out of her gloom—
>   And conquered her scruples and gloom,
> And we passed to the end of the vista,
>   But were stopped by the door of a tomb—
>   By the door of a legended tomb;

And I said—"What is written, sweet sister,
    On the door of this legended tomb?"
    She replied—"Ulalume—Ulalume—
    'T is the vault of thy lost Ulalume!" (91)

At this climactic moment, the poet or the poem itself through its mu-sical mechanisms remembers Ulalume—whose name seems called forth by the rhymes with the repetitions of "gloom" and "tomb" that precede it. The rhyme-enforced recollection creates a pathetic link, a reversed but (in the poem's world) veracious version of the pathetic fal-lacy. The landscape's surrounding gloom and his inner state finally rhyme. No longer can his volcanic soul and the titanic landscape of his imagination be contrasted to the crisped and seer autumnal setting of the poem. At the moment of recollection, the poet's fires go out and he reenters the experience of time and space shaped by the play of iden-tity and difference and structured by repetition that comes to signify loss:

Then my heart it grew ashen and sober
    As the leaves that were crisped and sere—
    As the leaves that were withering and seer,
And I cried—"It was surely October
    On *this* very night of last year,
    That I journeyed—I journeyed down here—
    That I brought a dread burden down here—
    On this night of all nights in the year,
    Ah, what demon has tempted me here?
Well I know, now, this dim lake of Auber—
    This misty mid region of Weir—
Well I know, now this dank tarn of Auber,
    This ghoul-haunted woodland of Weir." (91)

The poet remembers and the poem concludes by doubling back on itself to complete the rounding of this immemorial year. But at this moment all the figures of doubles in the poem, especially the poet and Psyche, his soul and his double, collapse. The outer setting and the poet's inner world become one; the poet and his soul, until this moment in dialogue, join to become a single voice:

Said we then,—the two, then: "Ah, can it
    Have been that the woodlandish ghouls—
    The pitiful, the merciful ghouls—

To bar up our way and to ban it
    From the secret that lies in these wolds
    From the thing that lies hidden in these wolds—
Have drawn up the spectre of a planet
    From the limbo of lunary souls—
This sinfully scintillant planet
    From the Hell of the planetary souls?" (91)

The poem ends in a univocal and monotonous recognition of error in which, finally, all hope is lost and something like beauty is left. The poet and his soul join in one voice to lament not the loss of Ulalume alone but both the loss of the memory of that loss and its return as well.

The return of the memory of loss entails a loss of its own, a recollection that is also a repetition of the primary loss, the loss of the fixed star's warm promise of transport and forgetfulness beyond the world of repetition, change, and death to a place away from "This sinfully scintillant planet/From the Hell of the planetary souls." Ulalume, represented by that impossible and evocative name, remains beyond possibility of recovery. She remains unfigured except as a "dread burden," both "the thing that lies hidden in these wolds" and, as the *OED* suggests, "The refrain or chorus of a song," a figure of repetition itself. The poem thinks longingly back not on her presence but on the presence of the poet's own momentary illusion that he might forget forgetting and live without remembering what he has lost. That he might escape, for more than a moment, his consciousness of time. The poem returns the poet to the ever-recurring rhythm of immemorial recollection in this hell of planetary souls where the poem leaves its poet and his readers. This is a secular hell, where no promise of salvation or surcease of sorrow remains credible. "Ulalume," with its childish lament, its melody of nearly senseless but beautifully rhythmic and rhyming grief, goes right to the heart of the modern, where it dwells in the aesthetics of bereavement without consolation, in the ever recollected but still immemorial burden of time and death that make themselves felt in the melancholy, beautiful, and regressive music of Poe's best poetry. Poe evokes Petrarchan traditions in his best poetry, but in doing so he marks the time of the beginning of humanism's end and the advent of a secular age for art.

CHAPTER 2

Poe and the Origins of Modern Poetry: Tropes of Comparison and the Knowledge of Loss

Poe's remarks on Hawthorne's failure to achieve popular success form a corollary to his ideas about the noncognitive province of modern art. These ideas about beauty had constituted the serious center of "The Philosophy of Composition," which he had published in 1846 in *Graham's Magazine*, a year before his first two reviews of Hawthorne had appeared. In these reviews, he famously advises Hawthorne to eschew allegory, which, Poe finds, "completely overwhelms the greater number of his subjects" and alienates the "popular sentiment" and the "popular taste." Moreover, Poe associates allegory with the fallacy that literary art might serve truth rather than beauty, which, as he argued in "The Philosophy of Composition," has nothing directly to do with truth. Poe writes:

> In defense of allegory, (however, or for whatever object employed,) there is scarcely one respectable word to be said. . . . The fallacy of the idea that allegory, in any of its moods, can be made to enforce a truth— that metaphor, for example, may illustrate as well as embellish an argument—could be promptly demonstrated.[1]

For Poe, the modern writer confronts a modern audience. The heterogeneity of this audience means that the grounds of agreed upon truths and common verities upon which allegory and metaphor as vehicles for truth rely and to which they refer is no longer the ground on which literary art can make its appeal.

Poe's longest review of Hawthorne's short fiction appeared in *Godey's Lady's Book* in 1847. It was his third review of Hawthorne and was occasioned in part by the appearance of *Mosses from an Old Manse* the previous year.[2] Here he revises his earlier, nearly unqualified praise for Hawthorne's artistry and originality in the two reviews of *Twice Told Tales* he had written a half-decade earlier by introducing his critique of allegory. He returns to a comment he makes in the concluding paragraph of his second review, where he mentions, nearly in passing, a "somewhat too general or prevalent *tone*—a tone of melancholy and mysticism" that characterizes Hawthorne's work (*ER* 577). In this, his final review, he expands this comment into a critique of Hawthorne's underestimation of the modern audience's taste for sensation and his overcultivation of an artful air of "repose" that Poe identified with the "'peculiarity' or sameness or monotone" of his tales. Most damning, Poe has come to believe, that Hawthorne is "peculiar and not original" (*ER* 587). Above all, he takes Hawthorne to task for his ill-conceived and untimely attempts at allegory. In fact, all Hawthorne's failings, including his failure to achieve originality, in Poe's estimation are aspects of his addiction to allegory. First and last, he is guilty of abusing tropes of comparison and substitution and for trying the patience of his readers. This, Poe explains, is why Hawthorne has failed to be widely appreciated:

> But at his failure to be appreciated, we can, *of course*, no longer wonder, when we find him monotonous at decidedly the worst of all possible points—at that point which, having the least concern with Nature, is the farthest removed from the popular intellect, from the popular sentiment and from the popular taste. I allude to the strain of allegory which completely overwhelms the greater number of his subjects, and which in some measure interferes with the direct conduct of absolutely all. (*ER* 582)

In Poe's antipathy to allegory, one senses his reaction to the modern transition to what Terence Whalen has called "a culture of surfaces," a culture that reflects the heterogeneity and massification of the literary audience. This makes allegory with its reliance on "deeper" or previously received meanings and other tropes of comparison like metaphor and simile (figures long associated with profound insight and the formulation of new knowledge) difficult to depend upon as purveyors of truth.[3] For Poe, allegory is nothing but "metaphor run mad," as he says later in this review, and its madness suggests its radical inappropriateness in the modern age in which a taste for sensation displaces the hunger for truth, at least so far as literature is concerned (*ER* 587).

Modernity for Poe alters the order of language and its relationship to truth, at least in art. Here again is Poe's antihumanism. The pressure of the modern crowd alters the human-centered, philologically and rhetorically grounded search for truths in or through art that was one of humanism's distinguishing projects. As Tony Davies puts it, humanism was essentially a linguistic project.[4] We considered in the past chapter the ways in which Petrarch hoped to heal his tormented soul through his poetic dedication to Laura as an emblem of divine love, and to poetry, as a figure for efficacious utterance akin to prayer. Poe's poetry offers an early reflection of and on an epochal alteration in the order of language and the regimes of meaning that signal humanism's end, or at least its reversion to darker potentialities that were, of course, present in the fascination with language and rhetoric from the first.

For Poe, the traditional order of linguistic and poetic signification, dominant since at least the Christian middle ages, alters in the modern world. He reverts to a skeptical position in which, it seems, no text, not even scripture or science, can be trusted to yield stable, universal meanings. Interpretive schema like the quadria, the medieval schoolman's method of deriving literal, allegorical, moral, and anagogical meanings from a scriptural text, seem at best curious artifacts of a now-dissolved orthodoxy. Science, on the other hand, offers practical power, but also, as Poe says in his "Sonnet—To Science," yields a world that seems antithetical to imagination and poetry. It tears the ancient, animating spirits from field and flood and wakes the poet from his "summer dream beneath the tamarind tree." No method or imagination yields deeper meanings or reliable enchantment in the art of a secular age. The pragmatic demands of the moment take precedence over all and all meanings may be—and already are—contested.

It is Poe's genius to assume these unpropitious conditions as a provocation for the modernization of art. In his estimation, the artist must address a marketplace where the taste for sensation predominates over the search for truths or the desire for utility, using but also altering poetry's traditional tools. In his poems and also in his tales, Poe, does not himself abandon metaphor or allegory, but he modifies these tropes of comparison to reflect the changes he recognizes in the order of artful signification, the corresponding absence of stable meanings rooted in subjectivity or unquestionable beliefs grounded in authoritative institutions. Indeed, for Poe, subjectivity in a secular age becomes like the age itself problematic, conflicted, and volatile. For Poe, these problematics of the self and of signification characterize the age in which he writes in ways that traditional allegory can no longer figure. Poe's response to these altered circumstances is not to abandon but to reinvent the tropes of comparison.

Skepticism, Death, and Metaphor

Poe's revision of comparison is a revision of an ancient poetic tradition. It participates in the ambivalence regarding the relationship of tropes of comparison to knowledge that begins with Aristotle's reworking of Plato's critique of representation.[5] Poe's own fascination with tropes of comparison risks becoming, like allegory, a sort of madness of its own. Consider the figure of the raven in the poem that becomes the occasion for "The Philosophy of Composition." By the end of the poem, Poe says in that essay, "the reader begins now to regard the Raven as emblematical," as an allegorical figure or, better, a metaphorical emblem for *"Mournful and Never-ending Remembrance."*[6] This might seem clear, but Poe's transformation of this lowly and "ungainly fowl" into a metaphor whose tenor is a meaning that is so exalted in the midcentury's popular imagination risks becoming ridiculous. The raven comes close to violating that appropriateness, that tastefulness and fittingness that Aristotle in book 3 of *Rhetoric* identified as the primary requirement of a successful metaphor. According to Aristotle, "Metaphor . . . gives style clearness, charm, and distinction as nothing else can: and it is not a thing whose use can be taught by one man to another. Metaphor, like epithets, must be fitting, which means that they must fairly correspond to the thing signified."[7]

In *The Poetics*, Aristotle associated metaphor's positive capacity to signify—the power of clarity, charm, and distinction—with the production and transmission of new knowledge, the filling in of gaps in discourse or experience, as when the poet supplies the verb for the sun's observed dispersal of its rays (for which no word exists) by comparing it, metaphorically, to sowing.[8] As we saw in the last chapter, Poe, in *Marginalia* sees the modern lyric as dependent not on clarity but on "the *indefinite* [which is] an element in the true ποιησις" or true poem (*ER* 1331). Poe's play with metaphors and other tropes of comparison suggests the ways a certain indefiniteness, a distancing of art from certain knowledge, comes to define literature in the modern era.

Here there is a little-explored affinity in the characteristic tropes of erotic poetry and philosophical discourse. Since at least the Song of Songs poets have attempted to produce, preserve, or convey knowledge of the beloved's body by deploying vividly sensual metaphors to give clarity and a distinctive presence in their discourse to the objects they desire or the truths they seek:

> A garden enclosed is my sister, my spouse; a spring shut up, a fountain sealed.
> Thy plants are an orchard of pomegranates, with pleasant fruits; camphire, with spikenard,
> Spikenard and saffron; calamus and cinnamon, with all trees of frankincense; myrrh and aloes, with all the chief spices:
> A fountain of gardens, a well of living waters, and streams from Lebanon.
> Awake, O north wind; and come, thou south; blow upon my garden, that the spices thereof may flow out. Let my beloved come into his garden, and eat his pleasant fruits. (Song of Solomon 4:10–16)

In poems like this, praise and mimesis come together. Metaphor re-presents or resupplies the absent lover's body, as in learned discourse it may illustrate, instruct, or persuade.[9] In pushing metaphor, in "The Raven" and elsewhere, toward the ridiculous, Poe signals his impatience with the common functions of signification, with the cognitive functioning of language in poetry. If poetry, as he says in "The Philosophy of Composition," is not the proper vehicle for truth, which, as he puts it, is an end "far more readily attainable in prose" (16), then what do the tropes of comparison in Poe's poetry do?

Poe's perversion of poetic comparison reflects poetry's modern place. Terence Whalen identifies an important aspect of Poe's engagement with modernity as a negotiation with a new identification of knowledge as an "economic good" in the "information metropolis," a good to which literature was expected to contribute. Whalen notes Poe's insistence, following Coleridge, that the poem serves pleasure and not truth. But one must also remember how strangely Poe's sense of pleasure mixes masochistic self-torture and demonstrations of sadistic mastery. Poe masters the familiar devices of comparison to seduce his audience even as his poetry frustrates their expectations. He engages and resists the literary tradition, the elements of which he reorganizes or recombines to fashion his own "originality," an

originality that he suggests Hawthorne fails to achieve through his reliance on outmoded allegorical techniques and assumptions that Poe
himself will modernize. Poe's use and abuse of comparison becomes an
expression of what Whalen identifies as his hesitancy "to assume his place
in a signifying environment where information has become the dominant form of meaning," yet it expresses his mastery of that environment at
the same time.[10]

In "The Philosophy of Composition," Poe explains that his poetry seeks
to convey a single melancholy tenor, beauty as sadness, which is a sentiment or emotion, but not quite a meaning. If Wordsworth said that the
art of the poet makes absent things present for tranquil contemplation, Poe
makes poetry dwell on the presence of absence and the turbulent pleasures
of self-torment.[11] His perversion of the tropes of comparison suggests how
he comes to make art by distancing poetry from meaning.

Since Aristotle's *Poetics*, the tropes of comparison are closely associated
with meaning itself. They share a logic of signification involving both resemblance and substitution with the more general functioning of any sign
or word, but metaphor and simile also have the capacity to disrupt assumptions or refresh perceptions, as Aristotle suggested, conveying newness
and knowledge very much like those gestures of explanation when one
might say, you've never seen a hippogriff but it's like a horse with an
eagle's wings.[12] In addition, metaphor and simile both work by logics of
representation as substitution—one sign comes to represent and replace
another. They are therefore the poetic elements most consonant with Poe's
poet's melancholia or protracted mourning, his tendency to dwell with loss.
Metaphor especially can make the missing object of desire present to the
senses as a work of mournful commemoration.[13] But Poe departs from these
ancient elegiac practices by representing in "The Raven" not the lost Lenore's
longed for body or voice but her radical and irremediable absence. The
talking bird does not represent Lenore, it comes instead to "emblematize"
her loss and the "mournful and Never-ending remembrance" that her loss
evokes. Poe thus pays homage to and parodies sententious sentimentaliza-
tions of death and consolation in Victorian culture. He deploys comparisons,
especially simile and metaphor, not to recuperate but to ratify loss. Death
becomes the master tenor of Poe's most memorable tropes.

Consider one of his more conventional uses of metaphor in "A Dream
Within a Dream." The poem begins with a parting "kiss upon the brow!"—
a sign of personal sundering. It ends with a metaphorical figuration of
time as loss and of classical skepticism about reality:

I stand amid the roar
Of a surf-tormented shore,
And I hold within my hand
Grains of the golden sand—
How few! Yet how they creep
Through my fingers to the deep,
While I weep—while I weep!
O God! can I not grasp
Them with a tighter clasp?
O God! can I not save
One from the pitiless wave?
Is *all* that we see or seem
But a dream within a dream?

This poem recalls Emerson's mood in "Experience." It may be that in revising an earlier poem, "Imitation" (1827), for this poem published in 1847, Poe decided to imitate Emerson, who wrote: "I take this evanescence and lubricity of all objects, which lets them slip thorough our fingers then when we clutch hardest, to be the most unhandsome part of our condition. . . . Dream delivers us to dream, and there is no end to illusion."[14] In Poe's poem, as in Emerson's essay, the sand serves as a familiar metaphor for time—grain by grain slipping away, and the sea with "its pitiless waves" redoubles the temporal figure and seems an apt reminder of mortal life's inevitable impermanence.

Poe's poem belongs near the origin of a series of modern skeptical crisis poems set by the seaside that includes Whitman's "Out of the Cradle Endlessly Rocking" and "As I Ebb'd with the Ocean of Life," Matthew Arnold's "Dover Beach," Valéry's "Le cimetière marin," and Wallace Stevens's "The Idea of Order at Key West." Poe's lines, however flawed ("While I weep—while I weep," seems melodramatic, even mawkish even for Poe), like Emerson's majestic essay, rigorously focus on the realization of loss and on doubts about life's value and experience's possibility. Poe never says "Ah Love let us be true to one another" or "*Il faut tenter de vivre*," nor does he sing of an ordering will that transfigures the world, or a maternal voice that soothes the poet with a single whispered syllable, "death, death, death, death, death," suggesting time's relentless passage. Poe's poet stands on the edge of oblivion and clutches at the substantial world, which, grain by grain, instant by instant eludes him. His metaphors are apt expressions of meaning's evasiveness and the fugitive quality of experience itself, which can never be made quite clear and can be known only as it is lost along with the moment that contains it.

Poe often makes loss the single tenor of his comparisons. This creates odd effects that characterize many of his poems. The first "To Helen," is a poem, like "Ulalume" and "The Raven" strongly marked by that regression toward the primal incantatory power of poetry familiar to Poe's readers. But "To Helen" takes Petrarchan nostalgia as far it can go by making a metaphor of loss an element of each of the similes that frame the poem. The shortness of the piece enables a complete citation:

> Helen, thy beauty is to me
> > Like those Nicéan barks of yore,
> That gently, o'er a perfumed sea,
> > The weary, way-worn wanderer bore
> > To his own native shore.
>
> On desperate seas long wont to roam,
> > Thy hyacinth hair, thy classic face,
> Thy Naiad airs have brought me home
> > To the glory that was Greece,
> > And the grandeur that was Rome.
>
> Lo! In yon brilliant window-niche
> > How statue-like I see thee stand,
> The agate lamp within thy hand!
> > Ah, Psyche, from the regions which
> > Are Holy-Land!

In this poem, which Poe always claimed he wrote as a child, one recognizes the exaggerated sonorousness familiar to readers of "The Raven" and "Ulalume"—for instance, the repetition of short *o* and *r* and long *o* and *m* in the first two stanzas. But here he also creates something new, something like an inverted blazon. Shakespeare, like many others, had long ago parodied the blazon, the bit-by-bit comparison of the beloved's features to beauty in nature, as in Sonnet 130,

> My Mistress' eyes are nothing like the sun;
> Coral is far more red than her lips' red;
> If snow be white, why then her breasts are dun;
> If hairs be wires, black wires grow on her head.[15]

Poe does not play this sort of game with the conventions of "false compare." His elegant sounding similes and metaphors play a different part by substituting the concept of loss itself for the beloved's beautiful bodily attributes that the reader might expect the poem to describe.[16] Poe's Petrarchan poem does not reconstitute the beloved's beauty bit by bit as a substitute for her presence. Instead, it forces the reader to focus on the entirety of beauty's loss and on Helen's irreparable distance from presence in the present that the poem and its reader occupy.

The first stanza establishes a structure that frames the poem by leading the reader to expect a portrait of the beloved and then leaving the frame empty. The poet makes an elaborate simile, a trope of comparison, by announcing its tenor, linking it to a vehicle and then elaborating its implication in the stanza's final line. The pattern runs: tenor ("thy beauty"), vehicle (is like "Nicean barks of yore"), elaboration ("That gently, o'er a perfumed sea, / The weary, way-worn wanderer bore, / To his own native shore"). Unlike the traditional comparisons that Shakespeare mocked, the intent of which was to make vividly present to the imagination the sensuous splendors of the absent lover's person and beauty, the erotic tenor of the comparison, Poe's poem moves from the present tense of the tenor (Thy beauty is) to the distant pastness of the vehicle (like those Nicean barks of yore) and elaborates those enchantments that Helen's beauty serves to recall and, by recalling, ratifies. In effect, Poe reverses the conventional terms of Petrarchan comparison. That poem does not serve to represent Helen's beauty at all. Instead, it makes her beauty represent the poet's recollection of loss and the melancholy disenchantment that modernity entails. Helen's beauty may remind the poet of those bygone ancient conveyances, but it also makes his distance from them emphatic, foregrounding his nostalgia rather than carrying him back from his own way-worn wandering to anything like home. In the second stanza, when Helen's "Naiad airs" do bring him "home," they only return him to a home that is figured, once again, as loss, emphasized by Poe's repetition of the past tense in these lines ("The glory that was Greece / And the splendor that was Rome"). Thus, the poet makes Helen, although apparently present in the poet's apostrophe, haunt this poem as if she were irredeemably lost. She is. His tropes make her beauty figure loss. For this reason, whatever eroticism there is in "To Helen" seems like necrophilia. The final stanza, which shifts the sound pattern of its vowels toward brighter *i*, *e*, and *a* sounds, translates the living Helen into a lamp-bearing effigy. More stone than flesh, sharply shadowed and motionless, she stands "statue like" in the distant, brilliant window niche, finally removed altogether from this world of ceaseless change to the static world of the poet's imagination. Radiant herself, she holds a lantern, translucent and figured by patterned and colored infusions (Agate), a lamp that one imagines can cast only shadowy figurations suggestive again of loss—what else in the West may the figure of Holy Land evoke but the definitive lost object of endless crusades? This lamp will light no one's way home. Helen, like the other figures of Psyche in Poe, like "Ulalume" and "Ligeia," represents not simply the figuration of death as a definitive final resting place but more a recollection of loss, a provocation of nostalgia and an occasion for self-torment. These, for Poe, define the force of poetry in the modern world.

By way of contrast, consider the patterning of metaphor and death in one of Petrarch's best-known sonnets to Laura, in which the poet struggles to comprehend the death of the woman he has long loved but never possessed:

> Those eyes of which I spoke with such emotion,
> The arms and hands and feet and countenance
> That had estranged me from my very self
> And made me different from all other people,
>
> The curling locks of pure gold glimmering,
> The lightning flash of an angelic smile
> That used to turn the earth to paradise,
> Are bits of dust that can feel nothing now.
>
> And I still live, which makes me sad and angry,
> Left here without the light I loved so much,
> In a great storm, a ship that is dismantled.
>
> Let my love song finish right here and now;
> Dry is the vein of my habitual art,
> My lyre now has turned to playing tears.[17]

The metaphoric vehicles return the tenor of the lost, beloved Laura's body—angelic though corporeal before she dies—momentarily to presence in the poet's and his reader's imagination, even if only so that the acute pain of her loss can be experienced one more. To experience her loss again, the poet must momentarily restore her presence. This is the work of Petrarch's comparisons. He struggles in his poem to overcome beauty's loss, to mourn it and ultimately to transcend it and return to the path of Christian virtue from which his love of beauty had threatened to estrange him. Poe's poet, by contrast, seeks to dwell with loss as a chronic state of being. He desires neither a momentary restoration of presence nor a recovery of self-possession. In his poetry he remains resolutely incapable of imagining any other state of being. Where the Petrarchan poet bemoans the beauty that lit his "bark" on life's weary way, he also remembers that his peace was shattered even while Laura lived, shattered by his obsessive confusion of erotic obsession and spiritual devotion. Nonetheless, Petrarch retains the capacity and the hope for spiritual devotion and an end to his self-estrangement. Poe's poet imagines his women, like Helen, at a distance, standing statuelike and untouchable, disembodied even in life, beyond desire, emblems of his own chronic spiritual homesickness and immemorial self-exile, his unrelieved nostalgia for the unimaginable fullness of a final return to a "holy-land" become unfigurable in a secular age. It is that lost plenitude that the woman's absent beauty finally represents.

Secular Truths and More Dead Women

Poe's tales are often as lyrical as his verses. In "Ligeia" and "Berenice," for example, Poe refashions tropes of comparison into blazons of loss. The eponymous characters in both tales, like the dead women in "The Raven" or "Ulalume," become the "dread burden" of the poet's art. These women exist only to objectify the narrator's sense of loss and communicate that melancholy to the reader. There is no mourning work that aims to preserve the beloved's memory or recover her presence. In these tales, as in his poems, Poe solicits and affronts his culture's sentimental pieties concerning death and love. As Theresa Rizzo puts it, Poe "perverts and challenges the religious foundations for the cult of mourning."[18] In fact, he does more. He perverts and challenges the work of mourning itself. Rizzo correctly identifies a twisted "victory over death" in "Ligeia." But Poe's perversion of this fundamental trope of Christian consolation, the resurrection of the dead, does not only figure a translation of Ligeia's soul into Rowena's body, but it fixes on a far more difficult to imagine substitution not only of soul for soul but of body for body. This impossible resurrection through substitution undermines any naïve beliefs about identity's stability in life or survival after death that the reader might entertain. Ultimately, Poe leaves the field of mortality to the conqueror worm of uncertainty. This is all the melancholy truth this uncanny tale affords.

"Ligeia" begins, oddly enough, with the narrator's catalog of amnesia, a list of facts about Ligeia and their time together that have escaped him: "I cannot, for my soul, remember how, when, or even precisely where, I first became acquainted with the lady Ligeia." Time and suffering have rendered his memory "feeble." A certain indistinctness of recollection seems determined by their ever increasing intimacy as well: "the character of my beloved, her rare learning, her singular yet placid cast of beauty, and the thrilling and enthralling eloquence of her low musical language, made their way into my heart by paces so steadily and stealthily progressive that they have been unnoticed and unknown." In fact, the knowledge he possesses of Ligeia seems peculiarly limited. Only by the incantation of the "sweet word" that is her name can he summon an image of her: "Ligeia! Ligeia! . . . it is by the sweet word alone—by Ligeia—that I bring before my eyes in fancy the image of her who is no more." And still her name, which refers to and represents her, does not confirm a plenitude of intimate knowledge, but recalls to him yet more things he does not know and has never known: "And now, while I write, a recollection flashes upon me that I have *never known* the paternal name of her who was my friend and my betrothed, and who became the partner of my studies, and finally the wife of my bosom" (all quotations 262). What does it mean that Ligeia's name, repeated and written as a token of remembrance, replacing and representing her, ultimately reminds the narrator of what he does not know about her?

The narrator's memory finally does seem to take hold on Ligeia's "person" when he writes, "There is one dear topic, however, on which my memory fails me not. It is the *person* of Ligeia" (263). And yet, as he constructs a blazon celebrating her perfection, she seems less a singular person and more, properly speaking, something like a rhetorical commonplace, a collection of conventional topoi or metaphors cherished by amorous poets since Petrarch:

> I examined the contour of the lofty and pale forehead . . . the skin rivaling the purest ivory, the commanding extent and repose, the gentle prominence of the regions above the temples; and then the raven-black, the glossy, the luxuriant, and naturally-curling tresses, settling forth the force of the Homeric epithet, "hyacinthine!" I looked at the delicate outlines of the nose—and nowhere but in the graceful medallions of the Hebrews had I beheld a similar perfection. (263)

Like the women in so many sonnets, Ligeia appears sundered into discrete impressions of separate body parts in the narrator's recollection, granted wholeness only as a function of the narrator's discourse that fashions or binds the increasingly recherché vehicles that describe her hair and nose (Homeric epithets and Hebrew medallions) into the semblance of a person.[19] Ligeia embodies the artfulness and artificiality of the Petrarchan tradition. Poe makes his narrator's series of stylized comparisons manifest the author's erudition and refinement for his credulous readers. But in so doing he makes his narrator displace rather than recall the image of his beloved's person.

Then things turn serious. "And then," the narrator says, "I peered into the eyes of Ligeia" (264). This portentous announcement shifts the tone and tenor of the narrator's discourse. He approaches the secret of that strangeness that, he claims, characterizes all beauty and which his courtly comparisons cannot convey. The topics and topoi of comparison, the rhetorical and referential resources of language itself, appear inadequate to such a task:

> The "strangeness," however, which I found in the eyes was of a nature distinct from the formation, or the color, or the brilliancy of the features, and must, after all, be referred to the *expression*. Ah, word of no meaning! behind whose vast latitude of mere sound we entrench our ignorance of so much of the spiritual. (264)

The narrator, in turning to Ligeia's eyes ("for which," he says, "we have no models in the remotely antique") turns from meaning—the intricate intercalation of signifier and signified, vehicle and tenor—to a meaningless "vast latitude" of mere sound. In this world "expression," that which presence requires as the intention behind or the inflection of meaning in language, is, for the narrator, a word without meaning except that it denotes everything we do not know, everything we cannot say. And in fact, before those eyes, in the presence of his beloved's remembered "expression," he again experiences the failure of memory with which the story began:

> There is no point, among the many incomprehensible anomalies of the science of mind, more thrillingly exciting than the fact—never, I believe, noticed in the schools—that in our endeavors to recall to memory something long forgotten, we often find ourselves *upon the very verge* of remembrance, without being able, in the end, to remember. And thus how frequently, in my intense scrutiny of Ligeia's eyes, have I felt approaching the full knowledge of their expression—felt it approaching—yet not quite be mine—and so at length entirely depart! (264–265)

His failure to capture Ligeia's expression—the key to her spiritual presence, to her unique identity, and to the meaning of his relationship to her—even while she lived epitomizes the experience of "Ligeia." The narrator's new expression of his loss becomes "thrillingly exciting," not as a present reenactment of his one-time possession of her but as another expression of his failure to possess her person in person, to know her expression even in the past. In this strangely negative way, death has not changed Ligeia at all. The narrator fails to grasp her presence even when she lived. Face to face with the woman he describes as an "opium dream," he finds, in her eyes, only loss and absence, the hint of an "expression" that always just fails to materialize or to make itself known or recollected.

Like Poe's "The Man of the Crowd," the tale Baudelaire thought captured the character of the modern artist, "Ligeia" names a character and a story that finally cannot be read.[20] Her expression, which of course can refer to the form or intonation of a linguistic phrase as well as to the contours of a face and eyes, cannot at last be grasped. Ligeia's expression functions not as the determinant of meaning or the inflection of identity, but as another instance of the continuous displacements that comparison and language both entail. This may not be the secret of life, but it is, perhaps, the key to comparison (what Baudelaire called "Correspondances") in poetry:

> And (strange, oh, strangest mystery of all!) I found, in the commonest objects of the universe, a circle of analogies to that expression. I mean to say that, subsequently to the period when Ligeia's beauty passed into my spirit, there dwelling as in a shrine, I derived, from many existences in the material world, a sentiment such as I felt always around, within me, by her large and luminous orbs. Yet not the more could I define that sentiment, or analyze, or even steadily view it. I recognized it, let me repeat, sometimes in the survey of a rapidly growing vine—in the contemplation of a moth, a butterfly, a chrysalis, a stream of running water. I have felt it in the ocean—in the falling of a meteor. (265)

"Let me repeat" is the key phrase in this peculiarly Poesque blazon—where things in the material world recall the lover's inability to grasp his beloved's expression and not her sensuous presence. The catalog of objects in the material world (rampant vines, moths, streams of running water) are indeed strange vehicles to denote a beloved's beauty. The list also includes "one or two stars in heaven," especially one that is "double and changeable," sounds from stringed instruments, passages from books, and the tag from Joseph Glanvill, "And the will therein lieth, which dieth not" that furnishes the story's epigraph and which the narrator repeats at intervals as the tale unfolds. Like the narrator, the reader expects to find the mystery of the story explained in Ligeia's particular expression. But that mystery quickly involves the reader in the narrator's obsessive rhythms of repetition, recalling the disruptive force of poetry's metrical artifice.

In the tale's repetitions and substitutions, Poe already hints that in the contest between will and death that Ligeia announces, the latter will always win. Absence prevails within the very gesture of representation that aims to recuperate presence.

In his lament for the lost Ligeia, Poe's narrator reverses the most common direction of metaphorical comparisons—always possible since all equivalences are commutative for if $a = b$ then $b = a$—so that the vehicle recalls the tenor. It is not that Ligeia's eyes and expression recall a growing vine (and how strange a comparison that is) but that the growing vine recalls Ligeia. The world offers itself as matter for metaphors and as a mnemonic device or a memento mori. A vine, a moth, a stream, the ocean, a meteor are each equivalent to, can each equally serve to recall the inscrutable expression of the lost Ligeia's eyes and the meaning of her expression which never becomes clear. Each thing or phenomenon becomes the vehicle of a metaphor that provokes the narrator not to recall her eyes but to relive the confused sentiment her eyes provoked.

This universal correspondence serves more to instigate further suffering than to proffer spiritual consolation. Do these correspondences exist in the world or only in the narrator's willfully masochistic mind, by the ingenuity of which he finds infinitely varied ways to make the world bear the single burden of his pleasurable self-torture. The narrator's imagination is essentially, as Poe would have it, poetic. The question, "Who knoweth the mysteries of the will with its vigor" implies a further question: of whose will does the poet speak? Does his heightened perception register the correspondences of the world, or does his perverse imagination create comparisons by the vigor of his will? This is an old question. Poe inherits it from eighteenth-century metaphysics and more proximately from the romantics, especially Wordsworth, who wrote often of the difficulty of distinguishing between the actual world and what the senses half-create.[21]

Poe offers positive knowledge about nothing. His sensibility is more radically pessimistic and more materialist than Wordsworth's. For Poe, the poet's forging of correspondences hovers on the brink of hallucination and assumes the violent proportions of an obsessive drive to reveal the fragility of meaning as a human creation in a world that provides no stable foundations for significance. Poe's imagined world exists without immanent meaning or discoverable correspondences except those the feverish or disordered mind can project upon the abyss.

In "Ligeia," Poe renders the agonized beauty of loss palpable in the rhythmical repetitions of his plot and the structures of difference and identity in his comparisons. Lady Rowena, unhappy substitute for and repetition of the dead Ligeia, serves this poetic function. She substitutes for the lost Ligeia, but she corresponds to Ligeia only in ways that stress difference and contrast rather than identity and positive correlation. Ligeia was dark, Rowena is blond; Ligeia has no antecedents, Rowena has a family and a title; Ligeia inspired childlike devotion and mystical adoration, Rowena provokes in him "a hatred belonging more to demon than to man" (272). Poetry is full of instances where the reliance on metaphor in elegiac verses leads to contempt for the vehicle because it can never be adequate to the tenor of the lost object.[22] But Rowena's inadequacies themselves inspire memories of Ligeia by sheer force of contrast: "My memory flew back (oh, with what intensity of regret!) to Ligeia, the beloved, the august, the beautiful, the entombed" (272). Like the narrator of "The Raven," Ligeia's narrator comes to experience the reminder of his loss as an elevating occasion for an ecstasy of self-torture: "I reveled in recollections of her [Ligeia's] purity, of her wisdom, of her lofty—her ethereal nature, of her passionate, her idolatrous love," and of her entombment (272). Rowena, like the body of the world itself, has the misfortune to become the vehicle or the occasion for these sentiments, the object upon which the poet's will works its desire, the abject, living figure that reminds the narrator of death and of the dead beauty who has come to represent death for him.

Rowena fulfills her office brilliantly—or is brilliantly made to do so by the narrator's imperious will, by the "fierce moodiness of his temper" which, he reports, she quickly learns to dread (272). When the Lady Rowena, like Ligeia before her, falls ill, she seems sick with nothing so much as repetition itself. After her first bout of fever and of perturbed half-slumber, "She became at length convalescent—finally, well. Yet, but a brief period elapsed, ere a second more violent disorder again threw her upon a bed of suffering; and from this attack her frame, at all times feeble, never altogether recovered. Her illnesses were, after this epoch, of alarming character, and of more alarming recurrence" (272). The rhythm of collapse and revivification increases and she seems at last to die, again, of nothing but repetition itself. The haunting scenes of her corpse reviving at intervals during the narrator's opium tinctured vigil, and his reveries of Ligeia, whom, he remembers, as herself possessing "the radiance of an opium dream," intensify the story's repetitive rhythms: "But why shall I minutely detail the unspeakable horrors of that night? Why shall I pause to relate how, time after time, until near the period of the gray dawn, this hideous drama of revivification was repeated . . . and how each struggle was succeeded by I know not what of wild change in the personal appearance of the corpse?" (276). The last phrase is certainly odd because by the story's end the wild changes in the corpse's personal appearance will be the only thing revealed at the ultimate moment where repetition and identity finally for a moment seem simultaneously to correspond and diverge.

The progress of the corpse, in each repetition, seems to distance it from life and to bring it closer to the finality of death, to "a sterner and more irredeemable death," culminating, at last, in a "dissolution more appalling in its utter hopelessness than any" (276). The shrouded figure on the bed, for which reanimation and dissolution seem part of the same process, becomes at last in the narrator's account not Rowena, not even a corpse, but "the thing that was enshrouded" as it rises and advances "bodily and palpably into the middle of the apartment" (276).

This moment of revelation returns the story at its end to Petrarchan figuration, or to Poe's perversion of the logic of comparison or of metaphorical substitution as simultaneously the murder and perpetuation of its object. This moment reveals the essence of Poe's poetics. The grave clothes fall away from the thing's head and "there streamed forth into the rushing atmosphere of the chamber huge masses of long and disheveled hair; and *it was blacker than the raven wings of midnight.*" Like the blazoned figure in a sonnet, like the living Ligeia in the narrator's early description of her, the dead lady never becomes fully present in the story, she remains until the end not a person, not the person of Ligeia, but a catalog of a body's parts: height, hair, and eyes. We know the story does not end with a final conquest of death by the will for all its vigor, since at the tale's beginning, which comes after this narrated end, the narrator conjures with a word the "image of her who is no more" (654). What means then this "thing" that stands among so many other things in the narrator's bedroom at the story's end? What sort of revivification might this be? In a story that seems so much about the logic of metaphor, what does this suggest about poetry itself? The thing with dark eyes and black hair that stands in Ligeia's (or is it Rowena's?) place at "Ligeia's" end is only one more repetition, one more metaphoric relay, one more vehicle that conveys the tenor of loss without arriving at a meaning or redemption.

The Logic of Metaphor and the Perturbation of Reason

"Ligeia," as Colin Dayan has observed, is a story of identity as a struggle for space. That struggle occurs in a field defined by what one might call the logic of metaphor, remembering that metaphor is both a trope of sub-stitution and a violation of logic's fundamental axioms. At the end of "Ligeia," at the moment when Ligeia's body occupies the space where Ro-wena's body had been, Poe stages a scene that breaks the ontological law ("whatever is, is"), ignores the law of noncontradiction ("nothing can both be and not be"), and violates the law of the excluded middle, ("everything must either be or not be").[23] Without these axioms, Aristotle affirms, knowledge—indeed thought, is impossible. But at the beginning of "Eu-reka," in the letter dated 2848 from the *Mare Tenebrarum*, Poe makes the lesson of "Ligeia" clearer. In a thousand years, he writes, it will become apparent that these axioms must be suspended before true thinking can occur. Citing the work of one "Miller" (John Stuart Mill") on logic, Poe makes his narrator comment on the proposition "Contradictions cannot *both* be true, . . . a tree must be either a tree or *not* a tree" as follows:

> Very well:—and now let me ask him, *why*. To this little query there is but one response:—I defy any man living to invent a second. The sole answer is this:—'Because we find it *impossible to conceive* that a tree can be anything else than a tree or not a tree.' This, I repeat, is Mr. Mill's sole answer:—he will not *pretend* to suggest another:—and yet, by his own showing, his answer is clearly no answer at all; for has he not already required us to admit, *as an axiom*, that ability or inability to conceive is *in no case* to be taken as a criterion of axiomatic truth? (1268)

Metaphor, as Aristotle already knew, is the trope that straddles thought's contradictions—it can produce new knowledge through comparison and undo the grounding of knowledge in logic, sometimes simultaneously. Poe presses this (il)logic of metaphor to an extreme.

In its tendency to undo the axioms of identity—making something itself and not itself at the same time—metaphor stretches and even vio-lates logic's limits.[24] Metaphor reflects and depends upon the fundamen-tal structuring of the linguistic sign, its production of identity from a play of differences and its doubled composition of signifier and signi-fied.[25] Language, like metaphor, plays with the limits of noncontradic-tion. Therefore, to comprehend its modality requires a logic slightly at odds with Aristotle's analytics. Ligeia's hair can be human hair and a ra-ven's feathers at the same time. Ligeia can take over Rowena's mortal body without ceasing to be herself in a way conventional logic cannot explain. In a sense there is nothing unusual here. If metaphor tropes difference into identity and identity into difference, then so does language. Both metaphors and the linguistic sign make something seem itself by comparing it to something else and make two things occupy the same place in the same moment. Metaphor, of which Plato was a greater master than Aristotle, is thus, paradoxically, the most antiplatonic of tropes. It appeals to the senses and it contradicts reason, it focuses attention on the body and finally refers to nothing but the restless, mysterious movement of the imagination from object to object in the phenomenal world. It may, as Aristotle suggests, produce new knowledge, but it does so negatively, by way of momentary bafflement. Rowena becomes the occasion for Ligeia's return because the willfulness of the poet's imagination at work in the world dwells upon their differences to make them finally the same, struggling against the limitations of his own and his readers' commonsense sense of what reason can conceive. Ligeia herself, that thing composed of comparisons, of starry eyes and hair "blacker than the wings of midnight" (277), that reappear as the shroud unravels at the story's end, has never, in life as this story represents her, appeared as herself except through the artifice of such comparisons. From the first she appears as the occasion for those immemorial metaphorical transports—her beauty "the radiance of an opium dream," her hair "setting forth the full force of the Homeric epithet 'hyacinthine!'" (263)—with which the narrator loves to elevate his style. His readers can be counted on to find these figures as romantically fanciful as the idea of the "misty-winged *Astophet*" presiding over the narrator's marriage to his soul's partner (262). The opulence of these rhetorical ornaments enwraps Ligeia as effectively as the shroud that entombs her and out of whose folds she reemerges having at last taken Rowena's place.

The oft-noted oddness of this ending is that Ligeia does not return through metempsychosis—her consciousness does not enter into Rowena's body. She replaces Rowena's body and soul by means that are impossible to imagine but uncannily familiar at the same time. The scene has been enabled by the logic of physical substitution, the strange logic of metaphor that already pervades the story. Rowena has served in the narrator's imagination as the negative mnemonic device or inverted metaphorical vehicle for the absent Ligeia whose place she takes. The narrator's abjection of the blond who substitutes for and recalls, at least by contrast, his lost raven-haired lady, deepens rather than resolves his melancholy. When Ligeia, in the story's final turn, appears in Rowena's place, the difference between the tenor and the vehicle of comparison, the signified and the signifier of the sign, and the dynamics of presence and absence these entail collapses. Ligeia's replacement of Rowena (and, again, the equivalence of metaphor suggests that such commutations should always be possible) depends upon the possibility that something can be itself and not be itself at the same time. The sensible world momentarily shifts on the axes of identity and comparison. The limits of conceivability alter, for an instant, to make space for the poet's expression of will.

The story ends with the narrator shrieking his certainty:

> "Here then, at least," I shrieked aloud, "can I never be mistaken— these are the full, and the black, and the wild eyes—of my lost love— of the lady—of the LADY LIGEIA!" (277)

However certain the narrator may be, the reader remains in a state of perturbation. The narrator's tale remains, in every sense, incredible. Poe's story undermines the stability of identity and the reliability of both meaning and logic. It suggests that such instability and unreliability are simply parts of the mortal condition. Ligeia, from first to last, is less a beloved presence or a lost object than she is an identity that relies on difference and provokes comparison, an occasion for the expression of the drive to make metaphors and, through them, to displace reason's limits and to loosen logic's bounds, to make of melancholy and the abjection of self-torture a universal state.

Indentured Dentures in "Berenice"

There is something like a transformative grammar in Poe's relationship to the Petrarchan traditions of courtly comparisons that he modernizes in his tales and poems. Poe's originality, as he says in "The Philosophy of Composition," is not a question of newness or intuition but an effect of shifting familiar elements into new arrangements to create novel effects (1381). Poe develops a poetics of reversal—akin to the psychology of perversity he describes in the "Imp of the Perverse"—which invert the foundational axioms of rational individualism upon which Locke laid the ideological cornerstone of the liberal Enlightenment. For Poe, the fundamental instinct that structures subjectivity is not reason or self-preservation, but the "overwhelming tendency to do wrong for wrong's sake," especially when doing wrong violates all the laws of enlightened self-interest (827). It is no exaggeration to say that perversity, taken to its (il)logical extreme, reverses the philosophical foundations of the democratic state, which founds itself upon the citizen's rationality. Such a reversal is already implied in Poe's theory of poetry and in his artistic practice as well. He reverses the common expectations that attach both to devotional, elegiac, and erotic verse. Self-torture replaces resolution in faith, consolation, or self-possession. Comparisons do not describe or represent the beloved or the world but endlessly repeat the loss of both. The most important sign of the beloved's presence is the corpse she leaves behind that marks her absence and becomes the melancholy fixture of the poet's imagination. In a secular world, Poe's poetry suggests, there is no conventional consolation, neither faith nor meaning can be trusted and only melancholy moves or elevates the soul, even if its effects are sometimes terrible or terrifying to behold.

Consider "Berenice" as an illustration of Poe's theory and practice. From the tale's beginning, inversions shade the comparisons the narrator makes to describe Berenice, and her teeth, the bits of ivory that become his fixed idea. Here the pearly teeth of the sonneteer's tradition become something uncanny and truly horrifying. "Berenice" is a tale like "Ligeia" that explores the mortal—and potentially deadly—relationships between metaphorical correspondences, the will, and the world. It sheds a truly ghastly light on what one might call Poe's theory of perverse will and its relationship to the making of comparisons, the basis of his poesis.

The narrator of "Berenice" seems intimately related to the narrator of "Ligeia." He too recites a tale of a dead or dying lover. He invokes a series of "inversions" that in this narrative come to seem like corollaries to Poe's poetic theory. Even before the narrator announces that "a total inversion took place in the character of my thought" during his marriage to Berenice (226), he specifies various reversals that have characterized his life. Of his room, which, like Ligeia's chamber, contains and concentrates the story's action, he announces, "Here died my mother. Herein was I born" (225). This odd narrative sequence, in which his mother's death precedes his birth, has been foreshadowed by the story's first paragraph:

> Misery is manifold. The wretchedness of earth in multiform. Over-reaching the wide horizon as the rainbow, its hues are as various as the hues of that arch,—as distinct too, yet as intimately blended. Over-reaching the wide horizon as the rainbow! How is it that from beauty I have derived a type of unloveliness?—from the convenant of peace a simile of sorrow? But as, in ethics, evil is a consequence of good, so, in fact, out of joy is sorrow born. Either the memory of past bliss is the anguish of to-day, or the agonies which *are* have their origin in the ecstasies which *might have been.* (225)

The narrator wonders how his imagination can have discovered, in the emblem of a benevolent deity's covenant, not the token of a divine presence, lending a unifying meaning to the multifariousness of the visible world, but a figure, instead, for the multiform wretchedness and manifold misery that, for him, constitute human life. The narrator projects a new meaning on what was imagined to have been the creator's symbol. God's original will—an intention both structurally and temporally prior to the narrator's reinterpretation of the divine sign—is lost, like the mother who was lost before her child's birth, like real agonies that stand for imaginary joyful "might have beens." This narrator drifts in a unidimensional chaos, moving, at birth, from "the night of what seemed, but was not, nonentity, at once into the very regions of fairy-land," moving, that is, from one chamber of imagination to another. The "regions of fairy-land" do not transcend the world's multiform miseries—the imagined night of non-entity. Poe's fairyland seems continuous with the Godless material world where the narrator and death both dwell, and from which there is no escape (225–226).

The narrative focuses the reader's attention on death from the beginning. The epigraph, attributed to an Arab poet, Ebn Zaiat, but appearing in Latin, casts an ambiguous light over all that will follow: *Dicebant mihi sodales, si sepulchrum amicae, visitarem, curas meas aliquantulum fore levatas*: "My friends told me that if I visited my lover's tomb my cares might be a little lightened" (225). Does visiting the dead alleviate the angst of living or make the living less careful of it? Is lightening care the aim of or the antithesis to poetry? Does poetry teach the reader to care for himself and for the dead he has loved? Or does the poet's desire for the beautiful melancholy of poesis lead him to recklessly sacrifice his lovers? Is the projective power of the imagination, as it forges correspondences with loss in the world, restorative or destructive?

Like the narrator of "Ligeia" the narrator of "Berenice" seems obsessed with the resources of language, the projective power of poetic correspondences and comparisons as they work in and on the material world. In fact, the materiality of language becomes the basis of his monomania. He describes a fixation on sound that counterbalances his multiform sensible sufferings. The attentiveness and intensity of interest with which he characterizes his "disease"—the reader is meant to hear in these syllables the root meaning of dis-ease, for, as the narrator says, his ruminations "were *never* pleasurable," (228)—sometimes lead him "to repeat monotonously some common word, until the sound, by dint of repetition, ceased to convey any idea whatever to the mind" (227).[26] And this, in essence, is his illness—a disruption of the normal movement from the materiality of the signifier—its sound—to the abstract level of the signified—its meaning. He dwells on the phonetic body of a sign that loses its power to signify. Even his theological studies—Augustine's *City of God* and Tertullian's "The Flesh of Christ"—do not teach him the spiritual lesson of transcendence, but illustrate spirit's failure to realize the living word. He quotes a "paradoxical sentence" from Tertullian, which "occupies" his "undivided time, for many weeks of laborious and fruitless investigation" (228): "Dead is the son of God—absurd, and hence believable, and he arose from the dead—certainly, because impossible." Tertullian separates the evidence of the senses and the testimony of reason from the possibility of belief, separating meaning from the physical evidence of the world in a way that the narrator of "Berenice," as modern subject, never can.[27] His ruminations never arrive at a meaning for what he sees. In those reveries common to mankind, the narrator writes, the world vanishes before the bewildering and pleasurable multiplicity of possible meanings, deductions and suggestions that reverie produces, until the occasion of these musings is "entirely vanished and forgotten" (228). Thought here still seeks to move from the sensible toward the intelligible, away from the material and toward the spiritual, and in that movement the object, the material vehicle of thought's movement, becomes dispensable. But for the narrator this movement is reversed:

> In my case the primary object was *invariably frivolous*, although assuming, through the medium of my distempered vision, a refracted and unreal importance. Few deductions, if any, were made; and those few pertinaciously returning in upon the original object as a centre. The meditations were *never* pleasurable; and, at the termination of the reverie, the first cause, so far from being out of sight, had attained that supernaturally exaggerated interest which was the prevailing feature of the disease. In a word, the powers of mind more particularly exercised were, with me, as I have said before, the *attentive*, and are, with the day-dreamer, the *speculative*. (228)

The narrator of "Berenice" cannot realize the metaphoric potentials of language, the meanings that tropes of comparison might unlock or reveal. He is without the capacity to speculate and can only attend to a world where correspondences fail to appear, a world whose objects, finally, correspond to nothing.

The narrator, like the poet in "The Raven," remains wedded to a world of appearances, a world in which an involution of self-torture takes the place of meaning as the province and object of poetry.[28] Berenice's husband, like Ligeia's, understands personal identity in terms that invert the terms Locke established. Locke's philosophy, like Kant's, enjoined care for oneself and for others as the law of reason. A certain "carelessness" of such weighty matters comes to impel the narrator's actions.

> And although to a careless thinker, it might appear as a matter beyond doubt, that the alteration produced by her unhappy malady in the *moral* condition of Berenice would afford me many objects for the exercise of that intense and abnormal meditation whose nature I have been at some trouble to explain, yet such was not in any degree the case. . . . True to its own character, my disorder reveled in the less important but more startling changes wrought in the *physical* frame of Berenice—in the singular and most appalling distortion of her personal identity. (228–229)

The narrator's carelessness does not correspond to the carelessness of the reflecting reader who expects to apply a moral drawn from Berenice's progressive decrepitude. No meaning will be forthcoming. The narrator seems incapable of productive reflection. He reduces personal identity to the sheer physicality of the body and the truth of his character emerges in and changes with the changes decay wrecks on Berenice's physique. This is a sort of doomed and negative reflexivity, a sensation without any proper reflection at all

"The Berenice of a dream," imagined "not as a being of the earth, earthy, but as the abstraction of such a being," and to whom the narrator "in an evil moment" persuades to marry him, is an abstraction that cannot survive contact with the poet (229). The alterations of her physical frame, her inevitably changing earthly earthy being, are what fix the abstracted narrator's attention on the "idea," which is not, as a Platonist might have expected, something represented by her teeth so much as it is something with which, in the narrator's imagination, her teeth are identified. The "realities of the world" affect him as visions while the "wild ideas of the land of dreams become, in turn—not the material of my everyday existence—but in very deed that existence utterly and solely in itself" (226). In Berenice's teeth, the commonplace ideas of reality and dream change places and the difference between them collapses. The narrator's abstraction of Berenice performs an inversion that alters abstraction's Platonic sense. For him, "abstraction" is an action—an expression of his existence in the world—that foregrounds the material meaning of abstraction's root verb, "to abstract," to withdraw, remove, or pilfer. For the narrator, the metaphorical meaning buried in the word abstraction becomes horribly literal and physically real.

This is the terrible, pointless point of "Berenice." She becomes, for her lover, identified with her teeth and her teeth become ideas, a catachrestic synecdoche linked to a metaphor that finally has no correspondent meaning or tenor. If the teeth are ideas, they remain inexplicable, a point the narrator emphasizes by switching into French.

> Of mad'selle Sallé it has been well said, "*que tous ses pas etaient des sentiments*," and of Berenice I more seriously believed *que tous ses dents etaient des idées! Des idées!*—ah *therefore* it was that I coveted them so madly! I felt that their possession could alone ever restore me to peace, in giving me back to reason. (231)

Both the plurality of the metaphor's tenor "*Des idées!*" and his obsession with "the alteration in their nature," suggest that these ideas, for which the teeth become vehicles, differ from Plato's unique, intelligible, eternal abstractions. These ideas have no intelligible content at all.

Poe's narrator indulges, once again, in a bizarre and inverted Petrarchism. For the teeth are not an attribute of the beloved that might recall her—like Laura's inviting lips or illuminating eyes, or like the teeth figured as pearls in so many blazons. They are abstracted from and contrasted to Berenice's illness ravaged body. The boney substance of the teeth does not seem to alter with time, but only a madman would confuse them with ideas. They correspond not to the dying woman's essential identity or longed for presence, but to the narrator's mad desire to reimagine a more stable world: "Not a speck on their surface—not a shade on their enamel—not an indenture in their edges—but what that brief period of her smile had sufficed to brand upon my memory" (230). Beginning this sentence the reader feels comfortably expectant of a conventional blazon, celebrating Berenice's idealized incisors. But, the end of the sentence delivers a surprising reversal. Not the beauty of the lady, not the teeth as material signs of spiritual incorruptibility, but their minute physicality, their shaded material imperfections and abysmal cavities (for what does the indenture of dentures suggest but a cavity as a mise en abyme?) abstracts the narrator's attention. "I saw them *now* even more unequivocally than I beheld them *then*. The Teeth!—the teeth!—they were here, and there, and every where, and visibly and palpably before me; long, narrow, and excessively white, with the pale lips writhing around them" (230). The teeth, surrounded by her pale, writhing lips, become ubiquitous signs of an ineluctably material world: "In the multiplied objects of the external world I had no thoughts but for the teeth" (231). In the correspondence of teeth and ideas, the teeth represent a pure materiality that corresponds to no ideal of spirituality or transcendence at all.

With the fit of abstraction upon him, the narrator visits the prematurely entombed Beatrice's sepulcher and finds her "still breathing, still palpitating, *still alive!*" (232). He then carelessly annihilates her in a mad attempt to stabilize himself and the world by abstracting her teeth from her "disfigured" body (232). All of this leads nowhere except to the final vision of "thirty-two small, white, and ivory-looking substances that were scattered to and fro about the floor" of his study when he recovers consciousness later. In the final instance the teeth are neither teeth nor ideas, they are ivory-looking substances with no meaning or connection to anything.

By collapsing the usual hierarchies of signification, by evoking and perturbing the correspondences between materiality and meaning, Poe suggests that the commonplace desire for stable truths and unchanging identities may be a sort of madness. The secular world affords neither. Berenice's defilement literalizes the blazon's metaphorical dismemberment of the beloved's body. By doing so, Poe suggests the terrifying potentialities of a willful imagination let loose in a secular world where all beliefs and meanings become questionable. With his inversions and perversions of Petrarchan traditions of comparison, Poe makes the irreducible materiality of existence and the absence of transcendent significance in the world available for the abstraction and distraction of the reader.

The Heart of the Matter

Poe's sense of the power poetry can discover in the significant instabilities of a secular world finds one of its most evocative expressions, not in his verse or his tales, but in "Eureka: A Prose Poem." The generic identity of "Eureka" is difficult to specify, as Poe's subtitle indicates. In his preface, addressed "to those who feel rather than those who think," Poe calls his work a "Book of Truths" (1259). In "the Philosophy of Composition," as we have seen, he separated the province of poetry from the realm of prose, liberating poetry from the burden of truth. But in "Eureka," he collapses his earlier distinction and asserts that "it is as a Poem only that I wish this work be judged after I am dead" (1259). A book of truths can be a poem because by the end of "Eureka," the universe becomes the province of poetry, in fact it becomes in its material existence itself a poem.

The revelation of the universe's truth depends, as Poe's dedication suggests, on feeling rather than thought. He begins by asserting that neither induction nor deduction can lead to truth, that the logic based on Aristotle's analytics is all delusion, that "there is, in this world at least, *no such thing as* demonstration" (1261). To explore this point, Poe introduces an element both irrational and illogical. That letter from the year 2848, recovered in a corked bottle found floating in the *Mare Tenebrarum* or Sea of Shadows carries the first part of Poe's argument. Its author writes that it has been "scarcely more than eight or nine hundred years since the metaphysicians first consented to relieve the people of the singular fancy that there exists *but two practicable roads to Truth,*" the deductive and inductive methods (1271–1272). Having archly dispensed with prior and posterior analytics, denying that there are self-evident truths or demonstration in this world, the future philosopher dismisses all metaphysics to say that, "consistency," the product of ardent imagination and intuitive leaps, furnishes the only road along which human understanding may advance.

"Consistency," an appeal to the aesthetic imagination, and not logic with its groundless axioms, offers "the great thoroughfare—the majestic highway" to the truth (1269). The poetic nature of consistency becomes clear when the future sage lists the axioms that logicians held dear, and by holding dear long prevented humans from gaining insight into their world. The first axiom denies influence at a distance—"a thing cannot act where it is not" (1266). The second is the familiar principle of noncontradiction, "a tree must be either a tree or *not* a tree" (1267). Poe lampoons belief in both these axioms as failures of imagination and impediments on the way forward of understanding.

We have already considered in Poe's poetry how tropes of comparison often are the signs of something lost that nonetheless remains active in the imagination and the world. Metaphor suggests in its very structure of substitution and displacement something that acts when it is not present. On the thematic level, in the elegiac and Petrarchan traditions of lyric, the poet refers to an absent lover who continues to occupy him even and especially after she dies, by furnishing the tenor for his tropes. We have also seen that the answer to the riddle—when is a tree both a tree and not a tree—might be when it becomes part of a metaphor. Berenice's teeth, for her lover, are her teeth and ideas, themselves and something else at the same time, until they collapse into pure matter. Moreover, consistency is a virtue of poetry as well as prose. Consider the Aristotelian virtue of "appropriateness" that the philosopher claims distinguishes successful metaphors and other tropes of comparison. There is a principle of consistency that allows the melancholy poet to express nostalgia by comparing Helen's beauty to "Nicean barks of yore," though logic alone cannot capture it. Metaphors and similes can seem right, though they violate the principle of physical resemblance commonly believed to govern successful compar-isons by forging or finding new correspondences in the world.[29] It is largely the principle of consistency that makes Poe's long elaboration of the Nebular Hypothesis (a view of cosmic dynamics—of centripetal and centrifugal forces—with apparent similarities to the big bang theory) and the surprising conclusion and uncanny apocalypse with which he concludes "Eureka" feel like they make sense—however out of the ordinary that sense might be.

The great revelation of the cosmic order at the end of Poe's long inves-tigation of matter's tendencies to attract and repel itself, of centripetal con-densations and centrifugal dispersals, which are the motive forces of both the universe's beginning and its end, comes in the form of a metaphor the poet fashions. Poe compares the eternally recurrent rhythmic expansions and contractions of the cosmos to the beating of a great human heart. He first calls this the "heart divine," but he finally identifies the universe not with divinity but with the single human heart, the particular organ of pro-pulsive life and compulsive desire that is within each and turns each in-ward gazing subject outward to the objects of the world. The human or cosmic heart is ultimately as mechanical as the nebular hypothesis that sets the stage for its appearance. Despite his evocation of a final "unity," where "without Attraction and without Repulsion" the universe becomes "Matter without Matter—in other words *Matter no more*," there is no meaningful spirituality in this revelation of a singularity as the end of repetition as the universe lapses into ultimate (in)significance (1355). Poe's apocalypse leaves no self or matter and, in its light, nothing matters any more. But this ulti-mate moment is revealed in turn to be a medial moment in a rhythm of eternal recurrence in which self, matter, and mattering appear and dis-appear and reappear again and again. Poe calls the universe a "Material Nihility from which alone we can conceive it [the universe] to have been evoked—to have been *created* by the volition of God" (1355). But in actual-ity there is no place in a material nihility for god's volition or for any form of transcendent power or meaning. The pattern of eternal repetition that the nebular hypothesis describes determines the divine will as a recurring moment in its endless, periodic movement rather than as a singular point of origin expressing a more stable being existing on a different plane like a volitional and transcendent deity. Though the narrator intones, "Let us endeavor to comprehend that the final globe of globes will instantaneously disappear, and that God will remain all in all" (1355–1356), the God who remains is not Aristotle's unmoved mover or first principle, nor is he con-ventional Christianity's anthropomorphic agent. This imagined deity is immanent in the cosmos and manifest in the eternal recurrence. This God is therefore immanent within time and mortality, not an alternative to them. This deity forms part of the phenomenal world of generation and destruction, and of becoming and passing away. This is a God without transcendence.

At this moment, the prose poem's narrator introduces a truly terrifying perspective in which the law of laws is "periodicity," time itself, and all that time entails for mortal beings:

> On the Universal agglomeration and dissolution, we can readily conceive that a new and perhaps totally different series of conditions may ensue—another creation and radiation, returning into itself— another action and reaction of the Divine Will. Guiding our imaginations by that omniprevalent law of laws, the law of periodicity, are we not, indeed, more than justified in entertaining a belief—let us say, rather, in indulging a hope—that the processes we have ventured to contemplate will be renewed forever, and forever, and forever; a novel Universe swelling into existence, and then subsiding into nothingness, at every throb of the Heart Divine? (1356)

Poe's use of words like "new" and "novel" only intensifies the mechanical repetitiveness of the endless recurrences of actions and reactions that he imagines, and which determine that nothing novel or new can ever happen. It is the eternal recurrence as infernal machine that the final metaphor of a "Heart Divine," endlessly beating in and as space, suggests. This is not the savior's sacred heart of redeeming devotion, nor is this the heart of all conquering love, it is the heart of matter, a profane body part that beats on independently of will or consciousness, a tell-tale heart of physical laws whose burden is the inescapability of time and death, for a death that must periodically be repeated is not even a release from time. It may, in fact, be time itself. This, for Poe, is the heart of the matter. Poe's last words remove any hope of escape from the infernal machine, for at the highest level of abstraction the individual meets only, once again, an abstracted part of him or her self, the image of a suffering that begins and ends with our self-torturing selves and finds no place for or peace in any other presence: "And now—this Heart Divine—what is it? *It is our own*" (1356).[30]

What can it mean to say that the universe is—literally? metaphorically?— our own heart? That it is somehow the unification of our multiform, varied and perverse desires? In Poe's poetic imagination, the universe exists only as we produce it as an imaginative correspondent to our own desire.

This is as far from Hegelian optimism concerning the ultimate reunification of spirit and matter at the end of spirit's world-historical journey as it is possible to be.

For Poe, this is the painful and beautiful truth that lyric poetry can convey. He writes that "Our souls no longer rebel at a *Sorrow* which we ourselves have imposed upon ourselves, in furtherance of our own purposes—with a view—if even a futile view—to the extension of our own *Joy*" (1357). In secular lyric poetry we confront and accept our own perverse imaginations, the projections of metaphor, the pleasures of self-torment. This expansion of the imagination, not edification, becomes the proper province of poetry.

At the end of "Eureka," Poe produces a mad version of Emerson's Orphic vision at the end of *Nature*. Emerson dissolved "the sordor and filths of nature" into a vision of the original "Man" out of whose consciousness "sprang the sun and moon" and whose force the reader can recover if he can conform his life to his own pure idea.[31] In Poe's vision, the universe conforms itself to us. It repeatedly reapproaches a final collapse into unity and death—a final, surcease of sorrow—but then it begins again. Even in this moment "Eureka" produces a vision of multiplicity, a non-Orphic imagining of something like "memories that haunt us in our Youth" and that "now and then speak to us with low voices, saying, "There was an epoch in the Night of Time, when a still existent Being existed—one of an absolutely infinite number of similar Beings that people the absolutely infinite domains of the absolutely infinite space" (1358).

There really is no singularity in the infinite regressions that populate Poe's image of infinite space with infinite numbers of similar Beings, a sort of mass of beings that suggests in itself the monotony of infinite repetition or eternal recurrence as well as a diversification of being into the incalculability of the crowd. This image of the absolute remains distant from any figuration of transcendence or univocal unification imaginable. It is an image of the absolute that is indistinguishable from the mass audience, the crowd of infinite numbers of similar but distinct selves that the modern poet confronts.

The universe, figured as the time-bound, "still existent" (perhaps one day existent no more?), infinite being's bodying forth of human joys, sorrows, and desires to an infinite number of similar but distinct infinite beings, discovers the cosmos as a metaphor for poetic self-projection and the crowd upon which it relies, or it willfully refashions the universe in its material existence into a metaphorical self-projection of the modern poet on a cosmic scale which is nonetheless without transcendence. There seems to be no way to tell a discovered correspondence from a willful refashioning, just as there is no way to distinguish the creator from the creation. This "infinity of imperfect pleasures—the partial and pain-intertangled pleasures of those inconceivably numerous things which you designate as his creatures," are, in fact, the heart divine itself, are "really but infinite individualizations of Himself" (1358). Each of these creatures, capable of pleasure and pain but only according to the dictates of a sort of thermodynamic law of emotional energy determining that "*the general sum of their sensations is precisely the amount of Happiness which appertains by right to the Divine Being when concentrated within Himself*," forms part of the divine being (1358). None of these manifestations of universal desire could build a world or become, however self-concentrated they might be, self-possessed or stable identities. Their highest consciousness comes not with an awareness of transcendence but with the sense that they themselves are composed of two forms of being in one place, something that makes each of them a logical contradiction and something akin to a metaphor: "conscious, first, of a proper identity; conscious, secondly, and by faint indeterminate glimpses, of an identity with the Divine Being of whom we speak—of identity with God" (1358). Each individual becomes a metaphor for this strangely nonsingular, non-self-identical divinity. This is not the God who introduced himself to Moses as the being of pure and eternal self-identity ("And God said unto Moses, I AM THAT I AM" Exodus 3:14). This deity is another absent presence diffused throughout creation as the great law Poe pronounces at the beginning of this prose poem, "*In the Original Unity of the First Thing lies the Secondary Cause of All Things, with the Germ of their Inevitable Annihilation*" (1261). This is a unity that is already a multiplicity, a corresponding god or law of the crowd, something Poe's poet refers to and embodies at the same time. What is left is a world that can only endlessly refigure the temporal rhythms of language and desire, the rhythmic schemes of a poetry of loss, a poesis that draws on and collapses, again and again, the mechanisms of comparison, the hierarchies of matter and spirit, and the structures of signification on which meaning depends. In the final analysis, this is a secular deity, a deity that may be an allegory for the secular crowd. That secular crowd is at the heart of Poe's curiously antique and strangely modern materialistic vision of the universe and of art. This is a god comprised of a mass of beings without omniscience, omnipotence, or transcendence, manifest in a cosmos as close to meaninglessness as one can get without falling into madness or the abyss. This is a poetry of truths, whose only edification is not to edify, in any conventional sense, at all. Poe's poetry exists to endlessly reform and repeat the passionate heart that produces it and its world for the poet and his readers.

The Power of Words

Consider, at last, the little read but lovely and haunting tale of desire, repetition, and poetry that Poe called, "The Power of Words."[32] In the story, Agathos welcomes a fledgling angel to the afterlife by explaining that omniscience forms no part of it. When Oinos says "in this existence, I dreamed that I should be at once cognizant of all things, and thus at once happy in being cognizant of all," Agathos imparts a morsel of other-worldly wisdom: "Ah, not in knowledge is happiness, but in the acquisition of knowledge! . . . But to know all were the curse of the fiend." Even, he explains, The Most High, because he is The Most Happy, must dwell in ignorance and remain doubtful of where to draw the line between the sensible and the senseless. In the afterlife, as in life itself, existence corresponds to desire and desire is a demand that cannot be met without loss of life. Life, for angels and mortals, constitutes itself around an absence that cannot be filled. This is life's agony and its joy. It is also the basis of creation, a creation *ex nihilo* that carries nothing within itself, a power that is available not only to the deity at the origin of the universe but is, in principle, the power of all spirits and speakers, a manifestation of the power of imagination, the energy of articulation, and the force of poetry "since the first word spoke into existence the first law." This, Agathos says, is "the *only* species of creation which has ever been"(823). The spirit knows that language cannot be reduced to meaning or made an instrument of representation. Language is a material impulse, a quantity of "energia" operating in the ether and on the world. The power of words speaks the universe into existence, creates things and makes them happen. Agathos describes a cosmos in which the correspondences of figurative language create relationships that endlessly circulate and endlessly commemorate loss. They can be traced, by analytical retrogradation, back to an originary pulse or movement, a word in the beginning, which, ultimately, Agathos demonstrates, like the heart divine in "Eureka," is our own. For "the source of all motion is thought—and the source of all thought is—" and Oinos finishes Agathos's sentence, "God." This actually seems the wrong answer. Agathos begins to explain, in response to Oinos's hasty introjection of God, something about "the *physical power of words*," when Oinos introduces another question which leads to the story's final answer and opens upon an infinitude of passionate, painful, pleasure:

> *Oinos.*—But why, Agathos, do you weep?—and why—oh why do your
> wings droop as we hover above this fair star—which is the greenest
> and yet most terrible of all we have encountered in our flight? Its
> brilliant flowers look like a fairy dream—but its fierce volcanoes like
> the passions of a turbulent heart. (825)

This might well be called Planet Petrarch, for it is the world of Petrarchan
figuration as Poe reimagines it. These comparisons memorialize not the
person of a lost beloved the poet might dream of recovering by representation, but the human heart's unfulfillable desires, the abandoned and
nearly forgotten figures of Agathos's passionate longing and poetry. "They
are! They *are!*" Agathos replies. "This wild star—it is now three centuries since with clasped hands, and with streaming eyes, at the feet of my
beloved—I spoke it—with a few passionate sentences—into birth." But his
repeated assertion of positive identity, "They *are!* They *are!*" only points
to the complexity of what the planet's landscape represents. These materialized metaphors are figures for desire that remove their tenor from
simple presence in the material world. These flowers and volcanoes become
vehicles of comparison in a world constituted by correspondence, the signifiers of life identified with unrequitable desire. Agathos continues, "Its
brilliant flowers *are* the dearest of all unfulfilled dreams, and its raging
volcanoes *are* the passions of the most turbulent and unhallowed of hearts"
(825). In the spirit world as in this, the poet revivifies abandoned metaphors
and nearly dead figures of speech, purifying the language of the tribe and
offering it to the reader as a vehicle for self-torture and pleasure. The death
of a beautiful woman turns out to be the most poetic topic because with it
unrequitable desire is born. The poet commits poetry to loss itself. He
turns his tropes to the reproduction of those painful absences that are, paradoxically, the basis of the only beauty and joy on which secular humans
can count. Death becomes the grounds for all. Death—the definition and
limit of life's sensible pleasures and pains—turns out, for Poe, to be the
tenor toward which his metaphors move. As in "Eureka" and "The Power
of Words," the common metaphor for mortality and passion, the suffering, beating heart of poetic creation itself, turns out to be what drives creation as the pulse of life whose systole bespeaks not transcendence but
mortal limitation and whose diastole expresses pain. For Poe, as for Whitman who learned much from him, "to die is different from what anyone
supposed, and luckier." And for Poe as for Whitman, death takes many
forms as it permeates the poet's life with the meaning of his many pains
and the occasions for whatever joy and beauty he can draw from them.

Love and Death in a Crowded World

Consider, by way of conclusion, Poe's second and lesser-known poem entitled "To Helen." This may be his most Petrarchan and his most modern work. It looks forward to Baudelaire's famous invocation of fugitive desire in an urban setting, "A Une Passante" (To a Woman Passing By). Poe begins invoking the tradition—with nods to Laura and Beatrice—by declaring the poet's love for a woman he has seen only once, years ago, among some roses in a moonlit garden:

> I saw thee once—once only—years ago:
> I must not say *how* many—but *not* many.
> It was a July midnight; and from out
> A full-orbed moon, that, like thine own soul, soaring,
> Sought a precipitate pathway up through heaven,
> There fell a silvery-silken veil of light,
> With quietude, and sultriness, and slumber,
> Upon the upturn'd faces of a thousand
> Roses that grew in an enchanted garden,
> Where no wind dared to stir, unless on tiptoe—(95)

Though the poet speaks of preternatural stillness, everything in the poem moves. The moon, the roses, and the woman—each a metaphoric equivalent of the others—seem both themselves and representatives of the poet's yearning. This poem is not explicitly about death, but one senses death's presence throughout. The "silvery-silken veil" of the moon's light, suggests both the orientalist opulence Poe so loved to evoke and the poet's nostalgia for lost secret pleasures. These, it seems, are memories of mere possibility, in a sense, memories of nothing at all, since he never knows this woman. The moon's light falls not only upon the face of the woman (for whose soul, in an equivocal image, the moon's light becomes a comparison) but also on the roses, "That gave out, in return for the love-light,/Their odorous souls in an ecstatic death." In an odd reversal, the sort of perversion of poetic tradition that Poe's sensitive readers will recognize, the woman appears mysteriously veiled like and by the moon that illuminates this scene with its changeable light; and the poet appears like the thousand roses who expire in an ecstasy of fragrant breath. These flowers stand as images for the woman and as images for Poe's poetry itself. To emphasize this point, the poem repeats the figure of the moonlight in lines that describe how it, "Fell on the upturn'd faces of these roses/That smiled and died in this parterre, enchanted / By thee, and by the poetry of thy presence."

As in "Ulalume," one might suspect that Poe here sacrifices sense to sound. How else to parse the lines that figure the moon, and the woman's soul, soaring and seeking "a precipitate pathway up through heaven." For certainly the direction of the motion here seems all in the wrong direction. The woman is still but the light moves earthward toward her face and the garden. This falling light suggests a fall from grace or a descent from heaven and not a pathway up toward both. But upon reflection, the tension created between the soul that desires to soar and the precipitate pathway downward that the universe offers seems perfectly apt. In this poem, it remains unclear whether this nocturnal vision leads the poet to refinements of spiritual imagination or tempts him to profane desires, a problem that Petrarch so frequently explored. The woman herself, as she receives greater detail in the poem's second section, appears not as a harbinger of tranquility or transcendence but as a figure, an odalisque, confined to the earth and constrained to suffer:

Clad all in white, upon a violet bank
I saw thee half reclining; while the moon
Fell on the upturn'd faces of the roses,
And on thine own, upturn'd—alas, in sorrow!

The poet's "Fate, (whose name is also Sorrow,)" brings him to the garden gate, makes him pause "To breathe the incense of those slumbering roses," and brings him face to face alone ("the hated world all slept / Save only thee and me") with the woman he addresses—though only in his verses ("Oh, Heaven!—oh, God! / How my heart beats in coupling those two words"), a woman whose sorrowing face and luminous eyes extinguishes and transforms, displaces and represents, for a moment, that world he says he hates:

The pearly luster of the moon went out:
The mossy banks and the meandering paths,
The happy flowers and the repining trees,
Were seen no more: the very roses' odors
Died in the arms of the adoring airs.
All—all expired save thee—save less than thou:
Save only the divine light in thine eyes—
Save but the soul in thine uplifted eyes.
I saw but them—they were the world to me. (96)

And those eyes, with their burden of sorrow and the light of an impossible possibility, become the originating pulse, the twinned impetus, for the poet's vocation: "What wild heart-histories seemed to lie enwritten / Upon those crystalline, celestial spheres! / How dark a wo! Yet how sublime a hope! . . . How daring an ambition! Yet how deep— / How fathomless a capacity for love!" As in "Eureka," the capacity for love and the capacity for imperfect pleasures, for pleasures "intertangled with pain" seem identical, this pleasurable pain becomes the poet's burden. He commits himself to the transcription and repetition of those wild heart-histories written on this woman's heart, as he imagines it, and on his own. Those eyes, whose lunar luminousness veils and reveals the world, become his world, his salvation and his precipitate hell: "They follow me—they lead me through the years. / They are my ministers—yet I their slave." Poe ends by evoking both a hope for deliverance through beauty and a commitment to the goddess most intimately linked with love:

> Their office is to illumine and enkindle—
> My duty, *to be saved* by their bright light,
> And purified in their electric fire,
> And sanctified in their elysian fire.
> They fill my soul with beauty (which is Hope,)
> And are far up in Heaven—the stars I kneel to
> In the sad, silent watches of my night;
> While even in the meridian glare of day
> I see them still—two sweetly scintillant
> Venuses, unextinguished by the sun! (96–97)

This poet's heaven is distant from both Platonic perfection and Christian hope. It is the secular realm of the modern, the crowded world of anonymous encounters whose mysteries he probes here and in his poetry and tales. Her venereal eyes illuminate the world of correspondences that double and displace, that constitute and reconstitute the world in language and the self in the world, the world of coming into being and passing away that no single point of illumination or singular vision can read or stabilize. These doubled eyes shed light on the crowded world of time and of loss that they momentarily hold at bay. The poet carries his confused longing back to that secular world, a longing he, like Petrarch, discovered in the figure of a woman touched by mortality and by the moon light, among the roses that bear the scent of poetry and death. With these quaint, completely traditional, even clichéd materials and devices, Poe seduces and baffles his readers and constructs a lyric origin for modernity.

PART II

Walt Whitman

CHAPTER 3

Whitman's Poetics and Death:
The Poet, Metonymy, and the Crowd

... where and how does lyric address meet cultural transmission?

—MAX CAVITCH, *American Elegy*

Death is not an event in life: we do not live to experience death. If we
take eternity to mean not infinite temporal duration but timelessness,
then eternal life belongs to those who live in the present. Our life has
no end in the way in which our visual field has no limits.

—LUDWIG WITTGENSTEIN, *Tractatus* 4311

Poe's Man of the Crowd was, as Baudelaire recognized, the type of the
modern artist in an urban environment. While the crowd in Whitman
seems less a figure of the contemporary marketplace and more a figuration of the poet's future, it is Whitman, in the poetry he published between 1855 and 1860, who seems most fully to become the man of the
crowd. He attempts to incorporate the crowd in his own poetic persona.
"I am large," the outsetting bard wrote in 1855, "I contain multitudes."[1]
Whitman did not seek to explain himself or the crowd or to make either
make sense: "Do I contradict myself? / Very well then . . . I contradict myself" (87). Instead, he created and sustained a lyric "I" that celebrated the
crowded modern condition and embraced its ultimate illegibility (the Man
of the Crowd *"lässt sich nicht lesen,"* does not allow himself to be read, as
Poe's narrator discovers). The Petrarchan longing for transcendence
through love that Poe translated into perpetual melancholy in the service
of a profane conception of beauty becomes, in Whitman, an insistence on
the voicing of "sexes and lusts" largely for their own sake. "I believe," he
writes, "in the flesh and the appetites" (51). Roland Greene identifies "Song
of Myself," from which these lines are taken, as a post-Petrarchan lyric

sequence.[2] Whitman, as much as Poe, reinvents the blazon, but he replaces the traditional brow, eyes, lips, teeth, and even the perfumed breath of the beloved with parts of the body and odors not usually referenced in romantic poetry. "The scent of these armpits," he declares, "is aroma finer than prayer" (50–51). Notoriously, Whitman tends to celebrate not his lover's body, but his own. This poet longs for no Laura and mourns not for Lenore. He dwells instead with the erotic thrill of reimagining himself, Walter, as "Walt Whitman, an American, one of the roughs, a kosmos, / Disorderly fleshy and sensual . . . eating drinking and breeding, / No sentimentalist . . . no stander above men and women or apart from them . . . no more modest than immodest" (50). There is little evidence that Whitman knew Baudelaire's *Fleurs du mal* (1857) (and even less that Baudelaire knew his American counterpart's work), but in 1865 Walt Whitman published a poem that echoes the eroticism of Baudelaire's great sonnet of a fleeting encounter on a crowded city street, "A Une Passante" ("To a Passing Woman"):

> Out of the rolling ocean the crowd came a drop gently to me,
> Whispering *I love you, before long I die,*
> *I have travel'd a long way merely to look on you to touch you,*
> *For I could not die till I once look'd on you,*
> *For I fear'd I might afterward lose you.*

> Now we have met, we have look'd, we are safe,
> Return in peace to the ocean my love,
> I too am part of that ocean my love, we are not so much separated,
> Behold the great rondure, the cohesion of all, how perfect! (263)[3]

Whitman, confronted with the modern crowd, gestures toward a transvaluation of erotic longing, a rejection of absence, and a refusal to mourn. Without the confrontation with a longed for and soon lost object, without desire, death, absence, and melancholy, the lyric poetry of Sappho, of Petrarch, Dante, or Poe would have lacked its raison d'être. Whitman's poetic language experiment in his early editions of *Leaves of Grass* modernizes and secularizes this long tradition of poetic self-expression and brings the lyric face to face with—or, more precisely, makes the lyric "I" internalize—the heterogeneities of the modern crowd as an object the poet might imagine himself possessed by and possessing. When he wrote, "I am large, I contain multitudes," he meant the reader to absorb this image of a self penetrated and inhabited by the masses, and giving those masses form. Again and again he explores the implications of the multitudes for lyric poetry in a secular age in which transcendence can no longer be assumed to exist as an end for poetry or art. "And I call to mankind," he writes in 1855, "Be not curious about God./For I who am curious about each am not curious about God,/No array of terms can say how much I am at peace about God and about death./I hear and behold God in every object, yet I understand God not in the least" (85). Instead he offers poems that turn from pursuing God to exploring "A word of reality . . . materialism first and last imbueing" (49).[4]

Yet Whitman also knew that death is a reality that poses particular challenges for secular poetry and for the modern imagination. Like the concept of God to which it is so closely linked, it strains human conceptual capacities. Inevitable and ubiquitous, death remains difficult to imagine without redemptive recourse to transcendental fables or Christian eschatologies that are difficult to credit in a secular age. "Have you guessed you yourself would not continue? Have you dreaded those earth-beetles?/Have you feared the future would be nothing to you?" In the poem that would eventually become "To Think of Time," Whitman seems to taunt his reader and himself with the inevitability of extinction. How can death be comprehended as a reality without despair? How can the poet, the outsetting bard of the material world, manage "To think the thought of death merged in the thought of materials," as Whitman came to express the problem in lines he added to this poem as he neared the end of his life ("To Think of Time" 552). Death and materialism, first and last imbuing in his poetry, comes to center Whitman's modern assumption of the lyric tradition and the modern crowd that had come to define poetry's context.

Death, Metonymy, and Translation

At times, especially in the poems he wrote before the Civil War, Whitman wrote as if death might be denied, as if it simply did not exist. Often he wrote as if death were not much worth worrying about. Max Cavitch, noting how little like mourning poetry Whitman's pre–Civil War verse is ("I keep no account with lamentations;/What have I to do with lamentation?" the poet asks in 1855) identifies in Whitman's early poetry "the intelligible workings of a universal temporality of becoming, in which death amounts to nothing. . . . Relax, Whitman says, time is a conservateur, not a thief."[5] Or, as the poet says, "All goes onward and outward . . . and nothing collapses,/And to die is different from what any one supposed, and luckier" (32). A poet can say that, but can the poet make that sentiment imbue his poetry? Cavitch identifies the conjunction of lyrical address with cultural transmission in Whitman's poetry, the bridging of the past, the present, and most important, the future in the poem's texture, and links that texture in turn with the poet's transvaluation of mortality from an occasion for lament to a pretext for celebration. Imagining a future for his words is one way the poet tries to make the bitter hug of mortality sensuous and sweet, but without beliefs that transcend material existence the continuation of the poet through the masses of his readers becomes itself as complex and difficult to figure as death. Whitman creates some of his most uncanny, transformative confrontations with language and his readers as he tries to imagine a future that would not be simply nothing.

The first long, dynamic exploration of death in Whitman's poetry occurs in the 1855 edition at the moment, in what will become "Song of Myself," when a child brings handfuls of grass to the poet and asks what the grass means. Harold Aspiz, writing on Whitman's "poetry of death," remarks that here "The persona [of the poem] first attempts to explain the meaning of death." He also observes that something sets this section apart from the rest of the poem, for it possesses a "distinctively naïve and wistful tone [that] may indicate that it was written as an independent piece then fitted in the poem's larger structure."[6] The poem does seem to pause here, but not so much to consider death's meaning as to take stock of how poetry's figurative possibilities can proliferate when the poet is unconcerned with arriving at a final meaning.

"What is the grass?" a child asks, and the poet responds with an array of metaphorical variations that continuously alter the tenor of the possible answers:

> How could I answer the child? . . . I do not know what it is any more
>   than he.
>
> I guess it must be the flag of my disposition, out of hopeful green stuff
>   woven.
> Or I guess it is the handkerchief of the Lord,
> A scented gift and remembrancer designedly dropt,
> Bearing the owner's name someway in the corners, that we may see and
>   remark, and say *Whose?*
>
> Or I guess the grass is itself a child . . . the produced babe of the
>   vegetation.
>
> Or I guess it is a uniform hieroglyphic,
> And it means, Sprouting alike in broad zones and narrow zones,
> Growing among black folks as among white,

Kanuck, Tuckahoe, Congressman, Cuff, I give them the same, I receive
them the same. (31)

Aspiz, having noted that little else in "Song of Myself" resembles the figurative wit of these lines, ignores the implication of this point by making
this part stand in for the whole poem: "In response to the child's challenge
to explain the meaning of the grass, the poet resorts to metaphor—a
rhetorical strategy that he follows throughout the poem in attempting to
interpret the meaning of death. The grass is itself a master metaphor, of
course, and as is the case with metaphors, it is defined by employing other
metaphors" (37). In fact, it is the recourse to metaphor and to these multiple attempts at definition that makes these lines seem part of a different
poem, or of a poem by a different poet.

Despite the proliferation of suggested metaphors between the leaves of
grass in the book's title and the poems that appear on the leaves of the book
(see, for example, "Scented Herbage of My Breast" which resumes this master trope), neither definition nor comparison—traditionally provinces of
metaphor—is a characteristic rhetorical strategy for Whitman. Compared
to Poe's romantic retooling of Petrarchan comparison ("How statue like I
see thee stand") or Dickinson's frequent play at definitions ("Hope is that
thing with feathers"), Whitman seldom concerns himself to define anything and even less frequently uses metaphors to furnish death or anything
else with apparent meanings. In this sense, these playful lines from "Song
of Myself" do typify the poem. In them, Whitman lists comparisons more
to explore metaphor's limits than to display the trope's sovereign power to
interpret or define the world. "I guess," repeated this frequently, undoes
the claim to knowledge implied by metaphor's linking of identity and
difference, definition and comparison. The grass, as Whitman figures it
here, does not become ultimately knowable in a flash of poetic intuition
or cognitive insight. Readers do not receive, nor does Whitman expect them
to receive, what Aristotle would have called new knowledge through
these surprising analogies. Their whimsical proliferation underlines that
point. The poet's inconclusive catalog of metaphors names the hanky, the
flag, and the hair of graves as tenors of the grass in a way that leaves the
meaning and nature of the grass undecided.

Metaphor as a vehicle of knowledge depends upon a flash of insight into
aspects of identities that cut across apparent differences. When successful, metaphors can possess a sort of self-evidence that transforms the world
of objects, for a moment, into what Baudelaire called, in "Correspondences," a forest of symbols.[7] By contrast, Whitman's shifting metaphors

and quizzical disavowals of certainty leave the material world and its differences intact: "How could I answer the child?" the poet asks, "I do not
know what it is any more than he." There is nothing coy about this statement. The grass may be a uniform hieroglyph, but who can say what its
meaning might be? Who can "translate" it? "I wish I could translate," the
poet says near the section's end, but that wish, in this section of the poem,
remains unfulfilled. Whitman's play with metaphors here seems less the
declaration of a seer than the statement of a poet in whose mortal vision
grass, in the final analysis, remains, literally, grass. By holding to the limits of that vision, by adhering to the material appearances of the world and
of life, especially when he writes of death, Whitman generates his unique
poetic power and makes his special contribution to the modernization of
lyric poetry.

I am suggesting that the key to Whitman's poetry and its implication
for lyric modernity lies not in its renewal of language's power to make the
world and death mean (to put, as Emerson says, "eyes and tongue, into
every dumb and inanimate object"), but in his realization that however the
poet may use them, the objects and people of the world remain "dumb,
beautiful ministers" that, mysteriously enough, furnish "their parts toward
the soul," though "We fathom [them] not . . ." ("Crossing Brooklyn
Ferry" 313).[8] Whitman does not find in the world, nor is he seeking, the
"picture-language" that Emerson hoped the true poet would discover
and which, he also hoped, would enable the realization of the material
world as a meaningful symbol for spirit ("The Poet" 452). Rather, at
moments like the moment of death's first major appearance in "Song of
Myself," Whitman happily explores the separation of language and the
world language represents from any single or determinate meaning at
all. This is the work Whitman makes his proliferations of metaphors in
this passage from "Song of Myself" do. What emerges in the poet's response to the child is not, at last, a metaphor, but a list of metaphors, a
conversion of the metaphorical into another version of metonymy,
which, as many critics have noted, is Whitman's characteristic trope.[9]
This is poetry that delivers no ultimate wisdom about death or life
except the repeated, ancient, pagan wisdom—as old as Gilgamesh—that
no mortal should expect to know such things or worry over much about
them.

Finally, in the lines that will eventually form section 6 of "Song of Myself," the metonymic linkages and not any metaphoric revelation finally
convey the reader and the poet toward a confrontation with death.

And now it seems to me the beautiful uncut hair of graves.

Tenderly will I use you curling grass,
It may be that you transpire from the breasts of young men,
It may be if I had known them I would have loved them,
It may be you are from old people, and from women, or from offspring
  taken soon out of their mother's laps,
And here you are the mother's laps. (31)

After the metaphor that compares grass on graves to uncut hair, these lines move by association, approaching closer and closer to sheer contiguity in their structure. That the grass "transpires" from the breasts of young men seems more literal than figurative—a prefiguring of the corpse that will be "good manure" by the poem's end (86)—and it becomes the mothers' laps not so much through metaphoric transformation but by the fact of pure proximity. It becomes the mothers' laps because the dead young men suggest maternal grief and because that is where young men conventionally lay their grieving heads. As if to underline its roots in accidents of association, the poem returns to the comparison between grass and hair with which it started only to explore the comparison's inadequacies and to put in play a new chain of associative possibilities:

This grass is very dark to be from the white heads of old mothers,
Darker than the colorless beards of old men,
Dark to come from under the faint red roofs of mouths.

O I perceive after all so many uttering tongues,
And I perceive they do not come from the roofs of mouths for nothing. (32)

By a process of contiguous association, from head, to face, to mouth, the grass over the buried corpses becomes the tongues of the dead, which seems as much a material description of the spears of grass growing from the corpse-composted soil as it does a metaphorical transformation of the scene. But the passage does not end with this startling image of massed, uttering tongues, a figure, perhaps, for the crowd of readers Whitman so frequently imagines and addresses in these early poems, beginning with the first edition's first lines ("What I assume, you shall assume" 27). Faced by this crowd, finding himself among these babbling tongues, Whitman conceives the desire not to silence or dominate these voices of the dead but to translate them into the present. "I wish," the poet says, "I could translate the hints about the dead young men and women, / And the hints about the old men and mothers, and the offspring taken soon out of their laps" (32). His wish to translate these "hints" suggests that he imagines the poem he writes to be simultaneously a site of inscription and an act of reading, through which the babbling tongues of the past, figured as a present, might again be made articulate, joined to the poet's voice and projected toward the future.

His choice of the verb "to translate" to join writing with the reading that perpetuates it, suggests a poetics in which self-expression and the incorporation of the other become inextricably intertwined aspects of the poem, though they also remain distinct, just as the translation remains distinct from its original. Translation, here and elsewhere in Whitman's poems about poetry, figures his ideal poetic strategy and suggests, as I will later discuss, his deepest thoughts about death as well. For in Whitman's imagination, the act of translation tends to indicate the death of the original that it also perpetuates. It substitutes for the original but also stands along side it, marks its passing and gives it new life in the same instant. By similar rhetorical means, Whitman translates death itself into something positive and links it to life as an ongoing process.[10]

Confronting Death

Translation may be the most familiar and the strangest literary activity. Like metonymy, it both resembles and differs from the transfiguring transformations of metaphor. Translation, like metaphor, involves substitution. Metaphoric substitutions, however, have a peculiar structure that translation doesn't share. To say, for example, that the grass *is* the handkerchief of the Lord does not simply replace the vehicle with the tenor but requires, conceptually, the persistence of both. Metaphor, in this light, is less a form of substitution (though it does substitute) than it is a mode of comparison that aspires to transcend and unite both terms in play by mapping one over the other.[11] As we saw in our consideration of Petrarch, metaphor can be made to recover, imaginatively, the lost presence of the dead lover by remapping the absent beloved's attributes onto the present objects of the material world. Translation, by contrast, displaces one sign by another, one language by another, moving from one place and time to another, and must, by definition, leave the original it perpetuates behind. The original is always lost in translation, no matter how faithfully rendered it may be. Translation (literally "carrying across") necessarily displaces what it conveys, always replaces and obscures, with an irreducible degree of violence, the signs of an original text with the signs of another text that purports to represent it.[12] While a metaphor can be used to fix or enhance a meaning by renewing the reader's sense of its tenor's present significance, the significance of translation emerges through the displacement of what precedes it. Translation's contiguous movement from one articulation of meaning to another, because of the inevitable alteration involved, suggests meaning's fluid instability and final ground-lessness. It entails the erasure or death of the original in the same gesture that represents and perpetuates it, giving it an altered life in the future.[13] For Whitman's poet, reading, writing, and death all involve forms of translation.

The first notable appearance of death in "Song of Myself" and *Leaves of Grass*, as a field of grass growing from the mouths of the dead and figured as their uttering tongues, furnishes the poet with an occasion for transla-tion and for self-perpetuation. The grass momentarily figures the crowd Whitman represents and incorporates, both as substitute and as part for whole: "And these one and all tend inward to me, and I tend outward to them," he will write of the crowd, "And such as it is to be of these more or less I am" (42). It becomes an opportunity for the poet to translate. Whit-man, the modern poet as man of the crowd, differs from Poe in this cru-cial respect. Death in his early poems represents no end at all, nor does it inspire perverse ecstasies of self-tormenting melancholy as it does for Poe and the Sapphic poets he emulates and inspires. Rather it is structurally incorporated into and translated by the expression and perpetuation of life, the utterance of poetry itself. The very form of poetry that Whitman in-vents, with its long, end-stopped lines, unencumbered by regular metrics or rhyme, seems to emulate the natural movement of the poet's breathing, his "respiration and inspiration," which he identifies with poetry in "Song of Myself" (27).

Poe, for Whitman, was both a model and mentor. But he was also a symptom of the age's morbidity against which Whitman sought to con-tend.[14] In *Specimen Days*, Whitman described Poe as the purveyor of "the lush and weird that have taken such extraordinary possession of Nineteenth-century verse-lovers." This, he does not hesitate to specify, is a pathology of poetic culture: "The inevitable tendency of poetic culture to morbidity, abnormal beauty—the sickliness of all technical thought or refinement in itself—the abnegation of the perennial and democratic concretes at first hand, the body, the earth and sea, sex and the like—and the substitution of something for them at second or third hand—what bearings have they on current pathological study?" (898). Poe's morbidity, his focus on death as an occasion for melancholy and self-torment, form part of what Whitman considered the illness of his age, an illness of idealizing substitutions, against which he prescribes a dose of "democratic concretes." It is Poe's substitutions for reality, his reliance on technique and refinements in his verse and especially on metaphorical substitutions for the material actualities of the body, sex, and the world around him, that most trouble Whitman.

His own lack of concern for technical refinements of comparison or substitution is evident in the mixed series of metaphors with which he introduces this topic: "By its popular poets the calibers of the age, the weak spots of its embankments, its sub-currents . . . are unerringly indicated" (898). If Whitman's age, given Poe's popularity, seems morbidly obsessed with death and mourning, Whitman's task is to confront the popular conception of death and to translate it into something different, something luckier, even if this sets him apart from popular poets and forces him to gamble that the uttering tongues that are the crowd he confronts will fail in the future to translate him and thus consign him to oblivion. For the poet, in Whitman's poems, oblivion is the only death that is absolute.

The ways in which Whitman's poetry enacts this difficult and dangerous project, to perpetuate himself by appeals to a popular readership whose morbid tastes he also wants to reform, no doubt contributed as much as his freeing of verse from conventional prosody to his early failure to win the vast, loving audience of which he dreamt. The popular audience expected not only regular meters and rhymes but also wisdom and solace, as in the traditional elegy, or sentiment and melancholy, as in the traditions of lyric deriving from Sappho. Whitman, especially in the earlier editions of *Leaves of Grass*, offered neither and this left him at odds with the crowds he wanted to woo. Consider Whitman's conventional use of metaphor in perhaps his most popular postwar poem, a poem he recited from lyceum platforms for over a decade after the Civil War. "O! Captain! My Captain!" is a fair example of nineteenth-century sentimentality in verse:

> My Captain does not answer, his lips are pale and still,
> My father does not feel my arm, he has no pulse nor will,
> The ship is achor'd safe and sound, its voyage closed and done,
> From fearful trip the victor ship comes in with object won;
>   Exult O shores, and ring O bells!
>   But I with mournful tread,
>   Walk the deck my Captain lies,
>   Fallen cold and dead. (467–468)

This, the final stanza, figures the ship of state safely at anchor after its tumultuous voyage through the war with its captain, the dead Captain, President Lincoln of course, still bleeding on the deck. The mapping of this familiar metaphor onto the nation's tragedy gives that tragedy a comprehensible and cognitively useful shape. The poem meets the reader's need for meaning at a moment of incalculable loss. But this poem, to a modern reader, seems inferior to Whitman's best work. Unlike the metonymically enchained metaphors that run through section 6 of "Song of Myself," and proliferate the grass's possible meanings, the ship and captain as master metaphors lock this poem's meaning in place and hold it there as the poem proceeds from stanza to stanza. The repetitions of imagery and sound, the incessant beat of iambic feet and internal rhymes, seem to mimic the poet's and the audience's uncomprehending horror and terror-stricken grief. But the poem still seems showy and fake, a melodramatic trick, a crowd-pleasing bit of histrionic emotiveness. For uncomprehending horror and grief conveyed through metaphor—incomprehension conveyed through the figure of comprehension itself and through a metaphor—like the ship of state—that is already a cliché and nearly dead—dissipates the poem's intended effect. The poem, in fact, approaches the ideal state of discursive prose. Its materiality as language disappears before the meaning it conveys (we don't care about the ship itself but only what it means). The overly familiar conceit remains at odds with the shocked, uncomprehending grief the poem means to convey.

Such melodramatic effects are rare in Whitman's poetry. Consider by way of contrast the brief epitaph that follows "O! Captain! My Captain!" along with "Hush'd Be the Camps To-day," in Whitman's final arrangement of his poems.

> This dust was once the man,
> Gentle, plain, just and resolute, under whose cautious hand,
> Against the foulest crime in history known in any land or age,
> Was saved the Union of these States. (468)

This dust was once the man borrows the language of the burial service in the *Book of Common Prayer* to present the sheer materiality of the body that here represents nothing but itself and the crimes of history. These lines, prosaic as they seem, convey grief through understatement, refusing conventional rhetorical gestures of ornamentation or consolation. The preservation of the union, under this "cautious hand," does not make the dust meaningful, but it makes the senseless loss of the man more poignant. The poet does not attempt any metaphorical transformation of the president's body to make death intelligible. He does not give the dust a shape through familiar, consoling images or narrative structures—the virtuous life is not imagined as a perilous voyage that ends in the peaceful harbor of well-earned rest, and the fallen president is not imagined as a type of Christ. Instead the poem confronts the reader with the brute fact of mortality as corporeal dissolution, from dust to dust, and stops there. A man lived, he accomplished a great and laudable thing, and now, a criminal act of violence has rejoined him to the dust of which all bodies on earth are composed. In these modest lines, as in Whitman's best poetry (though I am not claiming that these lines are great poetry), the mortal body and the earthly world stand undisguised and naked. In Whitman's epitaph, Lincoln's corpse becomes one more brute fact in the world of brute facts that the poet means to indicate and with which he is, as he says in "Song of Myself," mad to be in contact and intent on translating.

But can one translate what one cannot understand? In Whitman's great elegy for Lincoln, the pressure to discover meaning in death intensifies. "When Lilacs last by the Dooryard Bloom'd" seems to indicate an allegorical meaning that might make death comprehensible. This, in Whitman, is unusual. The star, the moon, the bird, the lilac figure something in the poem, yet it remains difficult to say exactly what they finally mean, except as figures in what Whitman calls "death's outlet song of life" (460), as when Whitman writes at the poem's end, "Lilac and star and bird twined with the chant of my soul (467)." Earlier in the poem, the poet even seems to tease the reader with an interpretation of the poem's metaphors: "Then with the knowledge of death as walking one side of me,/And the thought of death close-walking the other side of me,/And I in the middle as with companions, and as holding the hands of companions" (464). Max Cavitch notes that "When commentators inquire into the nature of these companions, they generally engage in a slightly irritating appeal to the flatly conceptual: for example, the thought of death is 'loss,' knowledge of death is 'process.'"[15] But knowledge, as Cavitch observes, "is a relatively rare word in Whitman, and when it does appear, it tends to be expressive of organic sensation . . . satisfaction with immediacy . . . and with the embodied self."[16] Kerry Larson sees Whitman's negotiations with his audience as founded upon an "impasse" between "knowledge and experience" that he stages in these lines, and sees Whitman generally moving "beyond a longing for referential stability to a vision of rhetoric so pure of interest as to be drained of any referential function whatsoever."[17] This seems to be exactly right. Which is why when "Lilacs . . ." arrives at its moment of consoling vision, it is not a moment of spiritual knowledge—not even really a moment of generative continuation as Cavitch suggests (though I agree that death is generative for Whitman).[18] The final dreamlike vision of Whitman's elegy is a vision of the stark reality of the war's heavy toll, a vision that confronts the reader with the accumulated corpses of the war, a mass death that compromises the centrality of the president's body in the poem and makes it another battle corpse among the myriads of war dead the poet envisions and finally, shockingly, refuses to mourn:

> While my sight that was bound in my eyes unclosed,
> As to long panoramas of visions.
> And I saw askant the armies,
> I saw as in noiseless dreams hundreds of battle-flags,
> Borne through the smoke of the battles and pierc'd with missles I saw them,
> And carried hither and yon through the smoke, and torn and bloody,
> And at last but a few shreds left on the staffs, (and all in silence,)
> And the staffs all splinter'd and broken. (466)

There is no false note of redemption here. Whitman's poet will not convert the carnage of these battles into a new birth of freedom, as did Lincoln in his elegy at Gettysburg or Julia Ward Howe in her injunction to departing soldiers to emulate Christ's self-sacrifice, "As he died to make men holy let us die to make men free." Instead, the war produces masses of "battle-corpses" that become white skeletons over time and the suffering of those who survive, which endures while they live. It is with this unredeemed and inconsolable suffering that Whitman confronts his readers:

> I saw battle-corpses, myriads of them,
> And the white skeletons of young men, I saw them,
> I saw the debris and debris of all the slain soldiers of the war,
> But I saw they were not as was thought,
> They themselves were fully at rest, they suffer'd not,
> The living remain'd and suffer'd, the mother suffer'd,
> And the wife and the child and the musing comerade suffer'd,
> And the armies that remain'd suffer'd. (466)

No doubt, these lines do sound the note of "memorial piety" and suggest "the improved sociability that begins with the recognition of the grievances of the living," as Cavitch suggests.[19] But like "The Wound Dresser," which these lines recall, the poem does not deny that the war primarily yields broken young bodies, death, and suffering, and little, in the face of so many dead, that seems like uplift or redemption, little to suggest that these corpses had not died in vain. In his later poems, Whitman, perhaps under Hegel's influence, will yield in his confrontation with death to a more transcendent vision. But in this poem, in 1865, the last lines seem especially ominous, since they suggest that such mass and senseless suffering has hardly passed from the scene.

A few years earlier, Whitman dealt with death in a more ebullient mood. In the poems he wrote before the war, he seldom dwells on bereavement. Indeed, in "Song of Myself," while he does not flinch in the face of death's material reality, he seems to forbid mourning. In 1855 he wrote, "And as to you corpse I think you are good manure, but that does not offend me,/I smell the white roses sweet scented and growing,/I reach to the leafy lips . . . I reach to the polished breasts of melons." Death and decomposition, in these lines, serve to renew the poet's and the earth's erotic life. He ends on a note of positive appeal that links life and death together: "And as to you life, I reckon you are the leavings of many deaths . . . / . . . O grass of graves . . . O perpetual transfers and promotions . . . if you do not say anything how can I say anything" (86). Death is not loss but one of the transfers and promotions that Whitman wants to translate into the song of himself that he offers to the secular world and the crowd of which he forms a part.

The grass is, as Aspiz notes, a "master metaphor" for Whitman's book. He constructs a number of relays or associative links that make the leaves of his poems seem like the grass he describes. This troping of death and literature becomes central in the "Calamus" poems that often seem like posthumous confrontations with an imagined reader in an unspecified future. In "Scented Herbage of My Breast," a central poem in this section, the leaves grow from the poet's corpse in its grave and the poet himself becomes excellent compost for a crop of future readers. The corpse is less a metaphor for the corpus of his book than it is a precise analogue for the reembodiment and displacement of the self into the crowd of future readers for which the book becomes a metonymy:

Scented herbage of my breast,
Leaves from you I glean, I write, to be perused best afterwards,
Tomb-leaves, body-leaves growing up above me above death,
Perennial roots, tall leaves, O the winter shall not freeze you delicate
    leaves,

Every year shall you bloom again, out from where you retired you shall
   emerge again;
O I do not now whether many passing by will discover you or inhale your
   faint odor, but I believe a few will;

Even here, pursuing a favorite conceit comparing his book to his body,
Whitman makes his figure oddly literal and concrete. For a poet to
compare his body to his book—as Montaigne claimed his *Essais* to be consubstantial with their author—seems less a metaphor than a specific statement of the conditions of life for an author whose work embodies him in
words that replace him. In John Irwin's words: "In the ideal transparency
of embodiment, the singer becomes his song, and the object its meaning.
For Whitman's song is an audible hieroglyph, a musical emblem."[20] But
why, for Whitman, does this insistent embodiment—like hieroglyphs
themselves—so often suggest entombment and an afterlife, the loss or
disappearance of the self as well as its persistence, the presence and the
inaccessibility of a great mystery? And why does Whitman, unlike Cham-
pollion who deciphered the Rosetta Stone, seem largely unconcerned
with what these hieroglyphs might mean? Consider the lines that follow
the lines just quoted:

O slender leaves! O blossoms of my blood! I permit you to tell in your
   own way of the heart that is under you,
O I do not know what you mean there underneath yourselves, you are not
   Happiness,
You are often more bitter than I can bear, you burn and sting me,
Yet you are beautiful to me you faint tinged roots, you make me think of
   death,

This thought of death, which Whitman's long sentence continues to elaborate, has little in common with commonplace thoughts of death in elegiac or sentimental poetry. Whitman warns his readers from the first that
death is different from what they supposed and luckier, though the bitter-
ness of mortality qualifies that last statement. He eschews both Christian
consolation and existential despair, but what does he substitute for them?
   In his most challenging poems about death, Whitman offers neither
hope for a final translation to a spiritual realm of personal immortality nor
despair at the prospect of the self's dispersal into the endless recirculations
of matter or the author's dissemination through the myriad "uttering
tongues" that might repeat his words and which are one of the tenors to

which the metaphor of grass refers. Life and death appear side by side or oscillate without overlap or equivalence. Neither life in death nor death in life seems to capture Whitman's thought. Rather, he presents life and death in their ineluctable contiguity, their purely metonymic association, their simultaneous presence (and absence) in the world and on the page, which makes them at once not the same and somehow indifferent. Addressing the leaves of the grave and the leaves of his book, Whitman writes:

> Death is beautiful from you, (what is finally beautiful except death and
> love?)
> O I think it is not for life I am chanting here my chant of lovers, I think it
> must be for death,
> For how calm, how solemn it grows to ascend to the atmosphere of lovers,
> Death or life I am then indifferent, my soul declines to prefer,
> (I am not sure but the high soul of lovers welcomes death most,)
> Indeed O death, I think now these leaves mean precisely the same as you
> mean,
> Grow up taller sweet leaves that I may see! grow up out of my breast!

Whitman remains indifferent to life and death, but death emerges as the figure and ground for the poetry through which he hopes to live. He urges his utterance into the world ("Do not remain down there so ashamed, herbage of my breast!") and discovers in his own body the compost and the vegetation for his organic self-expression ("Come I am determin'd to unbare this broad breast of mine, I have long enough stifled and choked"). And most impressively, "Through me . . . the words . . . to make death exhilarating." In his translations of death, Whitman does not claim to give death meaning but to make it exciting.

These moments in Whitman, frequent enough in the poems written between 1855 and 1860 to be familiar, remain uncanny and unsettling, and exhilarating as well. Though it may be precisely the wrong question, one of course cannot but ask what such an exhilarating association of death and life and poetry might mean ("Give me your tone therefore O death," Whitman writes a little later in the poem, "that I may accord with it, / Give me yourself, for I see that you belong to me now above all, and are folded inseparably together, you love and death are, / Nor will I allow you to balk me any more with what I was calling life," 269–270). What does it mean for a poet to take his tone from death and love and to alter the tone of both at the same time?

And what might it mean if the meaning of death were the wrong question? How is the desire for a certain tone—the hum of a valved voice in

Whitman's early words—different from a demand for meaning? In Whitman's apostrophe to death, he requests a formal, musical harmonizing, a sympathetic vibration, and not a meaningful understanding or a comprehensible content. Though Whitman addresses death he doesn't quite personify it. He does not, for example, make death a proper name, as poets from Donne to Dickinson and beyond do. He refuses to personalize it, since like the grass itself it is a ubiquitous, truly democratic, and ultimately impersonal (though what could be more personal?) phenomenon. Whitman imagines the accord between love and death as a common fact that may be experienced but cannot be grasped, difficult to individualize, exceeding understanding, although his early poems seek to articulate its beauty and to discover or create a livable and vibrant relationship to death's inescapable reality and its ineluctable presence. How does Whitman come to write poetry that so programmatically avoids generating meanings about lived relations, including love and death? The answer to that question involves what we might call the critique of metaphor's political economy, something Whitman translates as well and from a source some may find surprising.

Whitman's Cosmopolitanism and the Resistance to Metaphor

Despite the claims he makes to be the autochthonous poet of these United States, "My tongue, every atom of my blood, form'd from this soil, this air, / Born here of parents born here from parents the same, and their parents the same" as he put it in the so-called deathbed edition of *Leaves of Grass* (188), Whitman's knit of identity was always composed of threads that connected him to European traditions. "America," as he said in his 1855 Preface, "does not repel the past or what it has produced under its forms or amid other politics . . . accepts the lesson with calmness" (5). Whatever may be true of America, this is certainly true of Whitman. The acceptance and retooling of the past and its lessons is discernable in many of his poems and even in the form of *Leaves of Grass*. We noted above Roland Greene's observation that Whitman adapts the post-Petrarchan poem sequence to new and specifically modern ends. More broadly, in the language experiment of his poetry, Whitman also situated himself within a specific European intellectual tradition that assigned a political value to metaphor. This tradition, deeply suspicious of metaphor's protean power to produce ideological obfuscations, was part of an enlightenment strain of cosmopolitan utopianism. There is not only a poetics, but also an ethics implicit in Whitman's experiments with form and his embrace of the plain style in poetry. Considering the origins of his ethical prosody takes us away, for the moment, from the United States.[21]

The pose as visionary poet of a new social order that Whitman so often adopts originates in a fictionalized tradition of political prophecy that he found in his favorite French writers, Georges Sand and Le Comte de Volney. When Whitman assumes the bardic pose, purporting in 1855 to enlighten the teeming assemblage of the masses in a passage like the famous catalog beginning "I am afoot with my vision" (59) (this becomes section 33 of the 1892 edition), he borrows the figure of Sand's pastoral bard in the novel *Consuelo* and mimics the language of Volney's prophetic "Legislator" in his philosophical fable, *The Ruins: or a Survey of the Revolutions of Empires*.[22] Several critics have documented Whitman's specific borrowing from Sand and Volney (and the latter's influence on the former). Betsy Erkkila, for example, notes a genealogy of ideals that Whitman derived from these sources, including "the fundamental faith of the Enlightenment in reason, science, civilization, and progress," a cosmopolitan hopefulness about "the establishment of an international community," which Whitman identified with the United States—his teeming nation of nations. She and other critics also note that Whitman borrowed aspects of form, posture, and vision from these sources.[23] Volney, in particular, whose language Whitman "borrows" (to use David Goodale's term) helps specify the significance of Whitman's resistance to metaphor. Whitman knew that in a secular society even science, civilization, and progress were beliefs that, though grounded in material reality, were as vulnerable to challenge as any others.

Consider a passage to which Erkkila pays special attention in *The Ruins*, where a character called the Legislator, the Genius or the Apparition "lifts the narrator into a flight above the earth in order to reveal to him the 'science of the ages.'" That passage begins, "Suddenly a celestial flame seemed to dissolve the bands which held us to earth; and, like a light vapor, borne of the wings of the Genius, I felt myself wafted to the regions above."[24] Erkkila recognizes a similar moment in "Song of Myself" (it becomes section 33 of the final version), when the poet, assuming the guise of the prophetic legislator, rises and expands. In 1855 this passage read, "My ties and ballasts leave me . . . I travel . . . I sail . . . my elbows rest in the sea gaps, / I skirt the sierras . . . my palms cover continents, / I am afoot with my vision."[25] "Then begins," as Erkkila says, "the famous long catalog in which Whitman, like Volney, enumerates the multitudinous and heterogeneous forms of human life upon earth."[26] This catalog, this cosmopolitan vision of a secular world in which—given the varieties of human forms of life listed—no naïve belief in any single form remains credible, demonstrates Whitman's debts to the French writers and his engagement with secularism.[27] Volney suggests one source for Whitman's innovative reliance on metonymy and his adherence to the plain style at a moment when readers of poetry expected displays of wit, tropes of comparison, and elegant ornaments.

Consider the catalog's beginning as it appeared in 1855:

> By the city's quadrangular houses . . . in log huts, or camping with
>   lumbermen,
> Along the ruts of the turnpike . . . along the dry gulch and rivulet bed,
> Hoeing my onion-patch and rows of carrots and parsnips . . . crossing
>   savannahs . . . trailing in forests,
> Prospecting . . . gold-digging . . . girdling the trees of a new purchase,
> Scorched ankle-deep by the hot sand . . . hauling my boat down the
>   shallow river;
> Where the panther walks to and fro on a limb overhead . . . where the
>   buck turns furiously at the hunter . . . (59)

Whitman's list of sights from nature, commerce, the hunt, the countryside and the cityscape, continues for some time.[28] Most lines begin with an adverb (usually "where," occasionally "through") followed by small things observed, quite literally, in passing, which may be either nouns (a hayrick, a mockingbird, swimmers) or gerunds ("sucking juice through a straw" or "Looking in the shop-windows of Broadway") and modulate into a list of things that please the speaker:

> Pleas'd with the native and pleas'd with the foreign . . . pleas'd with the
>   new and old,
> Pleas'd with women, the homely as well as the handsome,
> Pleas'd with the quakeress as she puts off her bonnet and talks
>   melodiously (62)

Finally this single long sentence ends with a moment of what might seem like religious illumination:

> Walking the old hills of Judaea with the beautiful gentle god by my side,
> Speeding through space . . . speeding through heaven and the stars,
> Speeding amid the seven satellites and the broad ring, and the diameter
>   of eighty-thousand miles,
> Speeding with tail'd meteors . . . throwing fire-balls like the rest,
> Carrying the crescent child that carries its own full mother in its belly,

> Storming, enjoying, planning, loving, cautioning,
> Backing and filling, appearing and disappearing,
> I tread day and night such roads. (62–63)

This might have become, for a different poet, a moment of religious transcendence. For Whitman, however, the metonymic enchainment of cosmic phenomena and observed minutiae in the city streets works to remove the cosmos from the realm of transcendent spirituality and make it part of mundane experience rather than to elevate the mundane to the transcendental.[29] Walking with an embodied beautiful and gentle god occurs on the same material plane as collecting apples, strolling with other comrades, or speeding through space with the other phenomena of the visible universe. In fact, in treading this path—in using the ideas of movement and location to order his lists—the one thing Whitman avoids indicating is any ultimate meaning attached to his metonymical enchainments or any end to these unfolding sequences. Instead, not only his pleasurable mood but also his equitable repetitions suggest a democratic acceptance of all things and people as the poet finds them, quite apart from any meaning they may possess. He is like the crescent child who carries its own pregnant mother in his belly. He accepts this mise en abyme as the lot of mortal existence, the pinpoint particularity of subjective consciousness that carries within it the entire cosmos. This universal acceptance, in turn, suggests the word that Whitman himself so often uses, indifference, the equitable refusal to prefer or conclude.[30]

In a suggestive passage, just before this catalog (it will become section 32 of the final edition), Whitman wrote:

> I think I could turn and live awhile with the animals . . . they are so
>   placid and self-contain'd,
> I stand and look at them sometimes half the day long.
>
> They do not sweat and whine about their condition,
> They do not lie awake in the dark and weep for their sins,
> They do not make me sick discussing their duty to God,
> Not one is dissatisfied . . . not one is demented with the mania of owning
>   things,
> Not one kneels to another nor to his kind that lived thousands of years
>   ago,
> Not one is respectable or unhappy over the whole earth.
>
> So they show their relations to me and I accept them . . . (58)

To maintain this happy and democratic indifference, this pose of declining to prefer or to rank or to seek resolution, this refusal to judge, the poet submits to an unsettling discipline that holds everything equivalent and brackets difference—therefore bracketing meaning as well. Love, hate, affection, and violence, these cease to signify. They simply are.

We are close to the wellspring of Whitman's poetic project and to a crux in recent criticisms of his poet's pose by critics who find it simultaneously arrogant and enervating.[31] Yet, in light of Volney's lessons, Whitman's indifference seems neither cold nor abstract. Rather, this indifference, whatever its limitations, seems the necessary ground of democratic sympathy in a poet who finds himself confronted with the teaming masses and contentious crowds of modern life.[32] Adopting a poetic posture of disinterest in meaning, indicating a world of things and states to be taken in and not evaluated, Whitman makes the world available imaginatively as an object of sympathy and even identification through his poet to his reader. This sympathetic enlivening of the world occurs, paradoxically, through the power of metonymy, like translation, momentarily to objectify and fix, even as it enchains and displaces, the objects it names. For Whitman, metonymy's momentary objectifications often suggest death, the final contiguity to life and the ultimate translation. Whitman, "afoot" with his "vision," envisions a series of shifting, incorporative, sympathetic identifications that seem simultaneously posthumous and enlivening. He begins the final tally of this catalog with an affirmation:

> All this I swallow and it tastes good . . . I like it well, and it becomes
>   mine,
> I am the man . . . I suffer'd . . . I was there.
>
> The disdain and calmness of martyrs,
> The mother condemn'd for a witch and burnt with dry wood, her
>   children gazing on;
> The hounded slave that flags in the race and leans by the fence, blowing
>   and covered with sweat,
> The twinges that sting like needles his legs and neck,
> The murderous buckshot and bullets,
> All these I feel or am. (64–65)

Whitman's metonymies insist on the concreteness of each thing or event named, and become the site of a paradoxical tension between deadening objectification and enlivening identification. As James Perrin Warren remarks, "The act of observation gives way to the act of identification."[33] When Whitman's poetry succeeds, this tension remains taut and dramatic. The moment of transforming and erotic identification depends upon making the object present, as an object, while the poet remains indifferent to its meaning, indifferent to whether or not it be person or thing, a slave or a slave hunter, the wound or the bullet.

This is and should remain troubling, both ethically and aesthetically. I will have more to say about this problem in the next chapter. For now, note that no meaning, no comparison or analogy, no judgment impedes the transfer of erotic energy—the movement of sympathetic identification— from body to body and thing to thing upon which Whitman's language experiment, his poetic corpus and his attempt to embrace the teeming secular world and its agonies and transports depends. Agonies also come in indifferent series: "Agonies are one of my changes of garment," as he declares in a few lines more (65).[34] It is this resistance to metaphor as a vehicle of meaning, this foregrounding of metonymy as an enactment of indifference to significance that links Whitman to Volney and to the particular tradition of cosmopolitan Enlightenment skepticism that Volney represents.

Whitman's metonymic presencing of the world and his avoidance of judgment and meaning accord, as I have been suggesting, with the ethical materialism that he found in Volney's *Ruins*. They accord as well with Volney's linguistic and political theories. Volney's Legislator suggests that dangerous dogmas and illusory metaphysics grow from the common evil root of an easily abused rhetorical figure, metaphor. Metaphor seduces and perverts human judgment and sows discord in the world by abstracting the immediacy of experience and appearing to fix meaning. The Legislator declares to the masses arrayed in his vision:

> The first men, being children of nature, anterior to all events, ignorant of all science, were born without any idea of the dogmas arising from scholastic disputes; of rites founded on the practice of arts not then known; of precepts framed after the development of passions; or of laws which suppose a language, a state of society not then in being; or of God, whose attributes all refer to physical objects, and his actions to a despotic state of government; or of the soul, or of any of those metaphysical beings, which we are told are not the objects of sense, and for which, however, there can be no other means of access to the understanding. To arrive at so many results, the necessary circle of preceding facts must have been observed; slow experience and repeated trials must have taught the rude man the use of his organs; the

accumulated knowledge of successive generations must have invented and improved the means of living; and the mind, freed from the cares of the first wants of nature, must have raised to the complicated art of comparing ideas, of digesting arguments, and seizing abstract similitudes.[35]

In this view, the foundations of tyranny lie in religion and religion relies in turn upon the complicated constructions and abstractions of comparison and similitude, the creation of what Volney a little later calls "a perpetual round of metaphors," that become "fatal stumbling blocks to the understanding and to reason" precisely because they seem to infuse the stolid material of the world with brilliant, abstract meanings (*The Ruins*, 176–177).[36] These invented meanings become the foundations of discord. They shift attention from the sensible materiality of the human condition to the illusory realm of metaphysics and meanings. Upon these purely rhetorical foundations, priests and despots construct dogmas and make hieratic mystifications, using them to build the oppressive belief systems and institutions that perpetuate injustices and exacerbate human suffering. Whitman's embrace of the plain style in poetry is meant to redress these wrongs.

In lines he first published in 1860 and later used to conclude the first section of "Song of Myself" (1892), Whitman voices an antipathy to religion akin to Volney's:

Creeds and Schools in abeyance,
Retiring back a while sufficed at what they are, but never forgotten
I harbor for good or bad, I permit to speak at every hazard,
Nature without check with original energy. (188)

Like Volney, Whitman suggests that holding creeds and schools in abeyance, returning to the original energy of material nature, returns one as well to a language stripped or cleansed of falsely elevating comparisons and seductive ornaments. The plain talk that remains is rich in the metonymic enumeration of the peoples and things of the world, which it presents without the sedimentations of judgment and idealization, dogmas and conventions, rhetorical ornamentations and semantic distortions that begin with metaphor and distance humans from the material world and from each other.[37]

Such an original language should become a vehicle for renewed understandings, but it requires first a leveling indifference toward fixed and established meanings and values. To approximate this language, Whitman turns to the metonymic presentation of a fleeting, material present, expressing an urgent desire to embrace not the spiritual or transcendent significances of the world, but its material embodiments and transformations, bespeaking, most often, not love but sex, the "Urge and urge and urge,/Always the procreant urge of the world" that his best poetry describes and enacts (28).

This preference for sensuous materiality over abstract meaning is what is at stake in Whitman's poetry as a "language experiment" and this is what makes his poetry both secular and modern.[38] There is, implicitly, an ethics as well. Like Volney's Legislator, Whitman's poet holds that war and human misery result from bad signification. Among the three principal causes Volney adduces to explain the confusion of ideas he surveys, the first and most fundamental derives from the "figurative expressions under which an infant language was obliged to describe the relations of objects; expressions which, passing afterwards from a limited to a general sense, and from a physical to a moral one, caused, by their ambiguities and synonyms, a great number of mistakes" (181). The origins of human conflict and cruelty lie in the bad metaphors that vitiate plain language's primal power of indication and becloud its capacity to present a clear vision of the world and an accurate reckoning of its contents based on the poet's sympathetic relationship to it and to his audience. As an ethos in a society structured on violent injustices, this posture has clear limitations. But it also indicates the position literature comes more and more to assume in the secular world of contending beliefs that constitutes modernity.

In some ways this is not new. Without going back to Plato's distrust of sophistry in *Phaedrus* and *The Republic*, there was already, before Volney, a long tradition of linguistically based skepticism, a recoil from the troubling role that rhetoric can play in moral, ethical, and political deliberations. Montaigne, to take an example with considerable resonance for Whitman, during the religious civil wars in France, believed that "most of our sufferings are rooted in words. . . . How many and how terrible have been the wars occasioned by our doubt concerning the meaning of this syllable: Hoc."[39] "Hoc," of course, in the Gospels indicates the founding confusion of Christian mysticism, assigning to this material bread a symbolic and spiritual meaning as the body of Christ, changing the wine magically into the savior's blood. Jesus's declaration, "This is my body," makes of the bread the mystical incorporation of the Messiah, and opens the way for endless, bloody conflicts over what Jesus could have meant when he made such a statement (see Mark 14:22–24). In *Leaves of Grass*, Whitman often works to reverse this trope of transubstantiation by insisting that both the body and the soul be understood, without reference to any other plane of being or level of meaning, as objects metonymically enchained in and to the world of the senses, as when he writes "The scent of these arm-pits is aroma finer than prayer" (51).[40] The body's odor is finer than prayer because it keeps attention focused on the material world and the body's fleshy and redolent presence among the world's objects. It bespeaks a physical entity that one can embrace regardless of its meaning or lack of it.

Whitman uses metonymy to resist the pull of meaning toward abstraction. He bundles and inventories his perceptions and experiences of the world in lists or catalogs and leaves them for the reader to peruse. As an ethics, in a nation colluding in the inequities of slavery, violently expanding, and moving swiftly toward a cataclysmic war in which both sides were assured of their essential righteousness, this may seem woefully inadequate—as most any reasonable ethics in the face of political catastrophe and atrocity does. Many critics have noted his tendency to reproduce the political and ideological commitments of his era that contributed to the oppression of nonwhites and women. But those who condemn Whitman's reticence about these commitments should consider the fact that, as Michael Moon has said, at its best his poetry also "provides the means for making a critique of these commitments" in part by indiscriminately embracing otherness even—particularly—when that otherness is less than fully understood.[41] At his best, he also troubles some of the most profound or complacent assumptions of his era concerning spirituality, personal identity, sex, and death. His challenge to his culture's fundamental beliefs and its expectations for poetry is intimately linked to his insistence on metonymy and on the materiality of the sign, in which, as much as his pioneering free verse, his poetic innovation consists.

Metonymy, Love, and Death

Whitman's promiscuous juxtaposition of discrete objects produces a poetry of fraught contiguities that suggests, without explanation or elaboration, that all life is tinged with sex and death and all identity is caught in processes of transformative interrelation: "Always," as Whitman puts it, "the procreant urge of the world./ . . . Always substance and increase,/ Always a knit of identity . . . always distinction . . . always a breed of life" (28). In Whitman's vision, this urgent breeding of life leaves little space for elaborations of final meanings. He troubles any assumptions one might have about stable positions for the self or for the world of others the self encounters. As the poet says in the line after those just cited, "To elaborate is no avail" (28). Poetry for Whitman becomes a particular and especially intense species of naming or description, a lyrically epideictic form of rhetorical performance, one that brings the distinct objects of the world, including the poet, the poet's body, the body of the poet's work, along with the reader, into fluidly structured, contiguous, and transformative contact.[42] But what does that leave to be said about death, to whose ubiquity in the world Whitman's poet so frequently draws attention? Death remains beyond the limit of human experience, beyond mortal capacities to touch or describe, yet death remains a paradoxical presence in the world as well. Death is usually imagined to be the end point of all living transformation, an inert fixity that indicates, or perhaps, inaugurates, an eternity without change. Whitman's view of death, like his vision of life differs from the suppositions of his contemporaries. Once again, this difference finds expression in his tropes.

In his oft-cited essay on "The Metaphoric and Metonymic Poles," Roman Jakobson remarks that, "it is generally realized that romanticism is closely linked with metaphor, whereas the equally intimate ties of realism with metonymy usually remain unnoticed." Poetry, he continues, focuses on the sign, prose on the referent.[43] Whitman does not conform to this paradigm. While he does fix attention on the signifier he also insists on the presence of the signified as a material object (while ignoring that referent's meaning). This is part of Whitman's peculiar contribution to modern poetry, though it also continues a romantic tradition that Jakobson largely ignores.

Angus Fletcher links American poetry, and especially Whitman, to a tradition of realistic description characteristic of "low" romanticism. He redresses Jakobson's neglect of a poetic tradition that rebels against the romantic or symbolist fascination with the sign and aspires to capture a more immediate version of the real in both literature and life.[44] In Fletcher's often compelling formulations of his position, the essence of poetry as a modern form returns the poet and the reader to the pre-Socratic project of realizing a time bound, material and phenomenal world, fundamentally at odds with the transcendentalist's desire, still evident in some romantic poets, to reduce the experiential dimensions of the world to mimetic or metaphorical indices of abstract, timeless truths. Time, as Plato learned from Heraclitus, means flux and flux—the motion of things that come into and pass out of existence—affords no place for stable knowledge, no purchase for the certainty Plato set philosophers in search of.[45] Plato's idealism, like some forms of Christian spirituality that he influenced and which Whitman rebelled against as unsuited to his secular era, reduces the phenomenal world to a vehicle for the senses whose intelligible tenor is always elsewhere in the intellectual or spiritual realm of the timeless and changeless forms that can be understood but not sensed. Whitman rejects this Platonic paradigm—which has its part to play in the forms of lyric that derive from Petrarch and often bespeak longings for transcendence or salvation through love or faith. He detranscendentalizes the lyric.

Metonymy in the poetry Fletcher describes attempts to capture and to participate in the flux and flow of the phenomenal world. Such poetry, and Whitman's early editions of *Leaves of Grass* most notably, refocuses attention on objects qua objects, as they exist in this world, and unsettles all fixed foundations of belief that might assign those objects stable meanings. This focus on objects also makes Whitman's poetry tend toward "a meditation on human time" and a confrontation with mortality. For, finally, it is death that gives shape to human experience by marking that experience's inevitable and unbreachable limit. Death is also the point at which the body's own materiality comes undeniably to the fore, just before it dissolves to the dust from which it was compounded. Fletcher says that

> Poets cannot accept the ideality of Plato's timeless formulations, because these would abrogate death, change, and our becoming undistinguished atoms of momentary existence. Poets confront death, they celebrate life, and hence are forced into an imaginative method of refusing final truths and prescriptions. Even the allegorical poets seek this method, as we learn from Dante (Auerbach called him the poet of the real world) or Spenser, whose wild myth making always undermines the schematized prescriptions of allegorical "morals" and "messages."[46]

Such poetry, then, remains—as Plato himself put it—in the realm of "bare feeling" that philosophy seeks to transcend (*Republic* X §603–606).[47] This poetry dwells among and upon the sensible, pleasurable and painful vicissitudes of existence that philosophy attempts to escape, assuage or, at least, to silence. "The Law," Socrates says, "declares that it is best to keep quiet as far as possible in calamity and not to chafe and repine . . ." But the poet often makes grief and celebration his stock in trade, voicing "lamentations . . . and beating his breast" as Socrates says, and encouraging us to "feel pleasure, and abandon ourselves and accompany the representation with sympathy and eagerness." Plato complains that "we praise as an excellent poet the one who most strongly affects us in this way," for this sort of successful poetry spells trouble for the calm elucidation of true knowledge upon which Plato's authoritarian utopia depends (*Republic* § 605). Thus, the poet fixes the susceptible reader in the sensuous world of sensation, of strife, of doubt and opinion, of pleasure and of grief. Plato's philosophy and his ideal republic constitute a dream of a world reduced to timeless abstractions and transcendent meanings in which people turn away from the momentariness, the often insignificant concretenesses upon which the poet expands. In this sense lyric poetry like Whitman's continues the ancient traditions that Plato, at least in *Republic*, hoped to end.

In Whitman's poetry, it comes down to tropes. As Fletcher observes, much modern poetry that turns from the uplift of Platonic allegory to the earthbound exploration of materiality also turns away from metaphor, so long a poetic staple, and toward the prosaic and rooted flatness of metonymy tethered to the perceptions of a single, common self. For the experiential world, as such poetry usually describes it, originates in the perception of a single and common self, the perspectival experiences of what Whitman calls in the first line of the deathbed edition of *Leaves of Grass*, "a simple, separate person" (165). The metonymies of low romantic poetry tend to grow from the experience of this simple speaking self, often figured in the poem as the poet, however diffuse, however lacking in singularity, that figure of the poet in the poem might be. In this way, the lyric tradition and modern poetry become identified. Lyric, as I mentioned in the introduction, becomes the vehicle that—along with the novel—best registers the secular world of contending points of view. Fletcher, still working from Jakobson, observes that in such poetry "images of the surrounding world function as contiguous reflections, or metonymical expressions of the poet's self" (186). But, the self thus reflected in Whitman's poetry seems less a specifiable individual—unlike Wordsworth, Byron, Keats, or Poe who invent strongly individuated poetic personas—than a sort of metonymically entangled bundle of perceptions tied to an uttering tongue and addressed to an anonymous, contentious crowd of readers figured in the poem as the "you," he so frequently addresses.[48]

When he speaks of the "metonymical expressions of the poet's self," Fletcher has Whitman in mind. Moreover, these metonymies of the self in Whitman link his poetry to politics—or at least to an egalitarian ethics. Of Whitman's poetry, Fletcher writes, "Whitman's aim is less to express or depict persons exerting power over each other (which would yield allegory), than it is to express the adjacency of people, places, and things," an expression achieved through metonymy.[49] This may be his aim, but the reality of Whitman's performances is more complex.

> I celebrate myself,
> And what I shall assume you shall assume,
> For every atom belonging to me as good belongs to you. (27)

The very first lines of the poem he would eventually call "Song of Myself" announce the tension between autocratic assertion and democratic invitation that so often recurs in Whitman's self-stagings. Is the "shall" in these lines a command or a simple statement of the reality of equality expressed in line three? Is this rhetoric hortatory or descriptive? The tensed relationship with alterity characterizes not only Whitman's relationship to his imagined readers but also to the personified presence of his soul, which appears in the very next line: "I loaf and invite my soul." This personification of the soul is rather different from Poe's Psyche with whom the poet walks in "Ulalume." What does imagining a soul to be capable of loafing suggest? Consider one of Whitman's best-known and most anti-Platonic passages of poetry from "Song of Myself":

> I believe in you my soul . . . the other I am must not abase itself to you,
> And you must not be abased to the other.
>
> Loafe with me on the grass . . . loose the stop from your throat,
> Not words, not music or rhyme I want . . . not custom or lecture, not even
>   the best,
> Only the lull I like, the hum of your valved voice. (30)

Whitman makes explicit his rejection of the Platonic demand (fundamental to Christian belief and culture since Paul's Epistles) that the soul subjugate the body. But his poetic staging of this passage, in which body and soul both seem present and both seem materially embodied and erotically entangled, takes the unsettling of Christian dogma and any idea of the soul's immortality and self-identity to the limits of materialism. There is no hierarchy and fundamentally no difference between body and soul as material entities in this passage. The soul is imagined as another body, and, moreover, one capable of sexual intercourse and pleasure. Erotic transport replaces spiritual transcendence.

This oft-cited passage remains one of the strangest self-representations in literature I know. Here, as Rimbaud would say, Whitman realizes that I is an other, not identical to but agonistically and erotically self-engaged. In Whitman's passage, there is an "I" who speaks, a soul who sings, and another I ("the other I am") who must neither abase or be abased to the soul, but who seems to remain silent. This is no holy trinity. This passage speaks volumes about the conflicted nature of the self that Whitman's poetry embodies. Unlike Plato or Paul, Whitman refuses to imagine a resolution of the conflicts within the self by imagining a hierarchy of its parts—by elevating reason or soul over appetite or the body. He refuses to identify any essential self that takes precedence over the other parts and might fix the self's proper character or meaning as reasonable or spiritual. Instead of such hierarchy's, and the allegorical expressions they might ground, Whitman presents the self as a series of sheer erotic contiguities, purely metonymic contiguities.

For, again, Whitman not only refuses to subjugate body to soul, but he also imagines the soul itself as another body and a sexual partner:

> I mind how once we lay in June, such a transparent summer morning;
> You settled your head athwart my hips and gently turned over upon me,
> And parted the shirt from my bosom-bone, and plunged your tongue to
>   my barestript heart,
> And reached till you felt my beard, and reached till you held my feet. (30)

This erotic positioning of the soul on the body evokes a crucifixion but not a mortification. Instead, this moment of penetration results in ecstasy, a besideness of the self to itself. Whatever else this act is, it is sex and its consummation leads to something like spiritual transport, except that it seems neither exactly a transport and only in a strange sense spiritual:

> Swiftly arose and spread around me the peace and joy and knowledge that
>   pass all the art and argument of the earth;
> And I know that the hand of God is the elderhand of my own,
> And I know that the spirit of God is the eldest brother of my own,
> And that all the men ever born are also my brothers . . . and the women
>   my sisters and lovers,
> And that a kelson of the creation is love,
> And limitless are leaves stiff or drooping in the fields,
> And brown ants in the little wells beneath them,
> And mossy scabs of the wormfence, heaped stones, and elder and mullein
>   and pokeweed.

These eight lines pivot around the only metaphor in the passage, describing love as a "kelson of the creation," in the fifth line. But this image of love as the foundational centerboard of a ship imagines love as the foundation of a universe in motion. The figuration of this scene does not elevate the poet's vision beyond that materiality of creation. It turns his and the reader's attention from a vision of God as a brother to a vision of other selves as brothers and sisters and it culminates in the catalog of material objects, of rocks and wildflowers and weeds, that concludes the passage by returning the reader and the poet to the world.

Placing heaped stones, mullein, and pokeweed in conjunction with the hand and spirit of God does not exactly bespeak God's presence in the world. The equation of the poet's colloquy of the soul with intercourse and orgasm stands unmodified and unadorned. Whitman sings a world of nearly pure sensation expressed through metonymies whose only meaning is the objects and actions to which he refers. Stones and weeds represent only themselves. Whitman, in fact, explicitly brackets, as far as possible, the question of meaning altogether.[50] "I do not," Whitman says earlier, "talk of the beginning or the end" (28). Instead he talks of sex, which may be both a beginning and an end, a knit of identity, a continuation and a transformation. "To elaborate is no avail . . . learn'd and unlearn'd fell that it is so" (28). Sex is itself a form of contiguity, less a penetration to the depths than a friction between epidural surfaces. The urge for sex, the urge to brush against or penetrate or be penetrated by another, drives the world, its transformations, and Whitman's poem forward. Yet sex for Whitman, like the world sex drives, remains a matter of surfaces whose superficiality hides no higher or deeper meanings that humans will ever come to know. Union yields nothing by way of depth or meaning but manifests the ubiquitous propulsive energy of a cosmos that requires, and really will allow, no further elaboration.

Death and sex in Whitman's early poetry are equally ubiquitous and equally inexplicable. In "Scented Herbage of My Breast," as in so many of Whitman's pre–Civil War poems, beauty, death, and democracy constellate. For example, soon after the opening lines in which the poet, indulging in metaphor, compares the grass his corpse fertilizes to the corpus of works he bequeaths to the future ("tomb-leaves" or "body leaves," or book leaves "I write, to be perused best afterwards," 268–269), he announces his departure from emblematic language and his confrontation with death itself:[51]

> Emblematic and capricious blades I leave you, now you serve me not,
> I will say what I have to say by itself,
> I will sound myself and comrades only, I will never again utter a call only
>   their call,
> I will give an example to lovers to take permanent shape and will through
>   the States,
> Through me shall the words be said to make death exhilarating,
> Give me your tone therefore O death, that I may accord with it, (269)

Death, whose meaning as always remains unspecified, appears to have less to do with meaning than with an echoing common call, a harmonizing union that might give the self over to remaking the contending states (and its own conflicted states) into an embodiment of a common, harmonized amative will. Whitman's amativism seeks to enable an interpolation of lovers in all the states to become accorded with themselves and with death, with a vision of death as generative, as exhilarating and paradoxically full of erotic energy.[52]

Finding death exhilarating is different from finding death meaningful. Death, in Whitman's poetry, cannot be harnessed, metaphorically, to the machinery of comparison that might make death signify. Death remains beyond the limit of mortal knowledge or linguistic signification, and Whitman, therefore, constructs his poetry to remind the reader of the thing neither he nor they can know but which presses against their common life at every moment. Thus, when Whitman announces in lines that will eventually begin section 44 of "Song of Myself" that "It is time to explain myself . . . let us stand up" (79), he heralds not a great increase in positive knowledge but the enticing voids of mortal ignorance. When he asks, "The clock indicates the moment . . . but what does eternity indicate?" he offers no answer but seeks to "launch" himself and "all men and women forward with me into the Unknown" (79). Of this human condition, hurtling ever forward and confronted with the irreducibly unknown present and a future that always contains, somewhere, a crucial unknowable death, Whitman, at his best, becomes prophetic. Such prophetic poetry, as Harold Bloom has said, at its strongest, is a great unnaming, a refusal of the common vessels of meaning and a renewal of something that is not quite meaning, something that the poet can not quite name but only indicate.[53] "What is known," Whitman's poet declares, "I strip away" (79). What remains must remain a question without a final answer.

Whitman composes his first great poem, "Song of Myself," of such indications and questions. For example, near the end when he says, "There is that in me . . . I do not now what it is . . . but I know it is in me." And then "I do not know it . . . it is without name . . . it is a word unsaid, / It is not in any dictionary, or utterance, or symbol. / . . . It is not chaos or death . . . it is form and union and plan . . . it is eternal life . . . it is Happiness" (87), his reference to "eternal life" signifies something far different from the eternal life that Christian consolation imagines and which Christian poets refer to as spiritual salvation. It remains without a name and a part of the eternal, material flux of the universe, not a transcendence of it. Time and eternity, life and death do not mean here what men and women have commonly taken them to mean. They are different, as Whitman would have it, and luckier.

Whitman's poet keeps, with regard to this world, great indexes of things but "no account with lamentation, / What have I to do with lamentation?" (79). He reaffirms that he has no answers about this world or the next: "You are also asking me questions, and I hear you; / I answer that I cannot answer . . . you must find out for yourself" (83). Instead of answering questions, Whitman's prophet teaches the futility of dwelling on them. In lines from a poem in the 1855 edition that will eventually become "The Song of the Answerer," Whitman specifies the poet's limitation as a purveyor of knowledge: "He is the answerer, / What can be answered he answers, and what cannot be answered he shows how it cannot be answered" (130). Rather than answering questions, he corresponds to the questioner as an occasion for limitless self-reflection: "The English believe he comes of their English stock, / A Jew to the Jew he seems . . . a Russ to the Russ . . . usual and near . . . removed from none" (131). Near the end of the volume's first poem, the poet offers something like a communion supper ("Here are biscuits to eat and here is milk to drink" [83]), but this is not transubstantiation or symbolic nourishment but real, material sustenance for a renewed commitment to physical life ("You must habit yourself to the dazzle of the light and of every moment of your life" [83]). As Kerry Larson remarks, Whitman's apostrophe to the reader is "not so much communication as communion," but it is communion of a definitively material sort.[54] Consider a moment later, when the poet insists that the body itself is the only response to the body's death: "And I call to mankind, Be not curious about God, / For I who am curious about each am not curious about God, / (No array of terms can say how much I am at peace about God and about death.)" (85). These lines build toward one of the poem's grand climactic moments, in which the poet addresses death and mortality by making them, like himself and like the soul at the poem's beginning, embodied presences in a landscape populated and enlivened by metonymic transfers and translations:

> And as to you Death, and you bitter hug of mortality . . . it is idle to try to alarm me.
> . . . .
> And as to you corpse I think you are good manure, but that does not offend me,
> I smell the white roses sweetscented and growing,
> I reach to the leafy lips . . . I reach to the polished breasts of melons.
>
> And as to you life, I reckon you are the leavings of many deaths,
> No doubt I have died myself ten thousand times before.

I hear you whispering there O stars of heaven,
O suns . . . O grass of graves . . . O perpetual transfers and
   promotions . . . If you do not say any thing how can I say anything?
   (86)

Instead of pretending to speak for the world of continuous material transformations, Whitman claims that that world speaks through him, and
through him to his readers. He places his own utterances among and amidst
the various births and deaths, the transformations and promotions, the
multitudinous uttering things and tongues that form the fertile and inhu-
man human richness of the Earth, from which life comes and to which it
returns. He offers nothing at all about heaven or hell or the meaning of
either or of anything.

Death here becomes associated through metonymy, through sheer juxtaposition and not through metaphoric comparison or elevation, with the
endless erotic impulses of life. It becomes one more of those pulsations.
"Agonies," Whitman had written, "are one of my changes of garments"
(65). When Whitman's poet, near the end of his poem, poses as a preacher
("Do you see O my brothers and sisters? / It is not chaos or death—it is
form, union, plan—it is eternal life—it is Happiness"), his sermon unnames
each of these terms and breaks the vessel of its commonly comprehended
meaning. And it is the broken vessels of sacred and common meanings, the
open question of the meaning or meaninglessness of life's endless and
crowded contiguities, that opens in turn onto questions of democratic
union and ethics, the interrelations of self and other figured as the multitudes of future readers teeming in a secular and conflicted age, to which
the poet so often in his early poems returns and which he seeks to enchain
metonymically in his poems.[55]

CHAPTER 4

Whitman and Democracy: The "Withness of the World" and the Fakes of Death

Despite the distance he takes from meaning in his poems, Whitman's embrace of the crowd of readers he imaginatively projects is peculiarly intense. If he tends to deny the importance of meaning in his early poems, he does not turn his back on his audience but repeatedly seeks to embrace or grapple with his readers. No poet has ever imagined himself more closely tied to the modern crowd. These, for the poet, become not only his potential audience but also the body of democracy. While Whitman declared himself to be unconcerned with God, he often proclaimed his passion for democracy. "I speak the password primeval," he famously declared in 1855, "I give the sign of democracy;/By God! I will accept nothing which all cannot have their counterpart of on the same terms" (50). Yet democracy in Whitman seems, upon examination, less an article of belief than a question that must remain perpetually open to whatever it is that will come next. Democracy is the governing form of the secular state and seems as distant from fixed meaning as Whitman's poetry. As Jason Frank puts it, Whitman's "democratic aesthetics" calls "for an embrace of a world always in the process of becoming other than it is."[1] He projects democracy through the medium of the body—his physical and textual being—and he imagines that body in contact with the crowd around it, the people, objects, scenes who come or will come, now or in some unspecified future, to define and constitute his existence. Shortly after his declaration of commitment to democracy above, he writes:

> If I worship any particular thing it shall be some of the spread of my
>   body;
> Translucent mould of me it shall be you,
> Shaded ledges and rests, firm masculine coulter, it shall be you,
> Whatever goes to the tilth of me it shall be you,
> You my rich blood, your milky stream of pale strippings of my life;
> Breast that presses against other breasts it shall be you, . . .
> Winds whose soft-tickling genitals rub against me it shall be you,
> Broad muscular fields, branches of liveoak, loving lounger in my winding
>   paths, it shall be you,
> Hands I have taken, face I have kissed, mortal I have ever touched, it shall
>   be you. (51)

Democracy and death seem identified and entwined with the poet's mortal body—its returning to the dust to grow the self up into these others who shall be "you." There is a note of futurity here, as in the last lines of "Song of Myself": "I bequeath myself to the dirt to grow from the grass I love," (88). Whitman imagines a future existence as "mould" or "tilth," as part of the corpse-composted soil prepared as a place where the seeds of the future might take root and grow, a site where future readings and communions might occur. There is also a note of uncertainty, however, expressed in the ambiguity of the repeated verb "shall." This may denote a future certain to occur or an attempt to will that future into existence, a blurring of indicative and optative moods. What does democracy have to do with death and the future in Whitman's imagination?

Politics and death have long been associated. Consider *Gilgamesh*, the tale of a king who learns to accept and live his life and attend to his city's present and future only by learning that he can learn nothing about death. Whitman's poetry presents a similar mortal and prudential wisdom. Mohammed Bamyeh observes that in ancient political theory the opposite of death is not simply life but power and governance and that power and governance structure themselves through their orientation toward death.[2] Jacques Derrida, in *The Gift of Death*, sees the emergence of the individual and of democracy in the West resulting from and reflecting revisions of attitudes toward life's mysteries that structure the subject's relationship to responsibility and, ultimately, to death.[3] In the United States, as Russ

Castronovo has richly detailed, the dream of death and the erotics of democratic citizenship appear together in complicated constellations. Dominant among these is a fantasy of democratic citizenship that requires an abstraction from the body, which Castronovo says "incites a necrophilic desire to put democratic unpredictability and spontaneity to death" by rendering the complexity of lived subjectivity—its embodied existence as a specific and particular self—as private, thus excluding specificities of lived identity from the public sphere and structuring democratic discourse around their absence.[4] Castronovo has little in this context to say about Whitman, except to note that he stands as an exception to this "necro citizenship" because of his "insistence on . . . materiality, his belief that the dead are 'palpable' and continue to have emotional, social, and symbolic significance for the living" not as abstracted souls but as embodied presences.[5] Let us attempt to feel our way through the palpability of death and democracy in Whitman's poems.

Whitman's early poetry forms a moment in the modern revision of the ancient tradition that associates death and polity, but for Whitman, death is anything but a decorporealization of the self. For Whitman, *Leaves of Grass*—the constitution of his own body in and as poetry and his projection of it toward the future—becomes linked metonymically and incorporated with the bodies of his readers and, by implication, the body politic itself. His orientation toward the future is not a challenge to death but an example of death's expression in life—the "outlet song of life" the poet mentions in his elegy for Lincoln. As is often the case in Whitman's strongest poetry, this is not a spiritual but a material transaction. Michael Moon has observed that the "attribution of 'the body' in Whitman's poetry shifts between belonging to the author and belonging to the reader."[6] This shifting finds expression in the poet's celebration of a single separate self in the world, on the one hand, and on the other his indication of the self-articulation that projects him toward the future as an enactment of death, dissemination, and deliverance. Whitman bequeaths himself to his readers and the future to grow and proliferate like grass and to await the moment a future reader or readers might utter him again. To the future, Whitman says near the end of his book's beginning, "It is you talking just as much as myself. . . . I act as the tongue of you, / It was tied in your mouth . . . in mine it begins to be loosened" (84). Death and the reader become equated for Whitman and occupy the future together. In this way, again, death and life become confused. Both, in his imagination, decenter the self he sings, staging its dissolution and yielding to the other, becoming incorporated into the earth and translated into the other's tongue, the other's utterance, an alteration and perpetuation of the self the poet sings and celebrates.

Whitman consistently distances this protean death from common notions of loss or mourning. He worries little about spiritual survival or final extinction. It is his transvalued thought of death that allows him to relate the subject of democracy to the subject of his poetry. For Whitman, death describes and enacts the ineluctable displacements of self and world toward the future and those displacements, like the democratic future itself, remain for the present fluid and incalculable, a question whose answer, in a secular age, cannot be given in advance.

Whitman's poetry constitutes the poetic self he sings as part of the material and secular world he exists in and describes. As Angus Fletcher notes, in Whitman, "images of the surrounding world function as contiguous reflections, or metonymical expressions of the poet's self" of, that is, the poet's embodied presence.[7] The self in Whitman's poems is always figured as a body and imagined in physical contact or shifting identification with an environment that teems with other bodies, a modern, usually urban crowd that is always a figure for his potential readers as well. Through contact and identification with and through the poet's self, the poem projects the form, union, plan of the world. "It is," he writes near the end of the first poem, "not chaos or death. . . . It is form and union and plan . . . it is eternal life. . . . It is happiness" (87). But as a cosmic ordering, Whitman's intervention into the secularity of his world remains pretty minimalist: "it is without name . . . it is a word unsaid, / It is not in any dictionary or utterance or symbol" (86). His gestures toward unity and order in his poetry, like the self he sings, seem more metonymic bundles of disparate selves or contending possibilities than organic meldings of or grounds for unifying beliefs.

R. W. B. Lewis long ago described Whitman's poetic persona as just such a bundle of selves, a "typesetter, reporter, dandy, stroller in the city, political reporter," yet remaining the unsummed aggregation of all of these.[8] Whitman repeatedly stages the tension between the pull of identifications that transform the poet into whatever and whomever he beholds and the assertions of a single separate self who stands apart for a moment only to reenact his surrender to the world. Consider these lines, the last of which I touched upon in the previous chapter:

> I am a free companion . . . I bivouac by invading watchfires,
>
> I turn the bridegroom out of bed and stay with the bride myself,
> I tighten her all night to my thighs and lips.

My voice is the wife's voice, the screech by the rail of the stairs,
They fetch my man's body up dripping and drown'd . . .

All this I swallow, it tastes good . . . I like it well, it becomes mine,
I am the man . . . I suffer'd . . . I was there.

The disdain and calmness of martyrs,
The mother condemned for a witch, burnt with dry wood, and her
    children gazing on;
The hounded slave that flags in the race, leans by the fence, blowing,
    covered with sweat,
The twinges that sting like needles his legs and neck,
The murderous buckshot and the bullets,
All these I feel or am . . .
Agonies are one of my changes of garments;
I do not ask the wounded person how he feels . . . I myself become the
    wounded person . . . (65)

One might ask—and critics have asked—by what title or authority Whitman identifies his white male self with the burned mother and the hunted slave. I do not know that there is ever an answer to the arrogance of identification when it is posed in such stark terms. I also do not know whether any ethics or social life is possible without such identifications. What interests me here is that Whitman imagines transforming himself into the other rather than absorbing the other into himself. He does not digest what he swallows but leaves it alien and whole. Each identification transforms his sense of himself in a way that poses the question of identification's ethical limits even as it enacts the identification that ethics requires. Without imaginative projection, without imagining the other's feelings and desires, the categorical imperative to treat others as we would be treated remains an empty injunction.[9] Whitman's imaginative self-projections transform a list of apparently randomly chosen companions, sexual partners, oppressed men, persecuted women, and bereaved spouses into a series of incorporated but distinct, imaginative others that the poet ingests and transforms into constituents of the poetic "I" that they each alter in turn. Or, as Whitman's poet declares at the end of the long, famous list of the city's multitudes going about their varied tasks in what becomes section 15 of "Song of Myself": "And these tend inward to me, and I tend outward to them,/And such as it is to be of these more or less I am,/And of these one and all I weave the song of myself" (203). As Kerry Larson notes, where Keats saw the poet's capacity for identification with others entailing a loss of the self, Whitman insists "on an opposing perspective. . . . [He] no more implies the forfeiture of other selves . . . than the loss of his own." Larson goes on to stress "the dynamic implications suggested in Whitman's determination to preserve both sides of this exchange, for rather than merely urging or advocating the union of the many and the one, . . . [he] undertakes to act out this conjunction of interests" in his poems.[10] In the shifting constitution of this promiscuously incorporative, democratically inclusive, ethically alive and potentially embattled fabrication of a lyric "I" lies the secret of Whitman's poetry's power and the political stakes at its secular core.

Larson follows a hint from Donald Pease in his exploration of the odd composition of the self in Whitman's poetry. He notes that the opening lines of "Song of Myself" "eschew the ritual of invocation for a simple performative, 'I celebrate myself and sing myself.' The subject/object dualism conventional to address is here conflated for what appears as an inextricable fusion between the 'I' that speaks and the 'I' that is spoken, as if being claimed no permanence beyond the immediate moment it is uttered into existence."[11] Like Fletcher, Larson finds in Whitman a self linked to its environment through poetry. He notes that the "I" Whitman sings into being tends to disperse itself through the landscape as so many "words . . . loosed to the eddies of the wind," as in the benediction at the end of "Song of Myself." If, as Larson argues, Whitman's poet is always beginning and ending at the same time, then the close relationship of inception and death, erotic cohesion and final dissolution, frequently evident in Whitman's poetry begins to assume an explicable shape, or at least a comprehensible shapelessness. These catalogs seem, as Larson says, "as heterogeneous in content as they are undifferentiated in structure."[12] They manifest, he continues, the lowest grade of connectedness imaginable, figuring what William James called "a world of mere *withness*, of which the parts were only strung together by the conjunction 'and.'"[13] In James's view, I would add, this world of mere withness is occupied by a self imagined as a bundle of lives, a pluralism of existences rather than a single or unified entity: "Such a universe," James says, "is even now the collection of our several inner lives." He writes:

> The spaces and times of your imagination, the objects and events of your day-dreams are not only more or less incoherent *inter se*, but are wholly out of definite relation with the similar contents of anyone else's mind. Our various reveries now as we sit here compenetrate each other idly without influencing or interfering. They coexist, but, in no order and in no receptacle, being the nearest approach to an absolute 'many'

that we can conceive. We can not even imagine any reason why they *should* be known all together, and we can imagine even less, if they were known together, how they could be known as one systematic whole.[14]

James describes the self that Whitman's self-projections and catalogs had conjured a half-century before. This "I" is comprised of inner diversity. "I resist anything better than my own diversity," Whitman wrote in 1855, and, famously, "I am large . . . I contain multitudes" (87). This self is situated in and open to the diverse, secular world of the modern crowd, whose constituent selves comprise and reflect the poet's identities: "In all people I see myself, none more and not one a barley-corn less, / And the good or bad I say of myself I say of them" (45). The self in James faces the same challenge Whitman's poet faced: how to make of this teeming, contiguous chaos an ordered cosmos with which one could live. How can one imagine or project, even if only for a moment, a single separate self in a coherent and orderly world that itself lacks reliable or uncontested grounds for existence or belief. Is there any substance to the poet's self-declaration as "Walt Whitman, an American, one of the roughs, a kosmos" (50)? Can one be a citizen, a rough, and a kosmos in the same instant? No finite verbs intrude upon or shape this short list of identities. Finite verbs rarely appear in Whitman's most intense declamations and extended catalogs. What are a self and a world uttered with so few verbs, a song composed of metonymically enchained nouns and noun phrases and gerunds?[15] What do they suggest about the presence or absence of order in a secular world? What do they suggest about life and death or self and others or democracy and union?

There is already an element of death in this witness of the world.[16] The self-conscious subject stands apart from the world. "Apart from the pulling and hauling stands what I am . . . / Both in and out of the game, and watching and wondering at it," as Whitman says (31). The corpse, by contrast, is a thing among the other things. Consider Wordsworth's figuration of death as mere witness in the world in his mourning poem for Lucy:

A SLUMBER did my spirit seal;
   I had no human fears:
She seemed a thing that could not feel
   The touch of earthly years.

No motion has she now, no force;
   She neither hears nor sees;
Rolled round in earth's diurnal course,
   With rocks, and stones, and trees.[17]

In those lines from 1799, Wordsworth contemplates an impenetrable, time-bound world whose mortality he failed to imagine could touch his beloved but to whose mechanical and insensate movement she has now been conjoined by death. Death removes sense and self-consciousness, reducing her to mere withness among the rocks and stones and trees. Whitman, for his part, never forgets that the beloved body—his own among others—is always already addressed to death, always already an object with the objects of the world and, like them, slated to pass away, always is passing away from moment to moment—good compost before and after death—into the altering material world of the other bodies he addresses. "And as to you life," he writes in one of the several apostrophes that end "Song of Myself," "I reckon you are the leavings of many deaths, / No doubt I have died myself ten thousand times before" (86). Death becomes a familiar, indeed daily, hourly, moment-by-moment occurrence.

This vision involves something other than personal immortality or the transmigration of souls. Whitman describes a determinately impersonal and material recirculation of substantial being and he urges his readers to embrace it.

> And as to you Corpse I think you are good manure, but that does not
>   offend me,
> I smell the white-roses sweetscented and growing,
> I reach to the leafy lips . . . I reach to the polish'd breasts of melons. (86)

For Whitman's poet, the decaying corpse and the world to which it yields its substance become the living lover's body and the world he stretches to caress. All the world's objects and death itself are eroticized and oddly, impersonally made equivalent without quite being made the same. There seems no border between life and death, self and other, animate and inanimate, and no distinction between the desired and the abject. At moments in this poetry the world seems a vast charnel house and a moment later it seems teeming with multitudes and life. Among these oscillations the poet remains, in his address to life and death, indifferent.

This indifference toward death and life seems the most difficult aspect of Whitman's poetry to grasp or summarize. David Bromwich, taking a page from D. H. Lawrence, summarizes Whitman's vision of immortality as follows:

> Our usual mistake about immortality, as Whitman sees it, is to imagine
> our survival as the extension of a single entity. We can avoid this, he
> thinks, by supposing that we continue in time only as an author's

words continue in the minds of his readers. They create a benefit that is inconceivable to the benefactor. Our extension in space, through our moral relations with others, implies continuity of another sort. But to explain it, Whitman suggests that we can appeal only to what we know of existence (physical existence).[18]

The tentativeness of Bromwich's account is as commendable as its clarity. I think it nonetheless makes Whitman's treatment of death sound too finely rational, too moralistic, and too confidently final. Whitman's words, like the molecules and atoms of his flesh, like the words of the poems he utters, simply circulate, making the eddies of breath, the decomposition of flesh, and the poet's survival in the minds and mouths of his readers indifferent without quite being the same. The rigors of this view of things do not come easily to the poet or his audience. This is the difficult lesson he culls from Lucretius, as he will report it in "Democratic Vistas":

> Surely, this universal ennui, this coward fear, this shuddering at death, these low, degrading views, are not always to rule the spirit pervading future society, as it has the past and does the present. What the Roman Lucretius sought most nobly, yet all too blindly, negatively to do for his age and its successors, must be done positively by some great coming literatus, especially the poet, who,—while remaining fully poet, will absorb whatever science indicates, with spiritualism, and out of them, and out of his own genius, will compose the great poem of death. Then will man indeed confront Nature, and confront time and space, both with science, and *con amore.* (1012–1013)

Lucretius, as I remarked earlier, seems present in Whitman from the opening lines of his book in which he declares, "Every atom belonging to me, as good belongs to you" (27). Throughout his work, the confrontation with the fundamental materialism of nature, time, and change stripped of conventional belief or consolation remains a challenge for him as well as for the readers he imagines. For example, the poem that will later be called "To Think of Time" ends with a defiant thought of immortality: "I swear I think there is nothing but immortality! / . . . And all preparation is for it . . . and identity is for it . . . and life and death are for it" (106), but this assertion of immortality as an end also remains haunted by the possibility of ending in extinction that breaks into and breaks up the easy grammar of Whitman's line: "If otherwise, all these things came but to ashes of dung; / If maggots and rats ended us, then suspicion and treachery and death" (105). He seldom forgets that whatever he sees or feels of immortality's "exquisite scheme" (106), the reader, upon whom his future life depends, may not quite be able to make out; whatever he has to say of an "eternal soul!" shared with "trees . . . rooted in the ground . . . the weeds of the sea . . . [and] . . . animals" (106), the reader might not understand. (For indeed, such animism is not a comforting Christian belief but a materialist heresy.) Not understanding, the reader might depart and leave him unread. For the poet, that would be an ending in extinction indeed, a death without the erotic pulse that might associate death with poetry and translate it into disseminated life now and in the future.

For Whitman, life after death, like life, itself depends upon the circulation of matter as atoms or utterance. Life requires the seduction and penetration of the modern crowd of potential readers and the corresponding hum of their valved voice (30). As in Lucretius, this is immortality imagined as metonymic relay or translation—words mouthed or hummed in one throat sympathetically hummed or mouthed in another, the materiality of language's vibration passed from body to body, the tongue of the poet loosed in his mouth moving to the reader's and tying the two together. "There was never," Whitman says, "any more inception than there is now" (28): "Always a knit of identity . . . always distinction . . . always a breed of life" (28). This perpetual movement of inception, this ceaseless knitting and reknitting of identity and distinction, is the only immortality—indeed the only life—Whitman imagines.

To imagine life as eternal transformation and identity as an endless reknitting of the threads and the utterances of distinct existences is to imagine death not as the end of time but as the continuation of the material changes that mark time. The "sign of democracy" consists in this endless speaking of and being spoken by the others around the poet:

> Through me many long dumb voices,
> Voices of the interminable generations of slaves,
> Voices of prostitutes and of deformed persons,
> Voices of the diseased and despairing, and of thieves and dwarfs,
> Voices of cycles of preparation and accretion,
> And of the threads that connect the stars—and of wombs, and of the
>   fatherstuff,
> And of the rights of them the others are down upon,
> Of the trivial and the flat and foolish and despised,
> Of fog in the air and beetles rolling balls of dung. (50)

All is conveyed forward by the endless capacity of mere withness to add to its list or catalog first one thing, then another and so on, from the long-dumb voices of the present to the silenced voices of the dead, from those seeking justice to beetles rolling dung, knitting them all together and making them correspond in the poem at least for a moment.

These indiscriminate expansions of metonymy as withness differ from the hieratic orderings of sense and signification that metaphor implies. Withness does not fix or transport a meaning, as metaphor can, but attaches one signifier to another, then another, then another. Metonymy need not carry anything over from one element of the list to another or from one conceptual realm or world to another. It moves disjunctively through displacement from one momentarily embodied sign to another momentarily embodied sign within the world of things, including signs, that includes and constitutes the self. This real materiality of the self, and not its theoretical spirituality, constitutes the central and ineffable mystery of life as Whitman imagines it: "To elaborate is no avail. . . . Learned and unlearned feel that it is so. / Sure as the most certain is sure . . . plumb in the upright, well entretied, braced in the beams, / Stout as a horse, affectionate, haughty, electrical, / I and this mystery here we stand" (28). A mystery that is stout as a horse and braced in the beams seems a solidly material mystery indeed, one that not only stands apart from the world but is also structurally bound up with and to the world's things in their endless shifting through space and time.

Note in these lines the unfamiliar word "entretied," which neither *Webster's Dictionary* nor the *Oxford English Dictionary* lists as a word. Larousse doesn't contain it either, but Whitman's coinage suggests something close to the French *entretien*, a noun meaning conversation. *Entretenir*, a closely related verb, means—as a participle—well serviced or well maintained as well. It also, in English, suggests a plea or entreaty addressed to another, perhaps for deliverance. Whitman must have found the odd conjunction of entre and tied—the French preposition and the English predicate—suggestive. He stands not isolated in the world but tied up with and between things, stiffened as if by a carpenter's brace (and phallically as well) in the self-construction of the well-maintained "I" that appears in the poem's next phrase. The filaments of affiliation, the conjunctive elements running athwart and binding together its disparate parts, give this "I" whatever momentary structural integrity it possesses.

For Whitman's poet the construction of the self occurs less in the substantive elements—the noun phrases and long catalogs of nouns and noun phrases that make up so much of his most exciting early poetry—and more in the simple, tendentious act of joining these elements, bracing and weaving them together (another way of glossing entretied would be "woven" or "tied together") as the poet holds them for moment in suspension in his own imagination and figures them on the page as the enchainment of the self he sings with common being and erotic union that he entreats his reader to join and carry on. Because such a self shifts itself with every new contact dreamed or tie established or imagined, every new lashing of self to the other through plea, perception, or fancy, it remains open to the alterations of state—the passing out of one life and entering into another—that suggest death but suggest as well that death is no end to, but merely a continuation of, the always altering movement of the world. It is toward this materialization of life and death, of the self and its alteration that Whitman gestures near the end of "Song of Myself," when he writes, "And as to you life I reckon you are the leavings of many deaths,/No doubt I have died myself ten thousand times before" (86). Whitman's sense of life and of death, his sense of himself, is ultimately resistant to any finality of content or meaning and is not only open to but fundamentally constituted by change and displacement. Whitman depends for whatever coherence he may possess on the formal persistence of the signifier, the seemingly self-similar but always shifting indexicality of the pronoun "I," in its various iterations and through its unpredictable readings by those anonymous and future others to whom he addresses *Leaves of Grass*. In this way he invents a lyric self for a secular age.

Democratic Superficiality

Whitman's most profound mysteries are superficial, and they involve death and democracy. Wai Chee Dimock describes Whitman as "a poet whose commitment to democratic justice is, not least of all, a formal commitment, whose poetry, with its endless catalogs, its endless collections of attachable, detachable parts, one as good as another, one substitutable for the other, is perhaps as close as any poetry can come to being a generative grammar . . . a poetics governed by syntax."[19] This makes Whitman's "I" a poetic representation of the democratic "citizen," who, through varied embodiments and rearticulations of himself or herself, remains the referent of a shifting signifier—the universal cipher of the shifter, "I"—the constituent member of the republic's secular body politic. As has been often noted, liberal justice and democratic equality aspire to an abstraction of citizenship that ideally should achieve something like the precision of an algebraic formula—citizens X and Y are equal before the law and in the eyes of the state, and what pertains to one pertains to another no matter who or what semantic markers or existential accidents color the identities of X and Y in a given context or situation.[20] Whitman's poetry depends upon and also works against these abstract equivalences as it sutures the ubiquitous first-person pronoun into the shifting scenes of the multitudinous and embodied masses of the teeming modern world. For Whitman, these scenes and his inventories of them express what in "Song of the Broad-Axe" he calls "The loose drift of character," which he embodies so often elsewhere in his poetry:

> The loose drift of character, the inkling through random types, the solidification;
> The butcher in the slaughter house, the hands abroad schooners and sloops, the raftsman, the pioneer,
> Lumbermen in their winter camp, daybreak in the woods, stripes of snow on the limbs of trees, the occasional snapping,
> The glad clear sound of one's own voice, the merry song, the natural life of the woods, the strong day's work (332)

It is the effect of Whitman's best poetry to make moments like this—moments that should be madly and impossibly inclusive—seem for a moment perfectly natural and pleasing, like the sound of one's own voice, all part of the merry song of a day's work, and the dream of what Castronovo calls necro citizenship, to kill off difference. Whitman's anaphoras bespeak a radically democratic ideal, an aspiration to forge long metonymic chains linking his song with an often-apostrophized "you," addressed, potentially, to the specific reader and also to everyone else, knitting them into a union of equals in motion toward the future.

The frequently noted problem with all this, of course, lies in its residual capacity to become the reduction of the differences it seeks to utter, to reduce the particularities of separate identities to a blank universalism that does not include differences but requires their suppression.[21] When Whitman becomes bathetically patriotic or lapses into mannered gestures, he imaginatively constructs union at the expense of difference and his poetry loses vitality. But I think it is also true that Whitman's best poetry dramatizes this tension within liberal democracy's claims to universal inclusiveness by dramatizing the dangers of attempting to unify diversity under a single figure—the lyric "I" of the poem or the nation.

To see this requires attention to the profundity of Whitman's fascination with surfaces. What drives the poet's promiscuous impulse to touch and to catalogue, to contact and to name, to penetrate and to be penetrated is his sheer fascination with superficialities (for superficies are often all we have in the crowded world and the teaming nation of nations that Whitman struggles to depict). In Whitman's world, there are no psychological depths to plumb and no deep experiences to mine for lyrical richness. But there is a play of surfaces and the hum of the crowd—the touch of the body and the blab of the pavements. The rapid variation and displacement of those noisy surfaces most excite Whitman, not any profound similarity or deep and stable identity one might imagine they held in common. Whitman is no humanist. He imports these heterogeneities into identity itself in a way that pushes beyond humanism's limits and seems very different from and vastly more interesting than universalism's homogenizing claims. It is superficiality that makes Whitman a great poet and a modern bard.

I remarked at the beginning of the last chapter that Whitman's poet seems akin to Poe's Man of the Crowd. Yet the difference between the poet's relationship to the others he catalogs and the Man of the Crowd's fascination with the "tumultuous sea of human heads" is definitive. As Poe's narrator surveys the press of the diverse strangers in the city street, he begins to identify and classify them by type. He reduces the heterogeneity of the crowd to an orderly procession of clerks and shop girls, workers and idlers. His system breaks down and he becomes feverish and overwhelmed when he spots the old man whose "absolute idiosyncrasy of . . . expression" he cannot identify. Faced with the old man's inscrutable difference, the excited narrator finds himself driven nearly mad by a character he judges to be "evil," a character so lacking in transparency: that, as he tells us, "*Er lässt sich nicht lesen*," he will not allow himself to be read.[22] Poe's narrator obsessively deciphers the meaning of what he sees, desiring to master the crowd and render it transparent to control his own hysteria, to maintain the coherence of his own ego. When the opacity of the old man frustrates this desire to render the world legible and, thereby, to master its masses, the frustration drives the narrator to an abjection of difference, an identification of the illegible old man with deep crime and horror. Whitman's poet, by contrast, amidst the same overstimulating crowd, falls in love with hysteria and becomes mad to be in contact with the teeming masses of the world, to absorb them and be absorbed in turn, moved by an intense erotic fervor to join himself with what he sees, abandoning his own ego in the process. At the same time, he remains mostly uninterested in what any of it means beyond the thrill of the experience. Whitman's poet embraces what Benjamin called the "shock" of modern experience.[23] He wants only superficial sequences of momentary contacts and displacements held together, if at all, by structures of grammatical repetition, and then only for the moment they are uttered. Whitman celebrates the sheer contiguity of the world's objects and peoples and identifies them all with the poem's ever-shifting "I." "And these one and all tend inward to me, and I tend outward to them, / And such as it is to be of these more or less I am" (42). The metaphor of weaving here stresses the persistent, independent identities of the threads that compose Whitman's text and vision, not their melding into a single, universal, whole.

Whitman's poetry often generates its erotic charge by exploiting the friction between a superficial interchangeability and the particular details of difference. This is true even in the poem that will eventually be called "The Sleepers," perhaps the most perfect realization of Whitman's desire to render each equivalent to all and all equivalent to him. Here, for once, Whitman immobilizes the crowds so that he can better imagine absorbing and averaging them. But even here, as Whitman imagines the masses sleeping, he dreams a tension between difference and junction that plays on the surfaces of things like an erotic frisson that trembles on the skin: "The diverse shall be no less diverse, but they shall flow and unite . . . they unite now" (115). This is the dream, however impossible to realize, that impels the poet to imagine an unimaginable unity in difference, a knit of identity, one that generates no common term or meaning but enacts a promiscuous and provisional weaving together. Whitman writes

> The sleepers are very beautiful as they lie unclothed,
> They flow hand in hand over the whole earth from east to west as they lie unclothed;
> The Asiatic and African are hand in hand . . . the European and American are hand in hand,
> Learned and unlearned are hand in hand . . . and male and female are hand in hand . . . (115)

This is a dreamscape in which, "Elements merge in the night . . . ships make tacks in the dreams . . . the sailor sails . . . the exile returns home" (114). As George Kateb, perhaps the most enthusiastic champion of Whitman's democratic individuality as receptivity to others, says, Whitman "understands that his radical empathy is only a dream, that mobile identity is only a dream (and that only in sleep or death are people alike and equal)."[24] For Kateb, this openness to the potentiality of identification with others is one thing Whitman means by "soul." Kateb calls this heterogeneity of the self the "secular soul."[25]

The wishfulness of dreams provides the proper context for reading lines that can seem nightmarish in their sentimentalization of conflict, like "The call of the slave is one with the master's call . . . and the master salutes the slave" (116). To return to criticisms by those who, like Wai Chee Dimock and Philip Fisher, understandably find such a line repellent, the reader

Whitman most desires, the reader Whitman dreams might enliven his poem by wrestling with it and with him, might be expected to add "in your dreams" to the poet's dream of slavery.[26] By daylight, Whitman came to know slavery to be the period's most horrific failure of political equality, moral imagination, and ethical judgment, though he was far from certain what to do about it.[27] This dream of uncritical inclusiveness, Whitman also knew, cannot—should not—withstand daylight, though in his poetry, at moments, inclusiveness is all. As he wrote in 1855, in what becomes "Song of Myself," section 22:

> I am he attesting sympathy; . . .
> And am not the poet of goodness only . . . I do not decline to be the poet
>   of wickedness also.
>
>   . . . .
>
> What blurt is it about virtue and about vice?
> Evil propels me and reform of evil propels me . . . I stand indifferent,
> My gait is no fault-finder's or rejecter's gait,
> I moisten the roots of all that has grown. (48)

Whitman knew that this was a monstrous version of sympathy—a perverse parody of ethics—yet he offers it unapologetically as a provocation to his readers and their comfortingly thoughtless blurts of virtue nonetheless.

Whitman actively desired resistant readers, and he refers to them often in the early editions of *Leaves of Grass*. "I am," he wrote in what becomes Section 47 of "Song of Myself," "the teacher of athletes / He that by me spreads a wider breast than my own proves the width of my own / He most honors my style who learns under it to destroy the teacher" (83). "The Sleepers," in its contents and in its relationship to its imagined readers, rehearses both the fundamental necessity and the limited possibility of participating in the lives of others—including onanists, ennuyés, criminals, and frustrated lovers. Whitman emphasizes the repulsiveness of many of these sleepers—the dimension of abjection entailed by the desire to penetrate the superficialities of difference to some more profound sense of commonality, some more perfect sense of union. By dwelling on unsavory types and repellent situations, Whitman provokes the reader to struggle with the lures and limits of identification and identity. In this way, he fulfills the promise made near the beginning of what will be "Song of Myself: "Have you felt so proud to get at the meaning of poems? / Stop this day and this night with me and you shall possess the origin of all poems, / . . . . You shall not look through my eyes either, nor take things from me, / You shall listen to all sides and filter them for yourself" (28). To read properly is to read differently, to make something of the poem, which, without the reader would be nothing at all.

Whitman's poetry, at its best, demands that the reader live the irreducible tension between difference and identity, commonality and divergence, union and diversity, community and conflict, through the reader's relationship to the poet and, through the poet, to the world. "You shall possess," he promises his reader, "the good of the earth and the sun. . . . You shall no longer take things at second or third hand, nor look through the eyes of the dead, nor feed on the spectres in books" (28). In "The Sleepers," when Whitman writes, "I dream in my dream all the dreams of the other dreamers, / And I become the other dreamers" (108), he reminds the wakeful, athletic reader that this is only a dream, and that only in a dream is untroubled union possible. "I swear they are averaged now . . . one is no better than the other / The night and sleep have liken'd them and restored them / . . . The myth of heaven indicates peace and night" (114–115). Even in a dream, even in the myth of heaven as a tranquil, average resting place, identities persist. For while averaging is a strange and fundamentally abstracting mathematical activity, the elements averaged remain unaltered by the process and retain their differences. Each remains distinct from the average to which it contributes but in which no single figure finds embodiment. Whitman depicts the process of averaging, not its result. Embodiment remains concrete, an experience of surfaces and differences in the poem and in the experience of the world that the poem evokes as a hiatus in the world's fractiousness.

Perhaps the oddest moment and most suggestive equivalence occurs in "The Sleepers," when Whitman turns from erotic or masturbatory fantasies ("Darkness, you are gentler than my lover . . . his flesh was sweaty and panting, / I feel the hot moisture yet that he left me" [109]) to thoughts of flaccidity, old age, death and corpses: "my sinews are flaccid, . . . / It is my face yellow and wrinkled instead of the old woman's" (110). Here identification both works its equation and meets its limits, for when the poet confronts death and enters the grave, as he has entered the beds of living men and women earlier in the poem, he becomes not the body but the shroud that wraps and hides it, not the dead person, man or woman, but the veil that covers and signifies that person's absence.

> A shroud I see—and I am the shroud . . . I wrap a body and lie in the
> coffin;
> It is dark here under ground . . . it is not evil or pain here . . . it is blank
> here, for reasons.

> It seems to me that everything in the light and air ought to be happy;
> Whoever is not in his coffin and the dark grave, let him know he has
>   enough. (110)

If death seems an unimaginably dark blank of nothingness, life teams with
distinct objects. Everything in the light ought to be happy. But death here
also appears as an object in the light and Whitman's access to it is limited
to its surfaces, the shroud that marks the corpse's presence and hides the
body at the same time. Whitman's shroud marks the limits of identification, which must always work across the superficial materiality of appearances. The person's interiority remains a blank. The shroud, like other
things in the light, partakes of the concrete superficiality of the signifier
and stops short of meaningful depth or universal significance. Death, in a
secular world, like the crowd of individuals who surround him in the city,
remains profoundly superficial. This is one way that, for Whitman, death
makes no difference. Both death and life can be known only by the touch
of surfaces and touch, as he says near the beginning of "Song of Myself,"
"is about as much as I can stand." It is touch that Whitman says is always
"quivering me to a new identity" (55). Aboveground in the light and air or
below in the coffin and shroud, identification stops at a surface, but the
touch of surfaces suffices, for a moment, for both the poet and the reader
and the interchanges of both.

Reading without Meaning, or the Ethics of Democratic Modernity

No poet more frequently or aggressively addresses his present and future
readers. Yet, as Kerry Larson says, "the relationship between the author
and reader is not something Whitman works *from* but works *toward*."[28]
Whitman brags about his prowess in his opening salvo, "And what I assume you shall assume" (27), but he also frequently anticipates his failure
to achieve a relationship or to accord with his readers. In Whitman, reading
usually seems something different from the decipherment of meaning,
which suggests piercing to the depths or getting at the meaning of poems.
Reading for Whitman is, like the world in which it occurs, a play of
surfaces. Sometimes the poet associates reading with physical contact,
especially in the "Calamus" poems, such as "Whoever You Are Holding
Me Now in Hand":

> Or if you will, thrusting me beneath your clothing,
> Where I may feel the throbs of your heart or rest upon your hip,
> Carry me when you go forth over land or sea;

For thus merely touching you is enough, is best,
And thus touching you would I silently sleep and be carried eternally. (275)

Sometimes he associates future readers with his physical presence, a withness across time, as in "Crossing Brooklyn Ferry": "I am with you, you men
and women of a generation or a thousand generations hence" (309). Sometimes he associates them with present struggle, as when he declares, "I am
the teacher of athletes," and so forth. Often he associates reading precisely
with misunderstanding or the failure to make contact: "But these leaves
conning you con at peril,/For these leaves and me you will not understand,/They will elude you at first and still more afterward, I will certainly elude you" (271). At these and many other similar moments, reading
for Whitman seems to involve anything but an arrival at a correct meaning. Poetry, for Whitman, is not about meanings. "Not words, not music
or rhyme I want, not custom or lecture, not even the best" he declares in
"Song of Myself," "Only the lull I like, the hum of your valved voice" (30).
Poetry in a secular world is the enactment of a material presence made only
of words set amidst a world of objects without stable meanings at their core.

That verbal presence entails a certain absence as well. For Whitman,
language may be a prod and provocation, poetry may be an invitation or
an assault, but neither poetry nor language can be made to simply say what
it means. Consider these lines from "Song of Myself," which will form part
of section 25:

Speech is the twin of my vision . . . it is unequal to measure itself.

It provokes me forever,
It says sarcastically, Walt you understand enough . . . why don't you let it
    out then?

Come now I will not be tantalized . . . you conceive too much of
    articulation.
Do you not know how the buds beneath you are folded? (53)

The inequality of speech to the speaker's vision or to itself—its inability
to be more or less than ironic—the sarcastic self-interrogation, the conception of conceiving too much of articulation, these are the keys to Whitman's construction of a world in words. This world is the world he calls
the world of "Reality . . . Materialism first and last imbuing" (49) and in
which he seeks to utter what he calls "a word of the modern . . . a word en-
masse" (49), desiring contact with the masses of readers who fill his pages
even while warning himself that articulation possesses perils of its own.

The self that Whitman articulates appears coextensive not only with his book but also with the heterogeneous and conflicted contexts in which the book finds and, he hopes, will find its readers, the teeming mass of contentious opinions and fundamental strife that secular democracy in the United States was and is. For this reason, democracy as the dream of an articulation of the self with the world remains haunted by the figure of its own failure. The poet who seeks to give the sign of democracy remains haunted by failure as well. In this important sense, Whitman's occasional claims that he remains above the hurly burly of the crowds within which he also moves and apart from the multitudes that he also contains do not seem claims to a separate, abstract self but declarations that articulation has failed, and must, ultimately fail. Whitman is the poet of contact, but he is also the poet of contact's impossibility, of the impossibility of truly joining, here and now, physically or imaginatively, with those among whom one finds oneself living.

Consider the odd juxtaposition of "you conceive too much of articulation" with what soon follows it:

My final merit I refuse you . . . I refuse putting from me the best I am.

Encompass worlds, but never try to encompass me.
I crowd your noisiest talk by looking toward you. (53)

And then in the next sentence:

Writing and talking do not prove me,
I carry the plenum of proof and everything else in my face,
With the hush of my lips I wholly confound the skeptic. (53)

Where might one see the face or hear the hushing lips to which these lines refer? They exist only in the very writing that does the poet's talking and that the first clause seems to dismiss. Here again the poet contradicts himself. To read these lines simply as the affirmation of Whitman's self apart from the vicissitudes of words, apart from the possibility that skeptics will contradict and readers misunderstand him, is to forget that the multitudes he figures as part of his self-utterance figure a self that is, as he will put it in "Song of the Rolling Earth," itself "a word" among other words comprising the poet's poem, self, and world (363). And in "Calamus," Whitman explores the shifting identity in words that equate his body with the book the reader holds, whoever that reader may be whenever he or she may come to take him in hand.

Behind Whitman's brag, there is a modesty about meaning, a distance from "the talk of the beginning and the end" (28) and the attempt to fix meanings, which the poet explicitly eschews. There is an assertion of a physical presence apart from meaning yet remaining the incalculable occasion of all the meanings of the earth. Nothing could be more distant from the spiritual semiotics of Emerson's *Nature*, which hopefully asserted the world's metaphoric significance as a hieratic and hierarchical symbol of the spirit.[29] Whitman's best poetry works hard to avoid the dematerialization of world or word into meaning. If there is a loss of specificity here, it results not from an attempt to embrace the abstract but from a struggle to move as far toward the concrete as possible, to the very shroud enwrapping the final, impenetrable mystery of death but not beyond. That a final opacity may be the result indicates more about Whitman's modesty and his secular modernity than his often-alleged arrogance.[30]

In this light, Whitman's tendency to interrogate himself and his readers in precisely the same tones of exasperated affection seems significant. In "Song of the Rolling Earth" (1856), Whitman's poem moves from the words on the page to the earth itself, to the human body and to the poet's body as well. Whitman identifies all of these as words, but he reminds his readers that as words they cannot quite encompass or delimit the fluidity of existence that they nonetheless indicate:

A song of the rolling earth, and of words according,
Were you thinking that those were the words, those upright lines? those
    curves, angles, dots?
No, those are not the words, the substantial words are in the ground and
    sea,
They are in the air, they are in you.

Were you thinking that those were the words, those delicious sounds out
    of your friend's mouths?
No, the real words are more delicious than they.

Human bodies are words, myriads of words,
(In the best poems re-appears the body, man's or woman's, well-shaped,
    natural, gay,
Every part able, active, receptive, without shame or the need of shame.)

Air, soil, water, fire—those are words,
I myself am a word with them—my qualities interpenetrate with theirs—
    my name is nothing to them,

Though it were told in the three thousand languages, what would air,
soil, water, fire, know of my name? (362–363)

In these lines the self, as a word, interpenetrates the words of the world
though it remains at last nothing to or in the world but a name: "my qualities interpenetrate with theirs—my name is nothing to them." In the reference to the three thousand languages, one senses the pressure of Volney's
detranscendentalizing vision of the human cosmos as a babble of contending voices. In the characteristic balance between the power of utterance
and the impossibility of articulation, Whitman sounds most like himself.

No reader of Whitman could miss the odd descriptor "delicious" in
these lines which recalls, of course, the even odder use of the word at the
climax of a poem once entitled "A Word from the Sea" and now known as
"Out of the Cradle Endlessly Rocking" (1859). Whitman often seems more
inclined to taste words, to roll them around the surfaces of his mouth
and tongue, than to read them. Perhaps the most thrilling and chilling
lines in Whitman are these in which the word from the sea is told: "To
the outsetting bard." The sea whispers "the low and delicious word
death . . . /Creeping thence steadily up to my ears and laving me softly all
over,/Death, death, death, death, death" (393).[31] "Which," the poet says,
"I do not forget

> But fuse the song of my dusky demon and brother,
> That he sang to me in the moonlight on Paumanok's gray beach,
> With the thousand responsive songs at random,
> My own songs awaked from that hour,
> And with them the key, the word up from the waves,
> The word of the sweetest song and all songs,
> That strong and delicious word which, creeping to my feet,
> (Or, like some old crone rocking the cradle, swathed in sweet garments,
>   bending aside,)
> The sea whisper'd me. (393–394)

As in "Song of the Rolling Earth," the poet finds himself embodied not as
self-presence, but as a word in a world of objects that are words as well.
He discovers himself uttered by the world that speaks him into being—
"The sea whisper'd me." And the sea whispers him as *the* word that delimits
being and gives becoming its shape with death. This is a death that does
not end but continues along with life, like the repetitive motion of the
waves washing the shore, each moment of movement delivering itself con-
tiguously to its succeeding wave and to the shore, arriving as a word to be

tasted and savored more than just read—death, death, death, death, death. Whitman does not ask the sea to represent death as a metaphor or symbol. He hears the sea speaking a word without attaching any meaning to it or seeking to note or fix more than its material existence as an utterance.

Whitman's "death," like so much in his poetry, finally does not signify. It is not meaning, but the limit and condition of possibility for meaning. This, I take it, is the suggestion of a line from "Song of the Rolling Earth" like, "I utter and utter, / I speak not" which becomes only more uncannily suggestive in its context:

> The earth does not withhold, it is generous enough,
> The truths of the earth continually wait, they are not so conceal'd either,
> They are calm, subtle, untransmissible by print,
> They are imbued through all things conveying themselves willingly,
> Conveying a sentiment and invitation, I utter and utter,
> I speak not, yet if you hear me not of what avail am I to you?
> To bear, to better, lacking these of what avail am I? (363–364)

In these lines and what follows them, something like an aesthetic and an ethical vision for the poet and poetry emerges, and it is far less abstract or disembodied than attempts to harness Whitman's odd poetry to a familiar critique of liberalism or democracy can allow. Consider first that in these lines Whitman seems about to imagine the world as a living temple of symbols, a possibility that poets like Emerson, Baudelaire, and even Poe assume as part of poetry's continuous rearticulation of Petrarch's tropes of comparison. But he actually does something quite different. The world for Whitman stands apart from symbols. It offers no corresponding or expressive objects for the soul's discordant states, as it does for Baudelaire and Poe. It points toward no higher significances, as it does for Emerson. The earth, for Whitman, defines itself by what it is not and what it is not is any active verb imaginable:

> The earth does not argue,
> Is not pathetic, has no arrangements,
> Does not scream, haste, persuade, threaten, promise,
> Makes no discriminations, has no conceivable failures,
> Closes nothing, refuses nothing, shuts none out,
> Of all the powers, objects, states, it notifies, shuts none out. (364)

The repetition of "shuts none out," the peculiar intensification of what is after all the absence of any action, indicates that the earth's activity consists in its refusal to differentiate and its acceptance of all, its lack of signification, though it paradoxically furnishes signification's only ground, the ultimate indifference from which signification emerges:

> The earth does not exhibit itself nor refuse to exhibit itself, possesses still
>   underneath,
> Underneath the ostensible sounds, the august chorus of heroes, the wail
>   of slaves,
> Persuasions of lovers, curses, gasps of the dying, laughter of young
>   people, accents of bargainers,
> Underneath these possessing words that never fail. (364)

What can these words that do not speak but never fail portend? What can be the meaning of these word-sounds described in these disquieting lines as merely ostensible, merely apparent, that link, merely ostensibly, heroes, slaves, lovers, laughter, and dying?

"Ostensible," as adjective or noun, derives from the classical Latin *ostendere*, which meant to expose, to view, to exhibit. Its meaning developed from this neutral sense of the apparent to its familiar association in modern English with the untruthful and misleading, which has been its connotation since the eighteenth century. Whitman's use of the term here seems to hover between these two significances of the word, between the ostensible as that which appears or exhibits itself and the ostensible as that which misleads or disguises. The earth, however, is neither ostensible nor is it not ostensible—it does not exhibit itself and it does not refuse to exhibit itself. It remains "still underneath." And yet, despite all this seeming failure to differentiate or to signify, to appear or to represent, the earth remains both eloquent and dumb and never fails in being "still underneath," unmoving itself, but furnishing the grounds for movement nonetheless:

> To her children the words of the eloquent dumb great mother never fail,
> The true words do not fail, for motion does not fail and reflection does
>   not fail,
> Also the day and night do not fail, and the voyage we pursue does not fail.
>   (364)

Words that are eloquent from a source that remains dumb, words linked with motion, reflection, diurnal rhythms, and a voyage, words that do not fail. Whitman here places himself as the utterer of the words that speak not, but remain as dumb and eloquent as the earth, not symbols of transcendence or references to abstract ideas, but presentations of autochthonous solid masses. He speaks from the place of the unspeakable earth, but what can this speaking mean? Words, motion, reflection, time, and the voyage that, at last, does not fail. The word different from what anyone supposed and luckier, death, toward which all words, movement, thought, and time finally tend and from which they originate.

Here, then is the key to Whitman's secular poetics, which associates the political not with liberal abstractions but with an endless wrestling with concretions of alterity. Here is the reason that Whitman's metonymies arrest us not with inner states or profound meanings but with the nearly unutterable indication of life's teeming superficiality and of the fact that death remains just beneath these surfaces on which life occurs. Despite the lures of sentimentality or sententiousness (Whitman's poetry is good only when it avoids both), poetry, ethics, and politics for Whitman is a matter not of depth but of surface, not of profound identity but of superficial identification, of an irresolvable tension between the self and its others, love and indifference. What makes Whitman's poetry *poetry*, and often great poetry, is the manner in which it dwells with neither the political nor the ethical but supersedes both and infuses the world it imagines not with belief or meaning but with such erotic energy that all of life's significant oppositions, even life and death, begin to fuse, and the world's insignificance becomes suffused with energy and beauty.

Whitman's poetry moves his sensitive reader not to tears, as Poe hoped to do, but to nearly impossible moments of exhilaration, of visionary transport into, not out of, this world. At its best, Whitman's poetry takes the reader with the poet to the headland he imagines in the middle of "Song of Myself," where one may feel literally, if only momentarily, torn apart by the welter of worlds and words, the madness of mass contact with a heterogeneous crowd of prurient provokers, and the need to identify with even that which one finds abject or evil, and the desire to discover an erotic thrill even in the thought of death. At such moments, the reader feels borne along by the syntactical rhythms of Whitman's metonymies through the shifts of the self's multitudinous identifications and shifting identities until it all becomes too much and the reader resists.

This reader then will find herself or himself in the position of the poet who writes, "Is this then a touch? . . . quivering me to a new identity" (55), and chronicles the Orphic dismemberment of the poet, and by implication of the reader, and the momentary strangulation of the song that constitutes both:

On all sides prurient provokers stiffening my limbs,
Straining the udder of my heart for its withheld drip,

Behaving licentious toward me, taking no denial,
Depriving me of my best as for a purpose,
Unbuttoning my clothes, holding me by the bare waist,
Deluding my confusion with the calm of the sunlight and pasture fields,
Immodestly sliding the fellow-senses away,
They bribed to swap of with touch, and go and graze at the edges of me,
No consideration, no regard for my draining strength or my anger,
Fetching the rest of the herd around to enjoy them a while,
Then all uniting to stand on a headland and worry me . . .

I am given up by traitors,
I talk wildly . . . I have lost my wits . . . I and nobody else am the greatest
    traitor,
I went myself first to the headland . . . my own hands carried me there.

You villain touch! what are you doing? . . . my breath is tight in its throat,
Unclench your floodgates, you are too much for me. (55–56)

If Whitman has brought the reader along to this point on the worrying headland, then he and the reader stand at the perilous articulation point for poetry and for the secular crowd of poetry's modern readers as well, the impossible point from which strangers not only strangely matter to the self but actually constitute and threaten it at the same time. This is the point beyond which the threat of death becomes reality and the poet and the reader confront, for a moment, the wonder of the world from the position of a transfigured and transfiguring translation of death.

Here Whitman borrows from or translates the Dionysian origins of the elegiac tradition identified by Peter Sacks, but without the incipient spirituality and transcendence that Sacks notes in "the Orphic and Pythagorean adaptation of the Dionysian cults that most fully advanced a concept of the immortal soul."[32] In those cults, a troping of fertility charms become "mystical tokens endowing a guarantee of good fortune in the future life." For Whitman, the sprouts that take and accumulate after this Dionysian sundering represent nothing but the continuation of life through and with death in the material world. The mere fact of just continuing is what good fortune is without any belief in the promise of a future life after life in which the individual survives. From Whitman's point of view, irreducibly and courageously materialistic, the sundering of the poet's body by a crowd of readers and the dissolution of his physical corpse into good manure for future lives are, quite literally and indifferently, the same thing, and both are good.

The life of the poet disseminated (like Orpheus) through his work into the world and the death of the self, its decay and recirculation as compost and manure for new forms of life, become modalities of the same thing. Recall the special significance the Orphic myth must have had for Whitman, especially in Ovid's telling. After Eurydice's "second death," Orpheus renounces women and seeks only male lovers. He frustrates his audience of Thracian women, and in an erotic frenzy they tear him apart. His dismembered corpse lies on the ground while his severed head floats away on the river and, most important, keeps singing (*Metamorphoses* X, 1–66). As Susan Stewart glosses the Orphic myth, it reminds one of Whitman insisting on a face-to-face encounter within and across the limits of death. "In disobeying the interdiction against the face to face, Orpheus encounters the disappearance of his beloved and must attempt to fill her absence with compensatory song."[33] Remember that in "Out of the Cradle Endlessly Rocking," Whitman's great poem about his own poetic origin, the bird's song becomes full-throated only after the disappearance of his partner. Whitman learns the occult relations between poetry and death on that day. As Stewart puts it, Orpheus's "singing survives the sacrifice of his body, reaching into the future only as a consequence of this sacrifice. . . . The story of Orpheus underlines every poem."[34] It is not difficult to see that, understood in these terms, the story of Orpheus underlies Whitman's poetic self-making as well.

The self-sacrifice of the poet to the crowd both figures and explains the fortunes of death's luckiness for Whitman's poet. Death disseminates the self, or the self's body, and is indistinguishable from the continuation of a life imagined as endless alteration, self-contradiction, joinings and sunderings, endless change through song and in the articulation with and of the crowd of readers. These perpetuate the poet's words and sunder him from himself at the same instant. In Whitman's secular lyrics, death is no more other than the others to whom the poet addresses himself, to whom he gives himself up, and through whom he passes out of himself (dies) and becomes articulate with them (lives). "Death or life I am then indifferent, and my soul declines to prefer" ("Scented Herbage of My Breast," 269).

But what does that mean? In the context of Whitman's best poetry and especially in his first great poem, "Song of Myself," these moments of crisis and transport almost always involve a moment when not so much the poet as the poet's song threatens to cease to be:

I hear the train'd soprano . . . she convulses me like the climax of my
    love-grip;

The orchestra whirls me wider than Uranus flies,
It wrenches such ardors from my breast,
It throbs me to gulps of the farthest down horror,
It sails me . . . I dab with bare feet . . . they are licked by the indolent
    waves,
I am exposed . . . cut by bitter and poisoned hail,
Steep'd amid honey'd morphine . . . my windpipe throttled in fakes of
    death,
Let up again to feel the puzzle of puzzles,
And that we call Being. (54–55)

Throttled wind, fakes of death: "fakes," are the loops of a coil, as the *Oxford English Dictionary* has it, and here they figure the fashion in which death binds the secular poet to the world and loops in the reader as well. Impossible congestion cutting off the respiration, storms of bitter hail, and the music of the poem and the drama of the poet's and the reader's articulated performance, these are the excitements of poetry and the dangers of the world whose presence inspires and threatens the poet who sings it, like Orpheus, into moments of order without the benefit of certain belief in transcendence or creeds or schools. Being itself is ultimately, like death and the other things and people of the world, a word to be shared or articulated without fixed or stable meaning.

Here, in an important sense, is the key to Whitman's poetic trick, the momentary magic of his metonymies. In Whitman, again and again, the reader is asked to experience an overwhelming welter of metonymic linkages that nonetheless, despite the poet's resistance to signification, suggest significance but ultimately come to the limit of meaning at the limit of the poet's and the reader's imaginative energy. Past that limit lies the inaccessibility of death as a final transcendence or cessation of time, the inaccessibility of any world beyond this world. In this world, death finds its embodiment in the continued life of the reader's energy and utterance, which become relays for the poet's own. Addressing the future reader through death, Whitman writes, "I act as the tongue of you" (84). This is Whitman's ostensible secret and it is hidden always in plain view and often indicated by the poet. It remains hard to understand, and it makes Whitman's writing literature, in a modern sense, and secular.[35] Finally, Whitman has no message to convey. Birth and death, love and expiration, sex and grass, survival and extinction, life and death are forced into conjunction by the poet or found pressed up against each other in the teeming welter of the crowded world. These the poet places before the reader in his rhythmic lines that suggest order without actually imposing it. Whether that order originates in the world, in the poet's words, or in the reader's longing—a longing for political and ethical order that Kant knew was fundamentally aesthetic and essentially human—Whitman does not, and knows he cannot, say. And in not saying that, he says everything.

Whitman's poetry challenges readers to make sense of the overwhelming noisiness of a contentiously secular and crowded modern world in which the very wheels in the street seem to blab on the pavement and in which talk of conventional virtues becomes mere blurting. It is a challenge readers refuse at their own peril. For as Whitman suggests but cannot say, if there is life among the teeming deaths of the world, it is only because our own rage for order—to echo Wallace Stevens—suffuses the world with its own bright jets of joy, meeting the threatening din of the world's deadly order with the enlivening appeal of its own barbaric yawp. Whitman's genius was not only to invent a poetic form to order and disorient the world, but also to realize that the ethical and political survival of a democratic nation in a secular age may depend upon the ability to imagine the fakes of union where union has no substantial meaning beyond the vagaries and instabilities of a pressing and renewable urge for contact.

PART III

Emily Dickinson

CHAPTER 5

The Poet as Lyric Reader

If Whitman works to embrace and incorporate the crowd into the texture of his poetry and of the self who sings it, Dickinson seems to work equally hard to hold her audience, and sometimes even the world, at a distance. Sometimes she links her poetry to the epistolary impulse to address a single other as in "If you were coming in the Fall,/I'd brush the Summer by/With half a smile, and half a spurn,/As Housewife's do, a Fly" (F356).[1] Sometimes she seems to reject this world altogether to focus attention on the next as in "This World is not conclusion./A species stands beyond—/Invisible, as Music—/But positive, as Sound—" (F373). And among the many poems she wrote about poetry and the poet's office are a fair number that seem skeptical about the entire enterprise of writing verse as in "I would not pain—a picture—" which concludes "Nor would I be a Poet—/It's finer—Own the Ear—/Enamored—impotent—content—/The License to revere,/A privilege so awful/What would the Dower be,/Had I the Art to stun myself/With Bolts—of Melody!" (F348). In part because of the amazing variety of poetic expressions contained in the now-printed corpus of her nearly eighteen hundred lyrics, Dickinson has become the touchstone for debates about the nature of lyric as a genre, its status in the nineteenth century, and the validity of modern practices of close reading when applied to texts like hers.[2] Because I am interested in the modernity of Dickinson's poetry, some consideration of these debates will be necessary to move my readings forward.

In the broadest sense, I would say that Dickinson's poetry fits the broader definition of the lyric that Jonathan Culler has recently advanced. Unlike generations of critics, since the nineteenth century, who have associated lyric with the expression of the lyric "I," Culler identifies it with epideictic rhetoric, the mode that seeks to describe the world, and sometimes to praise or blame what happens in it. Culler's argument reminds us that many poems we consider lyrics do not obviously foreground self-expression. Many of Dickinson's most familiar poems, because of the presence of a lyric or perceiving "I" in them, seem lyrical in this sense. They make statements about the world that sometimes do and sometimes do not depend upon the speaker's presence in the poem. Her observation of a hunting cat, for example, describes a moment in the world's existence but does not depend directly on the poet's "I" in the poem: "She sights a Bird—she chuckles—/ She flattens—then she crawls—/ She runs without the look of feet—/ Her eyes increase to Balls—" (F351).

It remains the case, however, that whether one seeks to define lyric or to define the genre away, Dickinson seems to come to mind. The debates around "the new lyrical studies," whose proponents often seek to make distinctions between modern close reading practices, modern poetry more generally and the nature of traditional lyric poetry are a case in point.[3] They have certainly revitalized our sense of the nineteenth century and of Dickinson's place in it. But the urgency with which they have sought to redefine or reject the category of lyric and to typify close or lyric reading as an anachronistic imposition on her writing, an impediment to understanding her engagement with the art and culture of her period and its domestic and national politics, risks normalizing one of the idiosyncratic voices in world poetry.[4] To register the strangeness of that voice fully requires the sort of close reading that many adherents of the new lyrical studies abjure. And it indicates the ways in which Dickinson contributes to the modernization of the lyric, not least because she herself was a lyric or close reader of the discourses around her.

Alexandra Socarides's excellent study of Dickinson's relationship to the object world, *Dickinson Unbound*, illustrates the power and limitations of the new lyric studies. She finds the poet among the material artifacts of her household and sees her as "a writer who was absorbed in and influenced by nineteenth-century material culture, women's copying and bookmaking practices, familiar epistolary networks, and contemporaneous poetic discourse."[5] But her list of those objects that absorbed Dickinson's attention seems based on a questionable equivalence. The poet's engagement with "contemporaneous poetic discourse" is, I think, not best understood as being on the same level of intensity and implication as her sewing of the fascicles, her epistolary circulation of many texts, or her familiar tendency to deploy the same verses in different communicative contexts and for arguably different immediate ends. If we assume that Dickinson was a serious and dedicated literary artist, which seems beyond dispute, isn't it likely that her engagement with poetic discourse, with generic conventions and audience expectations (however large or small, real or imaginary, present or prospective that audience may be), her complex and sometimes vexed relationships to received literary and cultural meanings, beliefs, and practices would precede, explain, and motivate everything else she does, including her work on the material strata of her poetic production? There is a fine line in textual criticism between turning toward a richer understanding of poetic discourse and turning poetic discourse prosaic, for lack of a better term.[6]

Socarides herself is too gifted a critic and too good a reader to render Dickinson's poetry prosaic. Finally it seems difficult for a sensitive reader not to read Dickinson lyrically. In Socarides's description of what Dickinson was doing before she was misread, the problems of the status of poetic discourse and the practice of lyric reading determine her argument. "Dickinson," she says, "was actively appropriating and questioning the conventions of a wide array of poetic genres that were available to her—sequences, elegies, narratives, lyrics, and fragments, in particular—as well as pressing on the boundary between poetry and prose."[7] Again, lyric seems to be more than just an item among the other items in this series of poetic genres. As a mode or mood as much as a genre, lyric might play a part in or characterize any of the other items in the list. Lyric can be and often is narrative, elegiac, fragmentary, etc. Dickinson's appropriation and questioning of the conventions of each of these forms—including the epistolary—moves all of them in her work, which itself seems a sort of lyric reading, toward the condition of lyric itself, by which I mean toward the peculiarities of idiosyncratic self-expression that typifies the genre as an account of or a perspective on the world.

Lyric Correspondence

For Virginia Jackson, whose *Dickinson's Misery* has helped reshape Dickinson studies, the poet's manuscripts link her to personal events, daily

exchanges with particular friends and associates, and other forms of "social contingency." In her view, it is precisely this dense contextualization
that lyric reading obscures, for these social contingencies tend "to dis-
appear behind an idealized scene of reading progressively identified with
an idealized moment of expression."[8] Thus, if Dickinson appears to hold
her audience at arm's length, that appearance is a mirage of modern print,
which obscures the degree to which the poet embraced an audience of close
friends and personal associates.[9]

Rather than leave Dickinson isolated from time and society behind the
bulwark of the lyric, Jackson and others seek to engage her with other generic formations and social practices that would allow us to see her engaged in the flow of sociability and history. Rather than lyricize alone, they
remind us, she often corresponded with specific, living, present others. She
was not isolated from history but engaged, as Jackson puts it, in "the exchange between historical persons between whom the barriers of space and
time had not fallen."[10] As Jackson describes her project, she aims to revise
our sense of the lyric itself and to

> suggest another way of placing ourselves in relation to Dickinson's
> structures of address. Rather than considering the lyric "I" as a
> "speaker" . . . , a "persona" who talks to herself and so speaks for all of
> us, I want to examine what happens when Dickinson's writing directly
> addresses a "you," when that writing attempts to turn toward rather
> than away from a specific audience. In turning from the metaphor of
> speech to the act of writing, Dickinson's writing traced an economy
> of reading very different than the one that Higginson, and Mill, and
> Vendler projected for the lyric and most readers of Dickinson as a lyric
> poet have imagined: a circuit of exchange in which the subjective
> self-address of the speaker is replaced by the intersubjective practice of
> the writer, in which the writer's seclusion might be mediated by
> something (or someone) other than ourselves.[11]

Let us leave aside the degree to which Jackson here seems to ignore the
ways in which the metaphorics of speech in lyric, at least since the Renaissance, have often involved a dialogic practice of writing in which self-
address and the address to an other or an audience seem difficult to
distinguish. If Dickinson sometimes included her poems in her letters or
sometimes used verse as a missive—and therefore engaged in a sort of intimate communicativeness that a focus on the austerity of her lyrics in
print has caused us to miss—it is also true that her letters themselves are
often peculiarly lyrical in a specifically modern sense. They toy with and

frequently baffle her reader's expectations, because they toy with the conventions—reread the common language—that she and her readers share. They are modern in the sense that Poe and Whitman in their best poems are modern. They exploit and exacerbate the ways that close attention to language can make anything like immediate communication or un-ambiguous meaning seem elusive and rather like a modern poem.

One of the ways that Dickinson is a modern lyricist registers in the ways her poems manifest and read the continuous and concrete presence of an audience, however large or small, whose relationship to language and meaning the poet finds problematic. Like Mallarmé's Poe, she writes to distance herself from the language of the tribe, in a gesture that could be described as purification. She often writes in such a way that her conscious-ness of an audience puts even those with whom she is familiar in precisely the place, not of intimacy, but of distance, the place of a virtual mass read-ership with whom she plays elaborate games of linguistic misdirection and ironic self-staging. In this way, Dickinson works at the limits of a genre her works also typify, as Sharon Cameron has argued. The lyric mode be-comes in her work determinant of all other modes of writing, but not because lyric removes the poet from the world. Rather, lyric offers Dick-inson, as it did Poe and Whitman, a means of engaging with and resisting the discourses of the world on the fundamental levels of signification and significance, on the fundamental level of language and the materiality of the sign. She practices many genres, but she lyricizes all of them. The self she expresses through her deformations of utterance is as fragmented and performatively varied as any experimental modernist could imagine.

What must have it been like to receive a letter like the following during the momentous summer of July 1862, as the Civil War raged? The letter, which is familiar to readers of Dickinson, is to Thomas Higginson and be-gins with an apparent response to his request for her image: "Could you believe me—without? I had no portrait, now, but am small, like the Wren, and my Hair is bold, like the Chestnut Bur—and my eyes, like the Sherry in the Glass, that the Guest leaves—Would this do just as well?" This ironic self-portraiture manages to be vivid and distancing at the same time. How is it to be read? As a self-consciously literary performance, it reminds its recipient that it demands reading and challenges comprehension. The sim-iles, of course, deploy and mock the tradition of Petrarchan gallantry. They describe the poet and parody the conventions of poetic description at the same time.

This pleasant jesting then leads, without transition, to a more challenging passage, one that might lead an attentive reader to ponder the relationship of any representation to the life it represents: "It often alarms Father—He says Death might occur, and he has Molds of all the rest—but he has no Mold of me, but I notice the Quick wore off those things, in a few days, and forestall the dishonor—You will think no caprice of me—." Like the Petrarchan blazon, the "mold" is an image of a living presence and is meant to preserve that presence even after death. But in Dickinson's rendering, the life mask becomes death's representative—it becomes identified with the absence it was meant to remedy. It makes those who are still alive appear already dead, which dishonors the life it sought to represent. How is one to read this? What is Dickinson seeking to communicate in response to Higginson's friendly request for her image?

The letter continues to resist the communicative norms of the epistolary. After thanking Higginson for his tutelage ("I am happy to be your scholar, and will deserve the kindness, I cannot repay"), she offers the following as her first recitation, beginning, "I recite now—" "Will you tell me my fault, frankly as to yourself, for I had rather wince, than die. Men do not call the surgeon, to commend—the Bone, but to set it, Sir, and fracture within, is more critical."

This is as epigrammatically arresting as some of her best verses. It makes the reader want to quote: "I had rather wince than die," "Men do not call the Surgeon to commend the Bone but to set it." The statement that "fracture within, is more critical" makes one want to ponder. Is it the surgeon's task to heal the internal fractures of the subject's self-division or are these a version of that "internal difference—/Where the Meanings, are—" to which she refers in the poem that begins "There's a certain Slant of light," and that dates from this same year (F320). Whatever those internal differences in the poem are, they are revealed to "us" by that oblique illumination which gives "us" "Heavenly Hurt" and leaves no other trace or "scar." "None may teach it—Any," the poem adapts an arch distance from meaning and the reader, one which seems similar to the posture of the arch letter writer who pretends to recite her lessons for her master, yet offers him only ironies, a sort of self-division that hovers ambiguously between submission and rebellion in nearly every sentence, and perversely rereads his request for information:

> And for this, Preceptor, I shall bring you—Obedience—the Blossom
> from my Garden, and every gratitude I know. Perhaps you smile at me.
> I could not stop for that—My business is Circumference—An ignorance,
> not of Customs, but if caught with the Dawn—or the Sunset see

me—Myself the only Kangaroo among the Beauty, Sir, if you please, it afflicts me, and I thought that instruction would take it away.

This is a remarkable passage, one that reveals much less than it conceals about the self who writes it. It does, however, create a fascination in the susceptible reader (luckily Higginson was one such) and an irresistible desire for one sensitive to language to try to figure out what these sibylline utterances might mean. In case her reader has missed the fact that this is a performance, Dickinson makes her posture on the stage as clear as possible: "When I state myself, as the Representative of the Verse—it does not mean—me—but a supposed person . . . . Today, makes Yesterday mean."[12]

Clearly, one of the differences that produce meaning in Dickinson's imagination is the disjunction between the "I" and the figuration of the I that appears to speak the poem and the letters both. Another is the gap in temporality between the determining present and the experienced past. "*Je est un autre*," as Rimbaud would say some years later.[13] There is little resembling simple sociability or personal immediacy in any of this. In this and in so many other letters, the multiple turning aside of the reader's normative expectations, the disruptions of reading's normal processes, like Dickinson's slanted rhymes and familiar but often purposively disrupted metrics, suggest that rather than placing Dickinson, in any simple way, in a world of intimate and homey human contacts and communicative situations, her letters, like her poetry, repeatedly entice the reader into linguistic precincts that are far less familiar. These letters demand "lyric reading," and a form of lyric reading was required to produce them.[14]

Dickinson also lyricizes the material objects she sometimes includes in her letters by demanding they be read. Consider Virginia Jackson's intriguing analysis of Dickinson's occasional practice of including actual objects—a cricket or flower for example—as akin to what Michael Moon described as Whitman's practice of "producing metonymic substitutes for the author's literal corporeal presence in the text," Jackson writes:

> The cultivated perversity of Dickinson's mode of circulation consisted in disentangling rather than extenuating the cultural identification of personhood with writing. Like Whitman, she did so with what Moon calls metonyms, but unlike Whitman, Dickinson did not spin off substitutes for personal affectionate presence in print. Instead, she enclosed things in or stuck things to her writing. She distracted Thomas's [a reference to "Sceptic Thomas" in "Split the Lark" (F905)] gaze by giving him something else to touch.[15]

But, again, it seems true that in her poetry, like her letters, with or without the attached flora and fauna, she creates a perverse effect, not of distraction, but of focus on the materiality of her language—as distinct from the materials of her page or enclosures.

In Dickinson one often senses the presence of a legion of skeptical Thomases, potentially distracted or baffled readers, requiring diversion. The letters and poems both often seem to discourage and to require active acts of what Jackson calls lyric reading. Another way of putting this is to say that in these letters Dickinson's correspondents model for her the mass of the modern crowd she knows surrounds her, even in Amherst, a crowd she imaginatively courts and keeps at bay. Dickinson is in continuous negotiation with her readers, both virtual and real—which only seems paradoxical if one thinks that private publication, or no publication at all, precludes close attention to a readership and its expectations. Her intimates, as well as her imagined readers, share the expectations that structure the common discourses of her time. Dickinson's negotiation with those expectations in her letters as well as in her verse tends toward "transgression and boundary crossings," as Socarides puts it.[16] The boundaries she transgresses exist in the language she and her readers share and that she, as a poet and as a reader, works with and against. This is precisely what constitutes her art and where her affinity with the modern lyric lies.

Dickinson finds ways to lyricize her immediate context and history both. As Socarides says, she is still "the poet who has heretofore eluded, and perhaps always will elude, our grasp."[17] Lyric reading, far from being the modern critic's anachronistic deformation of the poem, turns out to be what the poet performs for her readers in her texts, including the material objects she attaches to the materiality of language already constituting them.[18] Like Whitman, Dickinson struggles to adapt the impersonal or shop worn language of her day to the task of describing the world around her and creating a personality or a persona in her poetry. In doing so, she resists rather than fulfills her reader's expectations about language and the self both—just as she toys with Higginson's demands for self-revelations in her wonderfully strange letters. Her playfulness makes her relationship to genre difficult to determine, or as Jackson suggests, perverse. She may be distracting her reader's gaze, or focusing it on the unstable limits of the self in language or the world. But, as her letters indicate, she makes the very objects of the world, like dead bugs and flowers, part of her text, both literary and lyrical.[19]

Biographical Fragments

It seems too obvious to remark that the artistic representation of subjectivity in Dickinson's lyrics has little to do with authenticity, if by authenticity one means a veridical relationship to an author. Giorgio Agamben, Paul De Man, W. K. Wimsatt, and many others over many years have identified the artifice of what Agamben calls a "comedic" or a dramatic performative voice or presence in the lyric that is at least as old as Dante and Petrarch and remains, in the lyric tradition, structurally distinct from the poem's author.[20] Poetry, however fictive, often dramatizes or represents agonies of conflicted subjectivity that relate to the desires and sufferings of living subjects. Certainly it has always done so. Nonetheless, studies of Dickinson have long tended to attempt to explain away the opacities of the poet's meanings by referring to the events—real or imagined—of her life.

Cristanne Miller argues against this tendency in Dickinson's criticism, which is older than the new lyrical studies, to tie her lyric "I" to her biography. In fact, the evidence suggests that even among her close associates, Dickinson's character and the meanings of her gestures and poetry could seem mysterious. In the late 1890s, just over a decade after Dickinson's death and during the tussle between Mabel Loomis Todd and the poet's sister, Lavinia, over Emily's literary remains, Emily's brother, Austin, who took Todd's side, remarked to Thomas Wentworth Higginson, "My sister Vin . . . had no comprehension of her sister, yet believed her a shining genius."[21] Austin meant the cut unkindly—meaning to undermine both Vin's rights to the increasingly valuable manuscripts she had discovered and was publishing and to advance Todd's interests, as she transcribed and edited his dead sister's poems into more conventional and easily assimilated forms. Nonetheless, he hits upon something that all serious readers of Emily Dickinson have felt: A susceptible reader has—and can have—nothing precisely like comprehension of this poet's work, and yet, the conviction of her genius and the work's beauty remains unshaken. Austin's vision of his sister as a normal, sensitive, and pious woman with a gift for expressing that piety in verse is one way to arrive at a meaning behind Dickinson's strange performances. Lavinia's insistence on the poet's sibylline mysteries is another. Like most readers, each constructs an identity for the poet behind the lyric voicing of the verses that give her fragments coherence and sense.

Emily Dickinson seems a perfect example of what Paul de Man called the anthropomorphism that characterizes readings of lyric poetry, in which the reader seems to discern the presence of a personality and voice through the impersonality of language and tropes that constitute the text.[22] We can have nothing like a meaningful comprehension of a poet's work without yielding to the desire to project an identity on or into her texts. This is no doubt a normal part of our hermeneutic endeavors, but Dickinson's peculiarities seem to exacerbate the problem—dare I say intentionally? We struggle to find the whole that makes her often fragmentary utterances cohere. In large part, I would argue, this is because few poets have ever taken the aesthetic possibilities of the fragment further than Dickinson, and the fragment, in its most extreme form, poses problems for comprehension that Dickinson is interested in exploring and exploiting.[23] Dickinson's long-standing popularity has often depended on a mode of reading her work that makes it indicate a coherent experience and subjectivity behind her fragmentary utterances. As Paula Bernat Bennett observes, "Part of Dickinson's greatness lies in the way she serves as a Rorschach for her reader's obsessions," which is to say that Dickinson's texts create in her sympathetic readers the sense that they reencounter themselves in them.[24] While one might say the same about a lot of literature, Dickinson's poems seem to have engaged their readers' imaginations in especially lively ways. She works to engage and to baffle the lyric reader's desire for intimate encounter and familiar conversation.

For generations of critics, and with especial intensity in the last decade, answers to the riddles of the poet's meaning—or, more accurately, attempts to domesticate the challenges to meaning she poses—have been sought in the poet's life, as if a sense of wholeness could be restored to her fragments by enriching the reader's sense of the interrelationships of her works and her life.[25] Who was the master addressed in those unsent letters? Who was the absent lover that Dickinson sometimes seems to address in her poems? What was her attitude toward the Civil War? Such questions have long been staples in Dickinson studies, though ultimately one is free to doubt whether they make much difference in reading her poems.

For example, moments in Lyndall Gordon's skillful biography of the poet and her family demonstrate the ways Dickinson's poems seem to simultaneously elicit a desire to glimpse the life behind them and remove themselves from any understanding that might be gained by looking into that life. Gordon cites the first two stanzas of "I tie my Hat—I crease my Shawl—" (F522), which narrates the poet's quotidian activities and duties ("I put new blossoms in the Glass—/ And throw the Old—away—" etc.), to end, in Gordon's citation, with "So much I have to do—/And yet—Existence—some way back—/Stopped—struck—my ticking through—"). She glosses the poem in familiar terms concerning the double and hidden life that an intelligent woman might live in Dickinson's time by identifying the poet with Jane Eyre, Maggie Tulliver, and Mrs. Browning. She ends then with an observation: "What's stranger in Dickinson's character are the silences surrounding almost every word in the climactic couplet about the nameless thing that 'struck' a tick-tock life."[26] For Gordon, the poem's strangeness emerges at the point where it breaks itself off from the catalog of familiar activities in a busy domestic life and emphasizes its own refusal to cohere by foregrounding an unnamed catastrophe that shattered the speaker's existence into fragments, thereby foregrounding its own status as a fragment and as a record of the experience of fragmentation itself. For Gordon, as a biographer, the poem serves primarily to draw attention to the biographical question implied by the last lines she cites. These help formulate for her the "unanswered questions" that constitute the "biographical absence" in Dickinson's work and become the occasion for her own.

But Dickinson's poem does not dwell upon this event. It continues to record what posthumous life must feel like:

> We cannot put Ourself away
> As a completed Man
> Or Woman—When the Errand's done
> We came to Flesh—upon—
> There may be—Miles on Miles of Nought—

The poem steadily shifts its focus from the unanswered biographical question to a statement of what it means, in poetry, to adopt the strategies of obfuscation and misdirection that for Dickinson seem to constitute her poetics:

> Of Action—sicker far—
> To simulate—is stinging work—
> To cover what we are
> From Science—and from Surgery—
> Too Telescopic Eyes
> To bear on us unshaded—
> For their—sake—not for Ours—

One finds here simulation, dissimulation, and self-protection, or is it protection of the others who could bear little to see what the stinging work of simulation conceals? Arguably, this work of (dis)simulation is the work of Dickinson's poetry itself. This is suggested not only by the burden of the lines I have cited, but also by a set of lines that appear in Johnson's earlier edition but not in Franklin's redaction:

> 'Twould start them—
> We—could tremble—
> But since we got a Bomb—
> And held it in our Bosom—
> Nay—Hold it—it is calm—(J443)

This bomb, the antidote to "Life's little duties," for Dickinson was poetry. Her verse often seems a weapon with which she could calm and protect her self, conceal and explore her perceptions of the world, and, at the same time, explode many of the cherished conventions and sententious certainties of her day. A weapon or tool, a "loaded gun" as she elsewhere suggests, that she could also pass on, as the imperative "Hold it" here implies, to the imagined reader, a reader whose presence is implicit in the "we" that dominates the poem's second half in both its versions. The poem ends in both versions by summoning its reader along with its speaker to the tasks of poetry itself:

> Therefore—we do life's labor—
> Though life's Reward—be done—
> With scrupulous exactness—
> To hold our Senses—on—

Poetry allows the speaker of this poem, and also the reader in that speaker's imagination, to continue to hold their senses on when pain or habit might dull perception, to keep the senses sharpened and attuned by disrupting the more common or merely habitual forms of sense in the world. In this sense, it might not much matter to the poem which of life's inevitable catastrophes motivates its mood. It is the mood itself, Dickinson suggests, that makes poetry intrinsic to survival.

In Gordon's treatment of these lines and of Dickinson, the poem threatens to vanish into the life—or dissipate into speculations about the life. It is especially evident in the ambiguity of the word "character" that Gordon uses above. For the "character" she refers to seems not to be the shattered character Dickinson creates who speaks the poem, but the poet herself, an individual of or with character, to whom Gordon gives a wholeness and a meaning that the poetry's insistent fragmentariness makes difficult to discern, or, in the poem's language, to dissimulate. The danger of any biographical approach to a poem, of course, lies in the poem's reduction to an index of a life. Gordon editorializes that life as a resistance to the domesticity the poem depicts by describing it as a "tick-tock life." She thus creates a trivializing intention for the poem's speaker. Yet "ticking" in the poem is not an adjective but a substantive that suggests the taxidermists stuffing of the corpse, which becomes a sort of ticking or cover, that arrests decay and the passage of time at once. Quotidian time seems a fragment of something like eternity, death and life in an instant conjoined for the instant that something called "Existence" stops. In all of this, the poem seems more exploratory than explicit, intent on dwelling with possibility rather than drawing reading toward a conclusion.

As a biographer, Gordon values the explicit and attempts to solve the riddle—or resolve the ambiguity—that the word ticking poses. What was that event that stopped Dickinson's "ticking," halting time or, perhaps, knocking the stuffing out of her? Gordon is certainly correct to do so. The pressure of this sort of question is inevitably part of the effect that Dickinson labored to create in her poetry. As Gordon writes, "the enigma she presents beckons: its teasing insistence suggests something to be solved."[27] But I also believe that believing that this biographical question, which the poem does nothing to answer, has an answer that might be found in the life of the poet seems strangely at odds with the poem's catachrestic mysteries. Dickinson works steadily to elicit and to confound our desire for meaning, our desire to know what may lie behind her odd verses. In this poem, by asserting that our mortal ticking (the superficial covering that gives our lives a form, as well as the movement of the clock that marks its duration) might at any moment be struck through or stopped reminds us that life may have no coherent meaning that might be abstracted from or survive such an event. The enactment of duration as reading, the steady attempt to hold our senses on the text, rather than the memorialization of the event that might finalize sense or define meaning is what this poem performs.[28]

There is something more here than the perpetual disagreement between critics and textual scholars, what Margaret Dickie calls the difference between editorial caterpillars and critical butterflies in her review of McGann, Cameron, and other recent writers on Dickinson.[29] That something more lies in the peculiar ways in which Dickinson's poetry elicits and frustrates exactly the sort of response and research that Lyndall Gordon's intriguing and ingenuous book (it is also very entertaining in its own right) so well exemplifies.

The fascination that Dickinson's life—whether understood as personal biography or societal context or both—holds for readers and critics of all sorts should perhaps surprise us more than it does. A dedicated formalist might suggest that this attention lavished on the life, entertaining as it often is, has seldom served to enrich our understanding of the poetry. But I would also add that our fascination with the stresses and strains of a generally quiet life lived in a quiet town is a tribute to the intense effectiveness of the best poetry Dickinson produced. The intensities of Dickinson's poetry are generated by the peculiarities of form in her verses and have little to do with the meanings—religious or romantic, ideological or political—that her poetry might seem to conceal. Dickinson's force has something to do with the odd way these poems elicit the reader's desire for meaning while refusing to deliver the meanings promised. It seems quite natural that critics and readers should search for this poetry's meaning in Dickinson's life, in the Civil War, in the war between the houses (her brother's and her own) or in the war within Dickinson's own heart and mind. But what if this poetry does not conceal anything, but endlessly explores the performance of desire, including the desire for meaning, and all desire's inevitable frustration? It might be worth asking what that would mean, to hold our senses on the inescapable fragmentariness of life and its expression rather than to pursue a coherence that fragmentariness both suggests and belies.

Fragmenting Language

Emily Dickinson's earliest surviving poem dates from 1850, when she was twenty years old. Like Poe's youthful effort "Romance," Dickinson's inaugural poem seems, in retrospect, to augur all that will follow. As Aliki Barnstone remarks, "Dickinson's early satirical work is a primer for later developments in her thinking."[30] The poem, however, reveals as much about Dickinson's poetic use of common discourse as it does about her thinking per se. Unlike Poe's poem, which declares the poet to be "young and steeped in folly" and to have "fallen in love with melancholy," Dickinson's verses announce nothing at all but embody an attitude that seems, well, Dickinsonian. That attitude, I will suggest, is what seems a prelude to some of the great poems to come.

Dickinson begins with a parodic invocation of the muse:

> Awake ye muses nine, sing me a strain divine,
> Unwind the solemn twine, and tie Valentine!

This, of course, is doggerel but amusingly jaunty in the echoes of its internal rhymes. The poem continues, or rather begins again after a graphic break that seems to mark this opening couplet as an overture:

Oh the Earth was *made* for lovers, for damsel, and hopeless swain,
for sighing, and gentle whispering, and *unity* made of *twain*,
all things do go a courting, in earth, or sea, or air,
God hath made nothing single but *thee* in his world so fair!

These lines, which echo so much romantic poetry, including especially
Byron, do not so much announce themes of isolation that will reappear in
Dickinson's mature work, as they enact them as ironic restatements of poetic discourse that remove the poet from the immediacy of communicative contact. She suggestively offers an impish sendup of Byron's well-known
verses, "So We'll Go No More a Roving." That poem was originally included as part of a letter to Byron's friend Thomas Moore to illustrate how
the ailing poet, "on the invalid regime," had been feeling past his prime
and "knocked . . . up a little":

So we'll go no more a roving
        So late into the night,
Though the heart be still as loving,
        And the moon be still as bright.

For the sword outwears its sheath,
        And the soul wears out the breast,
And the heart must pause to breathe,
        And Love itself have rest.

Though the night was made for loving,
        And the day returns too soon,
Yet we'll go no more a roving
        By the light of the moon.[31]

Dickinson's citation of these lines does not seem to be intended to communicate anything very definite. She borrows Byron's song rhythm and
some of his words, but one cannot be certain whether the lament in the
last lines is meant seriously or is included for the fun of the Byronic pastiche. The effect of the resultant rereading of Byron is quite funny and
should remind readers inclined to see Dickinson as morbid about her self-
isolation, as "the only Kangaroo among the Beauty," that loneliness for this
poet often serves as an occasion for her hopping playfulness and for the
manifestation of a mordant wit that leaves not only those around her but
the very language they inhabit fairly well chewed. Her poem continues:

The *bride*, and then the *bridegroom*, the *two*, and then the *one*,
Adam, and Eve, his consort, the moon, and then the sun;

the life doth prove the precept, who obey shall happy be,
who will not serve the sovereign, be hanged on fatal tree.

The poem continues this simple game of inventorying the coupled nouns that comprise a world of normal, even ritualized relations and chiding or threatening the swain to whom the poem seems addressed for not entering into this parade of natural seeming pairs:

Now to the *application*, to the reading of the roll, to bringing thee to
    justice, and marshalling thy soul;
thou art a *human* solo, a being cold, and lone,
    wilt have no kind companion, thou *reap'st* what thou has *sown*. (F1)

Less interesting than the content or the address of this poem (Dickinson miming the thwarted lover, the quest for the identity of a *bel homme sans merci*) is the poem's verbal texturing, the way she assembles her work from snippets of shop worn sentiment, overly familiar poetry, ceremonial language and twists them in a process akin to rereading into ironic forms by sly juxtapositions and disjunctive leaps. The purpose of this juxtaposition, or its effect in any case, seems less to generate new meanings in language than to distance language itself from easily determined significance, to create a gap between sound and sense, between the materiality of the signifier and sure access to a single signified or referent. There may in fact be a specific addressee—either a recalcitrant lover of Dickinson's or some other "swain" haunting Amherst—but the satirical irony of these romantic echoes does less to specify the addressee than to incorporate him or her into a general playfulness of poetic discourse that calls the possibility of any individuality founded on utterance (individuality founded through poetic utterance being one possibility or possible illusion upon which the lyric traditionally depends) into question. But this does not, I believe, make this poem unlyrical. Her rereading of the given expands the resources of the genre in ways that rely on the conventionality that Dickinson here transforms and modernizes.

This pointed but pointless playful interplay of rereading and writing is evident as well in the second poem, chronologically, in Franklin's editing (the third in Johnson's), which is composed almost completely of tags from Latin textbooks, folk wisdom, and poetic clichés:

Sic transit gloria mundi
"How doth the busy bee"
Dum vivamus vivamus
I stay mine enemy!

Oh veni vidi vici!
Oh caput cap-a-pie!
And oh "memento mori"
When I am far from thee

The poem continues in this vein for seventeen quatrains. Some of the best are

During my education
It was announced to me
That gravitation stumbling
Fell from an apple tree—

The Earth opon it's axis
Was once supposed to turn
By way of a gymnastic
In honor to the sun—

It was the brave Columbus
A sailing o'er the tide
Who notified the nations
Of where I would reside

And after two stanzas celebrating "Our Fathers" who "being weary" laid down on Bunker Hill, the following aphorism:

A coward will remain, Sir,
Until the fight is done;
But an immortal hero
Will take his hat and run.

And a final salutation:

The memory of my ashes
Will consolation be
Then farewell Tuscarora
And farewell Sir, to thee.

Virginia Jackson is certainly correct to say, "Whatever we make of these lines, it would be difficult to make them a lyric,"[32] if we mean by lyric the limitations of a single, original perspective. This valentine that Dickinson had sent to William Holland and that was reprinted in Springfield's *Daily Republican* is, just as Jackson says, too much "a pastiche from various sources . . . that is mediated by many, many things that are not the writer or the reader . . . a cultural grab bag of languages, texts, stories, myths, aphorisms, and bon mots." She continues, "most of them [are] fairly unmediated by anything we would recognize as a 'lyric' perspective."[33] I think Jackson is absolutely right about the ways in which these early poems "invite the reader to share their resistance to popular song's romance as well as the ABC's disciplinary tutelage . . . literally constructing the fantasy of a conspiratorial counter literacy mediated by sheets of paper converted to purposes that were not intended by the man who made them."[34] I would add only that it is Dickinson's achievement as a poet that she does not abandon, though she does complicate, the lyrical task of self-fashioning even in these moments of wit and play and pastiche as a way of making the lyric polyvocal and heteroglossic and of relocating originality not in the self but in pastiche, the rereading of the discourses that surround her.

I think she has here begun to pierce to the core of what her poetic practice will continue to perform—the realization that in the modern era, self-fashioning itself must be refashioned and, if possible at all, achieved through the sort of recycling of exhausted means and refurbished clichés that Jackson refers to as a "conspiratorial counter literacy." I think that phrase could aptly apply to Poe and Whitman as well, and may be one useful definition of the modern lyric. What Dickinson abandons, I think, is not lyric but the belief that anything like unmediated selfhood or undistorted communication or immediate intersubjectivity is any longer imaginable in art or in life. What she realizes is that the situation of the poet in a modern, secular era, changes the poet's relationship to self, to language, and to her audience. She discovers for herself one form the lyric might take after the end of art, the form of the rereading of the lyric tradition.

Dickinson's project in these early works seems less serious than the one Mallarmé attributed to Poe, to give a purer sense to the words of the tribe, or Whitman's self-declaration that the multitudes around him were within him and his poetry as well ("I am large, I contain multitudes"). Nonetheless, her playful antagonism to the shopworn cacophonies of the vapid sentiments she hears and reads all around her seems to be designed, in its modest way, to achieve something similar. When Proust criticized the opacity of language among the symbolists, Mallarmé replied by ridiculing the idea that sense in literature had much to do with art:

> All literature, outside of its own treasures, must, out of respect for
> those from whom it borrows, after all, for objects other than originally
> intended, language, present, along with its words, some sense however
> indifferent: it pays to distract the lazy reader, charmed with a superficial

glance that assures him that there is nothing he need worry about happening here.[35]

Mallarmé's rough style here is nearly as disjunctive as Dickinson's. He describes a borrowing from the language of the tribe that purifies that language and renders its sense a mere distraction. He writes later in the same essay:

> Words, by themselves, appear exalted as many facets recognized, the rarest or most valuable for the mind, the center of this vibrational suspension; which perceives them independently of their ordinary order, projected, as on the walls of a cave, as long as their mobility or principal lasts, being that which cannot be said in common discourse.[36]

Giorgio Agamben, referring to this passage in Mallarmé, describes a "dream of language" that he believes has possessed poetry since the moment the Italian humanists identified Latin as a "dead" language and borrowed its vocabulary and structures to revivify vernacular poetry: "it is a matter not of an agrammatical discourse but rather of a language in which the resistance of names and words is not immediately dissolved and rendered transparent by the comprehension of the global meaning."[37] In Agamben's view, words in poetry resist meaning—at least momentarily. They cannot be made simply to serve as lexical elements. Dickinson, even in these early poems where she seems to be just fooling around, resists the deadening formulas and received meanings of the language she hears all around her in an attempt to revivify the beauty and perhaps the power of the words themselves to conjure a self and world for that self to live in. This has little to do with communication, face-to-face or otherwise; it is more a matter of provocation. In part the poet's provocations of the reader helps "Distill amazing sense / From ordinary Meanings—" as Dickinson claims the poet does in the first lines of "This was a Poet" (F446). But it is also an exploration of how this "Entitles us—by Contrast / To Ceaselessly Poverty—" as she writes in the same poem's third stanza.

By resisting the common language of her time and place, Dickinson is too shrewd and honest a poet to act as if she can recover plenitudes of meaning that have been lost. Instead, she foregrounds and intensifies what Jonathan Culler calls the "indeterminacy of meaning in poetry," which "provides an experience of freedom and a release from the compulsion to signify. With its apparent gratuitous chiming and rhyming, its supplemental metrical organization and uses of lineation—in short its determination by a host of sensuous factors—lyric language works against instrumental reason, prosaic efficiency, and communicative transparency, quite independently of the thematic content of particular lyrics."[38] Whether this describes all lyric, it certainly describes Dickinson's verse with its famous peculiarities including hymnal stanzas, slanted rhymes, and idiosyncratic lineation and punctuation, as well as surprising and frequent disjunctions. In this important sense, she is a lyric poet and her richness comes from her indications of our common linguistic poverty and the glee that can accompany the release of language from common sense and immediate communication through perverse rereadings of its utilities.

This project, if I may call it that, emerges with her first poems and recurs continuously over the span of her career. She is still at work on the commonplace language of her tribe just a few years before her death, for example in poem (F1575), which Franklin dates to 1882, where again, she seems, perhaps, to be just fooling around:

Now I lay thee down to Sleep—
I pray the Lord thy Dust to keep—
And if thou live before thou wake—
I pray the Lord thy Soul to make—

One can parse these inversions of a common, childish prayer in a variety of ways. There may be a conventional intention here. Laying someone down to sleep (thee, notably, not me), the Poet prays that the Lord will keep the dust of the mortal body and wake the new made soul of immortality. But the strangeness of these lines, and especially the shifting from "me" to "thee" as the object of the pious sounding prayer, cannot be captured by this reduction of her words to sense. Nor can such a meaning capture the uncanny mixture of the simple childishness of the first line with the disturbing or at least dissonant echoing of the common burial service (dust to dust) in the second. Nor is it easy to make orthodox sense out of the substitutions of "live" for "die" or "make" for "take." What is this soul that life has left unmade and that awaits dying to be fashioned? If we only have souls after we die, can God be counted on to furnish them, and if so, why is the prayer even necessary?

The familiar words of this poem cannot easily be reduced to common sense, and it is this that makes this slight bit of verse, which a casual reader might mistake for doggerel, a poem, whether we can agree that it is lyrical or not. If lines like these do not purify the language of the tribe, they at least defy the common assumption of language's easy access to meaning, and especially to the meaning of that ultimate, common human experience, death and the self's relationship to what Christians traditionally assume all selves possess, a soul. It may be the case, as Agamben puts it, that the dream of Italian humanist poets, after Dante and Petrarch, was to quicken the dead language of the vernacular into a moment of "perfect self-referentiality," an evocation of a "pure language" that is "absent in every instrumental language" yet "makes human speech [and its instrumentality] possible."[39] But for Dickinson, as a modern poet, the case has changed. For her the dead language *is* the vernacular, the language she hears all around her, which she purifies of common meanings and instrumentality through acts of lyric reading and writing. The result is not perfect referentiality, but an intimation of the impossibility of perfect referentiality, a glimpse of what Dickinson calls, in another well-known poem, the "internal difference / Where the Meanings, are" (see "There's a certain Slant of light" F320). If, as Agamben puts it, "Thought lives off the death of words" (63), one wants to add that in Dickinson it is the words that live to be re-read and the meaning that, at least for moment, must be thought to die.[40]

CHAPTER 6

Dickinson's Dog and the Conclusion

Emily Dickinson still too often appears in the common imagination as a cliché effigy of the homespun poetess, an ethereal presence clothed in white and not quite of this world. She certainly did, as critics have noted, play with and off the image of the poetess popular in her day, and yet these affectations should not mask the fact that she is also among the earthiest of poets, an aspect of her work that is too little appreciated. She is among those poets who are most aware of what it means to try to get at the earth, at the shifting grounds of existence, that habits of perception and language itself often mask or conceal.[1] If Poe twists metaphors and Whitman enchains metonymies, Dickinson self-consciously practices the negating tropes of irony and catachresis. She invents a poetic style that depends on disjunction and solicits and resists the reader, as if her poems (perhaps like Sappho's) were fragments from lost genres of self-expression dating from an immemorial past that is somehow contemporaneous as well. For Dickinson, the lyric survives after the end of art largely as a gesture of fragmentation and a demand for reading. And while much ingenuity has been expended recently to normalize Dickinson, to make her whole so to speak, by linking her to her milieu and moment and by identifying her poems with the versifying letters and sentimental effusions of her day, even these efforts, as we have seen, tend to return to the peculiarities of her verse, those idiosyncrasies that make her, as Virginia Jackson says, "*sound* like 'Dickinson.'"[2] The best studies of Dickinson in her context, like Jackson's and Socarides's, can paradoxically sharpen our sense of what is most distinctive in her work. For what is most valuable in Dickinson is what is strangest. But what is strange in her is also familiar. Her poetry depends on the ways in which she renders the familiar strange and makes the world and the mind in it uncanny.[3]

Here we approach the dynamic terrain that Sigmund Freud once mapped in terms of two distinct but related concepts, the uncanny and the joke or *Witz* (the quip). Each of these involves, in a particular way, a form of unmasking or unveiling of its own. Freud related both these to the dynamics of the unconscious and of repression, the ground and also the potential undoing of signification and of meaning both.[4] Whether this is the same unconscious to which Dickinson refers at the end of "This was a Poet" ("Of Portion—so unconscious, / The Robbing—could not harm—/ Himself— to Him—a Fortune / Exterior to Time"), remains to be seen. And while I will not attempt a psychoanalytic theory of lyric, I am drawn to the power of Freud's two concepts, the unconscious and repression, not because they shed any light on the depths of Dickinson's personal psychology, but because they help clarify the linguistic peculiarities of the surfaces of many of her texts that make them so lyrically difficult to read. These terms help describe the unsettling experience of reading her poems.

Consider the well-known opening line of F314. "'Hope' is the thing with feathers." The initial effect of this line is akin to what Freud called the uncanny. There is here, in a small but significant way, the revelation of something scandalous, something that should have remained hidden, something known and yet forgotten, that comes back to light and consciousness through a momentary loosening of repression.[5] Similarly, in the joke book, Freud writes that jokes exploit "the free use of words and thoughts" so that "they may produce new pleasure by lifting suppressions and repressions."[6] Thus, Dickinson begins her poem with a joke. Here, her wit involves nothing very portentous, merely the reminder of what, when reading poetry, we often forget. In fact, one might say, the pleasures of conventional poetry—poetry that depends on sentimental responses or the affirmation of received wisdom—often requires this forgetting for the poem to work at all. We forget that the vehicles for many common metaphors—especially when their tenors are most ethereal or abstract— can seem grotesque and incongruous when we remember their literal referents. We forget (or repress, that is displace from consciousness) what we know about birds—that they are "things" with feathers—so that they can seem to convey the immortal singing of the soul, or the promise of god's love, or that hope which might have biblical origins in the flood and Noah's dove that descends on us from the sky or springs eternal in the human breast in Christian narratives and iconography. To call "hope" a *thing* with feathers is to render that most familiar Christian virtue uncanny, an ungainly and potentially unsanitary thing that does not descend from heaven or spring eternal in the human breast, but "perches in the soul." There is something pagan about this, perhaps because it recalls the grotesque definition by the "stranger" of "man" as a "featherless biped" in Plato's *The Statesman* (266e). Dickinson's metaphor reveals the forms of repressed possibility that any delimited meaning creates, since any clear meaning requires the careful delimitation of a signifying possibility from a vastly broader semantic range that any word potentially possesses. By recalling what the bird as a traditional metaphorical vehicle requires that we forget in order to make the featherless biped on its cramped perch a proper figure for the ethereal quality of hope, by restoring to our consciousness the actual feathers and habits of fowls, their fowlness so to speak, Dickinson makes the familiar virtue of "hope" seem strange—even a bit uncanny. At the same time, she causes the reader to doubt whether or not she is joking. Freud would say, she makes a "*Witz.*" She flirts with irony, the trope that opens up the field of signification that common usage tends to close, the trope of all tropes that most reminds the reader of reading's multivalences. Consider the whole poem:

"Hope" is the thing with feathers—
That perches in the soul—
And sings the tune without the words—
And never stops at all—

And sweetest—in the Gale—is heard—
And sore must be the storm—
That could abash the little Bird
That kept so many warm—

I've heard it in the chillest land—
And on the strangest Sea—
Yet—never—in Extremity,
It asked a crumb—of me.

All through the poem's short length these lines evoke and deform conventional Victorian sentiments and common Christian pieties about the cardinal virtue of hope. After the grotesque beginning, including the interesting evocation of the tune without the words that begins to make one wonder whether hope has any substance at all, the next quatrain and a half seem a largely familiar evocation of hope's perdurability. If it does not spring eternal in the human breast, at least hope seems to perch there, however awkward a roost that might be. But what does one make of the final couplet? It seems impossible to delimit its meaning. Does it suggest the unfailing fidelity of hope, which (like charity) asks nothing in return or the distancing of hope from the speaker's sense of possibility, since hope never seems to have had the least little bit, not a crumb's worth, to do with the speaker. Dickinson gives the reader no way at the last to decide between these possibilities. The poem, that began so strangely, wanders strangely off into irony at its end. This wandering, I would say, seems to be its point. The effect is close to funny (I think this is more than my own perversity) and, for a reader looking for hopeful comfort, unsettling.

To achieve this uncanny and ironic archness is what, I think, it means to sound like Dickinson. One's response to lyric poetry like Dickinson's, like one's response to a joke, is seldom improved by explanation unless one has been moved or intrigued by the poem or the joke from the first. (Those who have taught Dickinson to undergraduates will know what I mean.) Only those who already, on some level, "get it" may profit from the attempt to analyze or explain the poem's effect. In other words, the reaction to poetry like Dickinson's is irreducibly primary. If one doesn't react to the poem before the explanation, often involuntarily—however intellectually compelling or pleasing the explanation offered may be—one is not likely to "get" it afterward.[7] For jokes and art may be alike in one important way, one's aesthetic response and the analysis of that response exist on different experiential planes.

If, as Eleanor Heginbotham has noted in her book on the fascicles, Dickinson's poetry often seems to bespeak "active, timeless, spaceless, eternal existence," her language continuously emphasizes the materiality of her words, the potentialities of the signifier, rather than their spiritual import or the delimitation of the signified.[8] Dickinson keeps her readers off balance, as when she uses metrical forms that lead one to expect strong end rhymes and then substitutes slant rhymes or near rhymes instead. Often she plays off of familiar forms of language and suggests that they do not necessarily bear the burden of significance assigned them. This is the technique with which she is already experimenting in her earliest poems, "Awake ye muses . . ." and "Sic transit Gloria mundi." Dickinson's resort to such strategies, all of which have a joking aspect, often encourages the sort of "counterliteracy" that Victoria Jackson names.

Consider, as an example of Dickinson's wit, her riffing on one of the best known and most sententious love sonnets the nineteenth-century produced. Where Mrs. Browning wrote, "How do I love thee, let me count the ways," Dickinson responds:[9]

> Love—thou art high—
> I cannot climb thee—
> But, were it Two—
> Who knows but we—
> Taking turns—at the Chimborazo—
> Ducal—at last—stand up by thee—
>
> Love—thou art deep—
> I cannot cross thee—
> But, were there Two
> Instead of One—
> Rower and Yacht—some sovereign Summer—
> Who knows—but we'd reach the Sun?
>
> Love—thou art Veiled—
> A few—behold thee—
> Smile—and alter—and prattle—and die—
> Bliss—were an Oddity—without thee—
> Nicknamed by God—
> Eternity—(F452)

Dickinson's wit here consists in generating a sort of poetic grammar of reversal. Browning addresses her lover and offers the ineffableness of love as a vehicle toward an equally ineffable sublimity (all of her enumerations lead to inexpressibility and the sublime—"I love thee to the depth and breadth and height/My soul can reach, when feeling out of sight/For the ends of Being and ideal Grace" culminating in God and eternal life "—and, if God choose,/I shall but love thee better after death"). Dickinson, on the other hand, addresses love itself and brings it back to earth with the wondrously counterfactual, "Who knows but we," which distances the poem and its reader from love's transport by making it seem entirely conjectural. Where Browning ends with a vision of love's conquest of mortality, Dickinson ends with the babble of the words that love provokes from prating poets and nothing, really, beyond but death itself. And among those who, beholding love, "Smile—and alter—and prattle—and die—" Dickinson introduces a deity whose only act is to nickname all this "Oddity," "Eternity," in the absence of the beloved—whose presence remains distinctly ambiguous as the poem peters out in the series of subjunctives that structure its movement. In this poem, as in so many of Dickinson's most unsettling and uncanny lyrics, God and eternity are evoked, but they do not lead the reader to a realm of higher meaning but instead fold her or him back into this world of shopworn sense, exhausted prating, and ambivalent desire. Dickinson evokes transcendence, but most often she does so in a way that makes it seem distant and doubtful.

Consider another poem in which the longing for knowledge of God or for a transcendent realm that might lend meaning to mundane existence seems especially well marked:

> The Love, a Life can show Below
> Is but a filament, I know,
> Of that diviner thing
> That faints upon the face of Noon—
> And smites the Tinder in the Sun—
> And hinders Gabriel's Wing—
>
> 'Tis this—in Music—hints and sways—
> And far abroad on Summer days—
> Distills uncertain pain—
> 'Tis this enamors in the East—
> And tints the Transit in the West
> With harrowing Iodine—
>
> 'Tis this—invites—appalls—endows—
> Flits—glimmers—proves—dissolves—
> Returns—suggests—convicts—enchants
> Then—flings in Paradise— (F285)

It is difficult to know how to read such a poem, and again that seems something like the point. One could find that it registers a rather conventional Victorian piety about the fleeting quality of profane love in the terrestrial world compared to what awaits a believer in the celestial realm—a comparison of filament to firmament, so to speak. But close attention to Dickinson's words leaves one uncertain just what she means, for the poem conveys not certain sense but an ironically "uncertain pain" to its readers. This starts early, at the point where that "diviner thing" appears to be evanescent instead of timeless, as it faints upon the face of noon. This fainting belies the stasis noon often suggests by imposing a movement of fading or falling away upon it. The ineluctability of time's passing continuously blocks the glimpses of eternity that the poem seems to promise. It hinders Gabriel's wing and impedes his angelic flight, keeping him from returning, one supposes, to heaven. The central passages invoke the sun's diurnal transit from the warm East to the tinted West, and evoke the discomfiting uncertainty around which the poem assumes ironic shape. The poem finds its most disturbing expression in the phrase "harrowing Iodine," which describes the color of the setting sun as if it were the dressing on a terrible wound that aggravates the agony it promised to assuage. Whether or not this iodine presages a cure for the mortal condition is left uncertain. The unresolved mysteries of meaning in these lines is what, I think, the catalog of finite verbs comprising the last four lines suggests. These verbs qualify the force of "flings in Paradise" before the peculiarity of that grammatical construction has time or space to register. The quatrain that begins " 'Tis This" does not conclude by flinging the poet or the reader into paradise (not even like the refuse of existence or life's jetsam) but seems to make the "flings in paradise" just another item in the list of mental and physical actions and displacements. Paradise, in the poem, becomes another place where finite actions in mundane time occur. What does Dickinson mean by this? No one can reduce the poem's ironic indirections to say for certain. That distillation of uncertainty seems to be her pointed reply to the complacent beliefs about God and eternity in which her contemporaries—her family, friends, and society at large— affected to find comfort.

Given the unresolved ironies of Dickinson's verse, its enactment and solicitation of lyric reading, it hardly seems surprising that, as Eleanor Heginbotham observes, "wars of interpretation over intentionality" have been part of Dickinson's story—the story of her poetry's publication and reception—from the first.[10] Her often archly ironic performances seem calculated to elicit and frustrate the reader's desire for meaning. She inscribes confusions of intentionality and meaning within her poems. This may be most evident in her satiric repetitions of her great predecessors and contemporaries, Elizabeth Barrett Browning, Byron, Keats, Emerson and others, some examples of which we have been reading here.[11] These suggest the extent to which ironic performance constitutes the decentering center of her work. Irony, of course, of all tropes depends upon the reader to recognize its force. Her poetics, constructed around irony and catachresis, entails the characteristic play of intimacy and distancing between

Dickinson and her audience. This is another way of saying that Dickinson, widely famed as a reclusive poet, often writes with the intention of challenging an audience. Her wit is the sign of her participation in a secular age as a lyric reader who writes lyric poetry as well.

This was a Shaggy Dog

Wit is absolute social feeling or fragmentary genius.

FREDERICK SCHLEGEL

Dickinson's irony is an aspect of her wit and is the most telling sign in her poetry of both her sociability and her resistance to being domesticated, of the tension between intimacy with and distance from her readers that her poetry puts into play. Wit, as Schlegel's aphorism suggests, is essentially a social feeling, it cannot be imagined without an audience, real or virtual.[12] If Dickinson's poetry often works like a joke—a *Witz*, in Freud's terms—the question of what sort of wit a given poem might exhibit and what such wittiness might suggest about the social feelings in her poems remains open. Consider one of Dickinson's better known poems, which begins, plainly enough with a brisk narrative opening that seems to invite the reader to tag along on the poet's morning walk:

> I started Early—Took my Dog—
> And visited the Sea—
> The Mermaids in the Basement
> Came out to look at me (F656)

The poem invites the reader to accompany the poet on a walk with her dog to the sea. Nothing could be simpler. But the simple opening of the poem quickly becomes more complicated. The poet first introduces a familiar trope, a metaphor, figuring the sea as a house equipped with mermaids dwelling in its basement-depths. This fairytale figure might invite readers to wonder and delight. At this point, the mermaids seem more childlike and whimsical than witty, but in the next four lines she extends the comparison and the conceit gets more complicated. The poem shifts its point of view from the speaker's perspective to imagine the poet's appearance in the eye of another:

> And Frigates—in the Upper Floor
> Extended Hempen Hands—
> Presuming Me to be a Mouse—
> Aground—opon the Sands—

That frigates have eyes seems a bit surprising. The reader at this point begins to feel lead on and a bit confused. That the sea has a basement and an upper floor seems clear, but this shift in perspective, as the frigates—large battleships bristling with cannon—extend hempen hands (a metonymically framed metaphor that plays on the ropes or shrouds that control the sails) and gaze upon the shore (with what eyes?) cannot easily be assimilated to the first metaphor that compares the sea to a house on land. Mermaids in the basement are one thing, but battleships on the upper floors seem quite another. From the perspective of the frigates improbably lodged on the house's upper floors, the poet imagines herself but only as a mouse grounded—wrecked? Marooned?—upon the shore. Without worrying too much why a battleship might extend its hands to a mouse, one notes that this image suggests the smallness of the self in the face of the sea's sublimity. But that sublimity explodes the homely comparison of the sea as that cozy dwelling place of mermaids, with which the poem began. The next quatrain's crisply plosive initial "But" brings the reading (unlike the dog who has somehow disappeared) to heel. The next two quatrains develop a portentous and enticingly erotic refiguration of everything:

> But no Man moved Me—till the Tide
> Went past my simple Shoe—
> And past my Apron—and my Belt
> And past my Boddice too—
>
> And made as He would eat me up—
> As wholly as the Dew
> Opon a Dandelion's Sleeve—
> And then—I started—too—

The reader, carried forward by the sea's groping of the poet past her shoe, her apron, her belt, and bodice (one thinks of Marvell's "To His Coy Mistress"), begins to sense the presence of allegory here, a metaphysical figuration akin to the verbal wit that characterize the seventeenth-century lyric. That the personification of the sea as seducer supplants the earlier more innocent comparisons again might not trouble the reader overmuch: The house of the sea becomes the Sea as an importunate lover, and the beckoning frigates and the dog are all forgotten. But the expectation of a seduction also leads nowhere. The consummation of the sea's seduction doesn't quite occur and the promised ravishment dissipates into coy flirtation and a game of tag as the poet "starts" and the Sea, somewhat clumsily, follows:

And He—He followed—close behind—
I felt His Silver Heel
Opon my Ancle—Then My Shoes
Would overflow with Pearl—

Until we met the Solid Town—
No One He seemed to know—
And bowing—with a Mighty look—
At me—The Sea withdrew—

There may be a sexual connotation to the overflow of pearl and the withdrawal that ends the poem and the story (one thinks of Whitman's "Did it make you ache so leaving me"), but it doesn't seem a completely convincing reading. For one thing, the Sea, for all his mighty bowing at the end, reminds one as much of Hamlet's comically irritating peasant, galling the kibe of the nobleman he follows, as he does a powerfully seductive lover. The moment that promised erotic intensity or spiritual transport breaks apart—like the wave dissolved into sea foam in her shoe—the poem's erotic drive fragments and dissipates. The poem becomes, by the end, a lightly comic, merely mock-heroic story about getting one's foot wet by a wave. And what, by the way, has happened to that dog?

The sociability that recent critics have recovered in Dickinson's poetic practice often registers not only in the relationship of the poetry to its contexts and materials of production, but in her poetry's fragmented and fragmenting openness to and frustration of interpretation, its anticipatory toying with her audience, its demand for lyric reading. Dickinson's verses often lure the reader along from line to line and from image to image to come to the end without being able to say exactly what it all amounts to and where the trip arrives, except that it has entailed a pleasurable immersion in the poem's slants of language that tease and seduce the susceptible reader in nearly every line, leading her or him to expect a meaning the poem never quite delivers.

The poem's refusal to disambiguate the layered ironies that language can produce—the poet's intensification of those ironies—becomes itself a display of wit and a sort of joke, though not one usually designed to provoke laughter. Freud called this kind of joke a "concept joke," though in colloquial English, with due deference to Dickinson's brown Newfoundland dog, Carlo, we can call this sort of joke a shaggy dog story. The shaggy dog story holds its hearer suspended in uncertainty between the reader's reasonable assumption that there is a sense that will eventually come clear that he or she is currently missing and the suspicion that what he or she is hearing makes no conventional sense in its telling and has no pithy punch line or release of tension at its end. Such a performance simultaneously interpolates and provokes its audience. As Samuel Weber notes, having been the audience for a shaggy dog, the only recourse is a continuation of its agonistic performance, to expand the society the *Witz* constructs by repeating the story to another victim or audience and re-performing the gestures that promise meanings but create ironic uncertainties.[13] This is the task Dickinson criticism often performs. In this way, Dickinson's poetry not only anticipates an audience, it also demands a critical reading— like the ones she sometimes sought from Thomas Wentworth Higginson in her letters. Another way of saying this might be to say that we keep reading Dickinson and other writers who seem to dwell with irony, so that we seldom can be sure of their meaning, because that uncertainty becomes a reflection of our own secular state and a positive, if caustic, pleasure that we want to recreate and share with others. In this sense, Dickinson's poems are intensely personal and intensely social at the same time.

A poem like "I started Early—Took my dog" has the quality of seeming to be a fragment, a bit of experience or reflection set off from the flow of time for retelling that suggests a larger whole. Dickinson belongs to the poetic history of the fragment that includes Friedrich Schlegel's critical and philosophical fragments from the Atheneum and that looks back, as so much in romantic and lyrical verse traditions do, to Sappho. It was Schlegel who wrote, "In poetry too every whole can be a part and every part really a whole."[14] What interested Schlegel about the fragment as a mode of thinking and writing also, I think, drew Dickinson to fragmentation in her poetry. Fragmentation maximizes multiplicity in meaning, foregrounding irony by disrupting or minimizing disambiguating contextual elements and disrupting conventional expectations. It may be true, philosophically speaking, as Rodolphe Gasché has brilliantly argued in his foreword to Schlegel's fragments, that the logic of such romantic fragments, and even their irony, depends upon a Kantian transcendence, the intimation of a wholeness that cannot be cognized or fully grasped but can somehow be indicated. Schlegel's fragments evoke and depend upon a plenitude of meaning and significance that can be made present or intimated only in the broken form of their fragmented utterance. The fragments indicate the wholeness from which they originally derive.[15] Dickinson, in my reading of her, modernizes the fragment by creating poems that seem to bespeak a life without using the fragment to suggest that life's wholeness. They contain vividly sketched quotidian details about flowers and dogs and birds, but they intimate no reunification of Wordsworthian spots of time and no available world beyond our own earthly ends where conclusions might be reached. The broken forms of Dickinson's poetry and the play with shifting signification they often set in motion create in the reader the uncertain sense that maybe her or his life is fragmentary too. "We are," at last, "the birds that stay," as Dickinson puts it in another well-known poem, without access in this life to the "better latitude" that death as apotheosis might promise ("Tis not that Dying hurts us so—" F528) and without any certainty that that promise of a better latitude will ever be fulfilled.

'Tis not that Dying hurts us so—
'Tis Living—hurts us more—
But Dying—is a different way—
A kind behind the Door—

The Southern Custom—of the Bird—
That ere the Frosts are due—
Accepts a better Lattitude—
We—are the Birds—that stay.

The Shiverers round the Farmer's doors—
For whose reluctant Crumb—
We stipulate—till pitying Snows
Persuade our Feathers Home

The poem leads the reader to expect deliverance like the birds whose southern customs protect them from the cold harshness of a wintery life. But that expectation is disappointed. We remain forever the frozen birds that stay. She imagines humans ice bound and begging for crumbs, living off fragments as it were, until they die, as they lived, amid the snow of these medial latitudes and intemperate climes. The fragment itself becomes at times a rather bitter joke for Dickinson and her reader.

As Sharon Cameron writes: "The longing for coherence assumes that the whole explains the part. It likewise assumes that what the whole 'is' can be recognized. In distinction to these concepts, it is the genius of this poetry, or you could say its perversity, to decline—and in complex terms—precisely such assumptions."[16] In doing this, Dickinson emphasizes not just the difficulty of connecting past to present that her disturbing poem about self-fragmentation, "I felt a Cleaving in my Mind" (F867), evokes, but also the more fundamental fact that humans, of all animals, are aware of mortality and know that their lives can only be fragments because they know that unpredictably and inescapably their lives will be broken off.

I felt a Cleaving in my Mind—
As if my Brain had split—
I tried to match it—Seam by Seam—
But could not make them fit—

The thought behind, I strove to join
Unto the thought before—
But Sequence raveled out of Sound—
Like Balls—upon a Floor—

In the absence of naïve belief in the healing presence of an afterlife that furnishes wholeness to existence, this final sundering seems another example of the recollected sunderings that precede it, another of the temporal disjunctions of lived existence that persist as fragmentary moments of consciousness rather than the remembered experiences of a single, unified self. In Dickinson, the fact of existence orients itself toward the questions of meaning that remain questions and a hoped for wholenesss that death frames and fragments. Death and fragmentation suggest the irony and greatness, the terror and abjection of life. For Dickinson, this is the texture of life in a secular age.

In the absence of transcendence or of naïve beliefs that might lend life an air of purpose, a life can begin to seem an accretion of fragmentation and repetition. Against this, and as its expression, the work of making sense becomes a crucial task, the work of thinking through death becomes the work of life, a life that plays, as Dickinson puts it in one poem "Over and over, like a Tune," the work, one might say, of a secular lyric:

Over and over like a Tune—
The Recollection plays—
Drums off the Phantom Battlements
Cornets of Paradise—

Snatches, from Baptized Generations—
Cadences too grand
But for the Justified Processions
At the Lord's Right hand. (F406)

The snatches from baptized generations, cadences too grand to recollect except as fragments in this life in this broken world, might cohere, might achieve meaning if one could join the justified processions of the blessed in the presence of the Lord, but, of course, no one can count on that.

Whatever meaning the reader in a secular age might achieve depends only on what appears, however broken, to surface in recollection, a repetition, which, to be true to the complexity of the experience, cannot disguise its own fragmentation. "Dickinson's language is language that is broken," as Sharon Cameron puts it, in what is perhaps the most provocative meditation on the status of Dickinson's fragments. "What Dickinson's poetry epitomizes is the fracture of sense." But importantly, her fracturing of sense does not become senselessness; as Cameron specifies, it is open, not indeterminate. Instead, her most suggestive poetry opens on to an invitation to performance addressed to the audience she is always anticipating: "Say we are implicated in this speech not as its object or as the person addressed but as a consequence of its invitation to us to stand alongside of, although not in place of, the speaking subject. For the presumption of speech is not that it is *to* us, but that it is *ours*." It is this incorporation of "us," the anonymous mass of readers who figure an openness to a proleptic welter of possible readings, into the very texture of her poems that makes Dickinson's revival of the fragment seem so distant from transcendence and so bracingly modern and part of this secular world.[17]

The Sense of No Ending

For Dickinson, the absence of transcendence and the omnipresence of death are the characteristic topics on which her fragments center. Her interest in death may be one of the more clearly conventional aspects of her poetry. Death was different in the nineteenth century. On February 16, 1840, Emily Fowler, Emily Dickinson's friend in Amherst, wrote a letter to Mr. and Mrs. J. W. Hand in Washington that captures the way death in the nineteenth century could seem ubiquitous in ways that the twentieth century increasingly would try to conceal: "Death is all around us and yet we have been spared—Mrs Baker wife of the representative is just dead and Fanny Sellon one of my young companions is to be buried day after tomorrow—It has been a season of great mortality among us."[18] Certainly the omnipresence of death—as iconography and as experience— in nineteenth-century American culture (as in Europe as well), when most people died at home and funerals were front parlor affairs, and before the business of death became professionalized—is a familiar topic.[19] What is remarkable about Dickinson's verse, however, is how much poetic ingenuity she expended not on the familiar tropes of consolation readily available in more conventional verses, but on death's inscrutability, on the impossibility—as Emerson put it in "Experience"—of getting death closer to us, on preserving death's uncanniness from, for example, the denaturing passage of time. Emerson, nearly despairing, had written, "Nothing is left us now but death. We look to that with a grim satisfaction, saying, there at least is reality that will not dodge us."[20] Dickinson, more cold-bloodedly, offers the following gimlet-eyed scrutiny of the death-bed's ultimate moment:

> I like a look of Agony,
> Because I know it's true—
> Men do not sham Convulsion,
> Nor simulate, a Throe—
>
> The eyes glaze once—that is Death—
> Impossible to feign
> The Beads opon the Forehead
> By homely Anguish strung. (F339)

A poem like this looks forward to Wallace Stevens's lines summing up his view of an elderly woman's corpse prepared for burial, "Let be be finale of seem. / The only emperor is the emperor of ice-cream."[21]

Confronting the reality of death and doubtful of conventional consolation, Dickinson often turns her poetry to attempts at imagining the time of dying as the dying might experience it, and to considering the meaning of eternity without the comforting fiction of a celestial beyond in the bosom of a sheltering God. In poems about death, Dickinson again and again confronts the impossible challenge of imagining nonbeing from within the closure of existence, of trying to figure how one might sense the extinction of sense, of how one might express a moment in which consciousness and language are extinguished, a moment when one might say ". . . and then / I could no longer see to see" (F591) or "I . . . . / . . . Finished knowing—then—" (F340). In her fascicles, with their many poems about death, Socarides has suggested, Dickinson "investigates the inability of poetry to represent the complicated nature of loss as it exists at the very limits of comprehension. In doing so, she challenges the promise of consolation that the elegy aims to conjure, a consolation that depends precisely on the formal conventions of closure that the stop-again-start-again nature of the fascicles makes impossible" (80). This pressing against the formal conventions of closure is as evident in individual poems as it is in the fascicles, where the reader's inclination to construct narrative arcs or thematic developments is nearly irresistible. Dickinson repeatedly explores in her verse an experience of mortality to which no mortal has access—the experience of death. This experience has little to say about what death might mean, and Dickinson seems to want to suspend the thought of death's meaning indefinitely.

Like Whitman, Dickinson should be considered a great poet of "postmortem effects."[22] Apart from Whitman, no poet addresses readers more directly more often from a point of enunciation that is literally (if that adverb can make sense here) beyond the grave, as in this sampling of famous opening lines:

> "I heard a fly buzzed—when I died—" (F591)
> "I died for beauty . . ." (F448)
> "Because I could not stop for death" (F479)

These are among her most familiar postmortem poems. Like Whitman, however, Dickinson never seeks to get inside death, since like Whitman she realizes that death is where no self can go. Each of these poems is well known for its remarkable opening line. Each of them presents a narrative. And in each, there is weight of expectation clustered around the poem's ending that the poet works to elicit and then frustrate.

> I heard a fly buzz—when I died—
> The Stillness in the Room
> Was like the Stillness in the Air—
> Between the Heaves of Storm—
>
> The Eyes around—had wrung them dry—
> And Breaths were gathering firm
> For that last Onset—when the King
> Be witnessed—in the Room— (F591)

The first two stanzas introduce not only the startling posthumous formulation of the opening line but also a certain confusion between inner and outer, subjective experience and material reality, that will remain unresolved through the poem's end. The heaves of storm furnish a metaphor or a pathetic fallacy that projects the throes of death's final agony and the long intermittent "rattle" of failing breath. Clearly a portentous event, death itself—the King—is expected to manifest his presence at the ultimate moment. We readers, like those who keep the vigil in the poem, wait, breathless ourselves, to witness this:

> I willed my Keepsakes—Signed away
> What portion of me be

Assignable—and then it was
There interposed a Fly—

Here, then, is at last an event, but the interposition of the fly could not be
what we, the mourners, and the dying poet in the poem, have been wait-
ing for. But of course, that is precisely what turns out to be the case, as the
insignificant insect takes the place of the awaited King and performs his
office as well by marking the threshold of extinction:

With Blue—uncertain—stumbling Buzz—
Between the light—and me—
And then the Windows failed—and then
I could not see to see—

I have always found these lines fascinating, as the housefly, with its stumbling buzz, becomes large and even lordly enough to block out the light,
to cause the windows and the eyes to fail, to emerge in the place of the
King as death's agent and personification while remaining a common fly.
Here again, one can understand this as a confusion of the dying subject's
inner state with the outer world as the boundaries between self and world—
the constituents of consciousness—dissolve, as the corpse that housed
this self will soon dissolve into earth. Remarkable as well is the last line,
with its odd recursive formulation of not seeing to see. This is Dickinson's
way of imagining, in a sensual world, what the end of sense might be like.
But it also seems like no end at all, since, of course, not seeing to see still
depends on seeing. Like a little shaggy dog story, this short poem leads
the reader into a narrative that promises culmination and ends, in fact, no
where, or, in fact, refuses to end at all except in an impossible suspension
of sense and time in endless recursions.

Dickinson's well-known riff on Keats's famous conclusion to "Ode on a
Grecian Urn" also suspends what the poem might be expected to end.
Keats, of course, suggests that art triumphs over death and consoles
mortals doomed to die. He offers this as an envoi for the ages:

When old age shall this generation waste,
        Thou shalt remain, in midst of other woe
Than ours, a friend to man, to whom thou say'st,
        "Beauty is truth, truth beauty,"—that is all
                Ye know on earth, and all ye need to know.[23]

In a fashion that recalls her earliest pastiche poems, Dickinson offers a
homelier version of Keats's high-minded sentiments that ends by calling

their efficacy into question by raising doubts about the consoling permanence they promise.

> I died for Beauty—but was scarce
> Adjusted in the Tomb
> When One who died for Truth, was lain
> In an adjoining Room— (F448)

As readers of the poem recall, these two introduce themselves and, discovering "We brethren, are" "as Kinsmen, met a Night—," they converse—on truth and beauty one supposes—between the rooms that are their graves. One might expect, given the august nature of Dickinson's pretext here, that this conversation will furnish sustenance for eternity and edification for the living. Instead the reader gets another intimation of mortality as a process without a revelation, a process with no certain end, "We talked between the Rooms—/ Until the Moss had reached our lips—/ And covered up—Our names." For Dickinson, death ends not in apocalypse but in oblivion, but it does not do so punctually.

Dickinson's best-known poem, "Because I could not stop for Death—" also shifts the grounds out from under the reader at the very end. The amusing personification of death as a suitor who keeps company with the speaker on a carriage ride through existence, leads us to expect, since immortality rides along, that the end of the poem will coincide with a revelation about the life to come. Instead, after putting labor and leisure away and passing the school and fields, the poet becomes aware, around the "Or" of the middle quatrain, that she and her companions have, in fact, ceased to move or, perhaps, have slowed to near stasis while the sun and the world proceed to leave them behind ("We passed the Fields of Grazing Grain—/ We passed the Setting Sun/ Or rather—He passed Us—"). The poem culminates with a confusion of movement and stasis that finally leads nowhere and leaves us there:

> We paused before a House that seemed
> A swelling of the Ground—
> The Roof was scarcely visible—
> The Cornice—in the Ground—
>
> Since then—'tis Centuries—and yet
> Feels shorter than the Day
> I first surmised the Horses' Heads
> Were toward Eternity— (F479)

The only verb moving in these last lines is "paused," which, of course, does not move at all. We and the poet remain pausing with death and immortality behind a team of horses whose heads are toward eternity but who seem to have stopped moving. Eternity remains a surmise that is unlocatable in all the centuries that continue to elapse. Eternity, in Dickinson's poem, remains enmeshed in time and suspending time at once. Once again, death seems, for Dickinson, another sort of shaggy dog, a sort of conceptual joke or *Witz* that she lures her reader repeatedly into following to an ending that refuses to conclude.

Helen Vendler remarks that to "Dickinson, Death was the unintelligible riddle," and draws attention to two poems where the riddle of language seems to indicate the limit of life as well.[24] Consider the following poem that Vendler quotes in full:

> The Brain—is wider than the Sky—
> For—put them side by side—
> The one the other will contain
> With ease—and You—beside—
>
> The Brain is deeper than the sea—
> For—hold them—Blue to Blue—
> The one the other will absorb—
> As Sponges—Buckets—do—
>
> The Brain is just the weight of God—
> For—Heft them—Pound for Pound—
> And they will differ—if they do—
> As Syllable from Sound—(F598)

Vendler remarks that the conventional ruminations on consciousness in the first two stanzas exist only to set up the riddle of the final quatrain, and her commentary on those last four lines is suggestive: "The Brain is said not to contain the Divine nor to absorb it—merely to equal it in weight. But do we not feel a difference between the two weighed things? Yes— and the difference is language. God, through Nature, utters Sounds, but human language alone is voiced in Syllables."[25] This gets at some of the strangeness of what Dickinson is doing here, but there is more to be said about the odd deflection from language to syllable. A syllable, unlike the more commonly evoked linguistic unit of the word, exists right at the limit of significance. Often a syllable in isolation has no meaning at all. Moreover, to differ syllable from sound is strangely involved as well, since a syllable is itself a sonic demarcation, though it suggests, at its limit, the grapheme that represents it as well or the concept to which the word syllable refers. We are here, to borrow from the line that concludes Vendler's introduction, very close to seeing, by an odd slant of light, the "internal difference—/Where the Meanings are—" ("There is a certain slant of light" F320). We are close, that is to say, to achieving an illumination about the point in language where difference becomes paradoxically indifferent and meaning becomes portentous just as it is about to vanish altogether. There is a similarity, Dickinson seems to want us to see, between this riddle in language and the riddle of death itself—they both bring us to the limit of the cognizable, which is where she often wants to situate her poetry. Often, for Dickinson, death and life both seem like cognitive or conceptual jokes or shaggy dog stories. And nothing could be more serious.

Considering the importance of "process" in Dickinson's poetry, Charles Anderson remarks that in her poetry, as in life, the end of all processes is death. He writes, "'Conclusion' is the goal of all living things, according to one poem; they can only hope 'At *most* to be perennial.' Escape from death through seasonal renewal is merely temporary, and it does not save the individual. At most it can serve as a symbol, recalling that larger escape from time into immortality man yearns for."[26] Anderson here brings Dickinson close to the effusions or disseminations—the self-bequeathal to the grass and to the future reader—that Whitman explored in his poems, however different from Dickinson's they are. Yet, where Whitman seems to want to clasp the reader, the world, and the future crowds he imagines to his expansive chest, Dickinson often seems about to turn the reader away or to hide herself behind her layered ironies. And yet, she lures the reader on by evoking a yearning for meaning and transcendence that her poetry in fact works to frustrate or to show that in this world these yearnings must remain unfulfilled.

As Anderson says later in the book, "her best poems on death were not inspired by personal experiences. . . . They sprung instead from the inherent ambiguity of the grave." "Few poets, he added, "saw more clearly the boundary between what can and what cannot be comprehended."[27] He concludes:

> In nature's cyclical process the year goes down to death. If this were
> also the end of time, as the snowstorm's illusion and the sun's eclipse
> suggest, then man would escape into eternity. What seems like process
> with the limits of the temporal scheme, according to her system of
> images, may well turn out to be something quite different in the

limitlessness of eternity. There motion may become inseparably fused with motionlessness, in what she called nature's "changeless change," but this is beyond the mortal poet's grasp. . . . For her it was an endless carnival of entertainment.[28]

For Anderson, Dickinson's baffled, sometimes amused sometimes appalled witnessing and recording and enacting of such moments in nature arrives at no meanings but the pleasure and terror entailed in their contemplation and repetition, and in the endless carnival of mortality as comic or tragic entertainment. This, as Anderson says, and not any more conventional consolation becomes her "ecstasy," and it is one she engages to share with her audience in her peculiar secularization of the lyric.

Conclusion, or the End of the Book

Dickinson seems an appropriate place to end this book because, in an important sense, she approaches the limit of what the lyric in a secular age can achieve. She interrogates sense, the world of everyday discourse and common meaning, while remaining on the near side of coherence. Like Poe and Whitman, she poses challenges to comprehension. She demands what we have come to call lyric reading. Dickinson in her verses often seems to pose riddles to which one can never hope to find answers, in part because finding an answer would spoil the fun or blunt the pain she is asking we enjoy. She makes the reader's role in making meanings—the difficult sociability of interpretation—central to her poetics even as she repeatedly sets up the search for meaning to fail. Readers have long complained that Dickinson does little to help them to understand her poetry. The work that her early, heroic editors did to smooth her prosody and clarify her sense was, misguidedly, meant to offer some help in this direction. Even after Thomas Johnson's brilliant editorial act of recovery in reconstituting her peculiarities on the printed page, a critic like Charles Anderson could lament the disarray of Dickinson's corpus, existing as it does in a heap of scraps, manuscripts, letters, fair copies, a few published poems, many variants, and the notorious fascicles, and complain of the burden all these fragments place on the critic.[29] More recently, Sharon Cameron has taken up this disarray, especially the many variants in the fascicles, more positively in her exploration of what it might mean had Dickinson, long acknowledged as the portfolio poet par excellence, been exhibiting not the mania of a literary pack rat but a calculated use of her art to explore what the choice not to choose among possibilities of words and the possible meanings of a poem those words might yield: "Not choosing in Dickinson's poetry . . . results in a heteroglossia whose manifestations inform every aspect of the poetry."[30] This to my mind suggests another aspect of Dickinson's indebtedness to Emerson—and after Nietzsche I think she may be Emerson's most inventive reader—and to the odd disjunctions of human temporality and subjectivity that Emerson noted in "Circles" when he wrote, "Our moods do not believe in one another."[31] Dickinson seems intent on not choosing among her moods in a given moment or over time. In this way she lives the agon of discourse that Emerson defined as the circular logic of conversational exchange and the "Valor," which "consists in the power of self-recovery,

> so that a man cannot have his flank turned, cannot be out-generalled, but put him where you will, he stands. This can only be by his preferring truth to his past apprehension of truth; and alert acceptance of it, from whatever quarter; the intrepid conviction that his laws, his relations to society, his Christianity, his world, may at any time be superseded and decease.[32]

This, I note, is merely a negative formulation of the positive principle that Emerson articulated in "Self-Reliance," where he inveighed against that foolish consistency that makes self-contradiction a taboo. "Speak what you think now in hard words, and to-morrow speak what tomorrow thinks in hard words again, though it contradict every thing you said today."[33]

The secular self, without untroubled access to transcendental principles or ends, as Emerson learned from his great precursor Montaigne, does not persist in time. The desire to be true to oneself must take the absence of a stable self and the changes of the ephemeral self as a given, whatever the consequences for one's inevitable and necessary social articulation.[34] The secular self tends to belong to specific moments in time—and to specific engagements with others—and can lack in duration what it possesses in intensity. Dickinson, in her poems and in her treatment of her manuscripts, builds a lyric poetry that is frequently dedicated to exploring the disjunctions of the self and its experience, especially as the heteroglossic language of her moment and tribe prescribes and deforms both. She opts for the discrete and discontinuous instants of the self's experience of time and her own repeated efforts to deform her language to make both self and expression seem new. In doing so, like Emerson's circular or self-reliant speaker, she imagines the self not in isolation but engaged in negotiation with the selves around her. It is this secular engagement, this difficult sociability, to which recent studies of the cultural contexts and material

manifestation of Dickinson's work draw our attention. I have been interested here to note how evident this engagement with a crowd of readers
ranging from perhaps one to the world is in the poems themselves, and it
is figured in and as acts of lyric reading.

Dickinson often chooses to emphasize human limits in her lyrics, focusing her wit on death and the disruption of subjectivity. She focuses as
well, in the distortions of popular forms and sentiment that constitute her
verse, on what Benjamin called, in "On Some Motifs in Baudelaire," "the
crowd." Dickinson, like Poe and Whitman, writes verse that responds to
the crowd, the audience, and its discourse. For, once again, as Benjamin
observed, the crowd for the poet was the figure of the modern audience
for printed verse.[35] And though she resisted common forms of publication,
which she described in one poem as "the Auction / Of the Mind of Man—"
and refused to reduce her "Human Spirit / To Disgrace of Price" (F788),
she wrought her poems with the commonplaces of the public sphere, the
common beliefs and sentiments of her compatriots, in mind. She knew, as
well, that these common discourses implicated her and that the only possibility of self-recovery or self-realization for her lay through her poetic
struggles with and within them.[36] Some critics, like Betsy Erkkila, have
read a political or ideological engagement in Dickinson. Erkkila writes:

> Living in a time of major political, social, religious, and epistemologi-
> cal breakdown, perhaps best signified by the political collapse, blood
> violence, and on-going social questions raised by the Civil War,
> Dickinson turned to writing not as a retreat into privacy but as a
> higher order of culture and a powerful means of talking back to, with,
> and against her democratic age.[37]

Whatever Dickinson's actual politics might have been, Erkkila clearly recognizes her engaged desire to talk back to her era. Her fascination with
oft heard words and familiar phrases, the most basic materials of her art,
constitutes as well the inherent sociability, the grounding and the possibility, of the always-altering self and its appeals to the anonymous others
that her lyrics construct.

This sort of sociability figured in Dickinson's negotiation with the
crowd of readers who embodied the welter of meanings, the heteroglossia
of her secular age. Like the similar engagements in Poe and Whitman,
Dickinson's poetry suggests that the modern lyric subject is the antithesis
of that universal and endlessly perfectible Enlightenment individual that
harkens back to Locke and Kant and grounds the triumphant ideology of
liberal capitalism during this period.[38]

Critics in the United States, since Louis Hartz's *The Liberal Tradition in America: An Interpretation of American Political Thought Since the Revolution* (1955) have been much exercised by the persistence of the "liberal subject" that emerges with the European Enlightenment and is marked by its unique dedication to reason and perfectibility, upon which virtues Westerners founded their imperial claims to universality and world dominance. Whitman and Emerson in particular have often been charged with being agents of this form of politically noxious individualism.[39] Recently, Colleen Glenney Boggs has drawn attention to a countertradition to this triumphal imperialism of the liberal subject by considering the "crisis of taxonomy" that figures in representations of animals in nineteenth-century American literature—especially in works by Poe and Dickinson (though also, importantly, in works by Frederick Douglass).[40] I mention Boggs's innovative work here, near the end of this book, because it reminds us that there is always a countercurrent that accompanies modernity's ideologies of sweetness and light, however hegemonic liberalism's Enlightenment discourse might seem. We have too seldom paid attention to this countercurrent when reading our major nineteenth-century writers. I mention Boggs's work here as well because the presence of the animal, as Derrida has noted, is one way of describing what separates the certainties of philosophy from the mysteries of poetry.

Derrida may have had Emily Dickinson (or Poe, or Whitman) in mind—though he needn't have—when near the beginning of *The Animal That Therefore I Am* he says that "thinking concerning the animal, if there is a such a thing, derives from poetry. There you have a thesis: it is what philosophy has, essentially, had to deprive itself of. It is the difference between philosophical knowledge and poetic thinking."[41] Such poetic thinking is thinking that one might not even be able to call thinking, in a traditional sense, since it is the thought of thought's limitation. One way poetry—as exemplified by Poe, Whitman, and Dickinson—presents such a thought is that, like our associations with animals, it raises the question of meaning and of meaning's relationship to communication, to the possibility and impossibility of response from an other and of mutual comprehension.[42]

Poe, Whitman, Dickinson, near the threshold of modern poetry, take the language we still speak (Mallarmé's "language of the tribe") and alter it, not necessarily purifying it, but inflecting it with alterity and thereby reminding us of the uncanniness of language and speech both, a scandalous recollection of what the too great proximity and familiarity of speech and language often conceals. (Already we are close to Heidegger's Ursprung here, the origin of the work of art as unveiling, but what was or is behind that veil is something that cannot be simply stated.) Dickinson, whose poetry one male critic once described by saying, "it sometimes seems as if . . . a cat came at us speaking English," poses these fundamental questions of thought and meaning, these fundamental questions of forming and deforming the substance of communication and sociability, in many of her poems.[43] Blackmur describes Dickinson by deforming the romantic topos of the singing bird, a thing with feathers, that so often figures as the origin of poetry (Keats's Nightingale, Shelley's Lark, Whitman's mockingbirds, even Poe's Raven come to mind). Dickinson is not the only cat among the songbirds, any more than she was the only Kangaroo among the beauty. But she is the cat who worries the conventional canary. In her we get poetry that comes from the source of poetry, which might be the cat's difficult to parse meow rather than those bird songs we might mistakenly believe are easier to translate or understand. This is poetry that finds, again and again, the limit of the poetic and of the human as well, where the question of what it means to be a human among and addressed to other humans might be reencountered and reenacted with the greatest and most familiar strangeness we can imagine.

These modern nineteenth-century poets, Poe, Whitman, and Dickinson, perform the dislocations, conflicts, and doubts that emerge in their negotiations of literary existences in a secular era defined by the heterogeneities of the modern crowd. We remember Kierkegaard and Nietzsche when we recall the dark side of the modern, but we seldom recall that Nietzsche's primary provocation for his attempt to reconsider and revalue the European Enlightenment project began with his reading of Emerson's essays in what one might call the American axis of European modernity.[44] Poe's influence on modern European poetry and Whitman's contributions to modern prosody find a place under this rubric as well. The darker side of secular modernity, the critical interrogation of universalism, knowledge, and power—of the nature and limits of the human itself and above all of language as the medium of communication and sociability—finds a generative impulse in Emerson's essays and in the poetry of Poe, Whitman, and Dickinson. In them, we find reformulations of language and of the self that we assume language constitutes and communicates to others.

They enact, in their texts, the self's secularization, its unmooring from common certainties and beliefs upon which any self must still rely. This is the movement of secularism as uncertainty. This is poetry that belies traditional consolations and offers little purchase for any stable self at all. Their work complicates still widely accepted assumptions that nineteenth-century American literature is simply complicit in the dominant culture's ideological project. What I offer here is in an important sense a historical reading, linked as it is to the problems and pressures of modernity. But it is also, like the literature in question and the lyric in general, in an equally important sense distant from what history has often come to mean as a determining construct or disambiguating context in literary studies. History here does not help us to understand what these poems mean, it gives us a background for appreciating the ways that these poets call common or univocal meanings into question, which is one important function of the lyric in a secular age.

ACKNOWLEDGMENTS

A veritable crowd of readers and interlocutors, friends and colleagues and family helped me with this book, sometimes without knowing they were doing so. Thanks to Geoffrey Bennington, Joel Burges, Morris Eaves, Rita Felski, Kenneth Gross, Jennifer Grotz, John Irwin, Rosemary Kegl, Kerry Larson, James Longenbach, Bette London, Elissa Marder, Krystyna Michael, and Russ Sbriglia for reading parts of chapters as they evolved and for conversations—in passing or extended—on lyric poetry, literature, and life. For reading larger pieces or the whole damn thing, special thanks to Michael Levine and Ezra Tawil, friends, colleagues, and brothers in arms, and to Sharon Willis, my best and most discerning reader. Paul Fess listened to the argument and lent heroic and indispensable assistance with the final preparation of the manuscript. Special thanks as well to the sympathetic and acute readers at Fordham and to Richard Morrison, who remains one of the truly great editors. Gregory McNamee provided invaluable help with the copyediting and markup. I had opportunities to present parts of this book in lectures or seminars at the University of Rochester, the University of Essex, and Southern Methodist University as well as at the American Comparative Literature Association. Thanks to those audiences and colleagues for listening and responding with the sort of questions that help a critic realize what he's doing. Thanks as well to the graduate students in my seminar on secular lyric who played their part in helping to hone these arguments. Undergraduates in my nineteenth-century poetry classes helped me realize that I wanted to say something about Poe, Whitman, and Dickinson. Heartfelt apologies to every one of them for the faults that remain, which are wholly mine own.

The University of Rochester provided generous financial assistance in the final stages of publication, for which I am thankful. For emotional and physical sustenance, for food, wine, and affectionate conversation that seems to always restore my spirits, I am deeply grateful to Morris and Georgia Eaves, Bette London and Tom Hahn, and Nigel Maister and Jennifer Grotz. My immediate family, Marta and Chris Carpenter, Krystyna

Michael, and Paul Fess, provide warmth, good humor, and—in their per-petual youth—a distressing measure of passing time. Mila Carpenter, my first and best Facetime friend, and Andzej Fess, who looks me in the face with only mild surprise, I am so happy to be among your welcoming party and to salute you upon your arrival into this secular world. I wish it were in better shape. Sharon, of course and always, to whom I owe so much, I look forward to the rest of our lives together, and I hope to spend a good part of it enumerating the debt.

INTRODUCTION. THE SECULARIZATION OF THE LYRIC:
THE END OF ART, A REVOLUTION IN POETIC LANGUAGE,
AND THE MEANING OF THE MODERN CROWD

1. Edgar Allan Poe, *Poetry, Tales, and Selected Essays*, ed. Patrick F. Quinn and G. R. Thompson (New York: Library of America, 1984), 38. All references to Poe, except where otherwise noted, refer to this edition and hereafter appear in parentheses in the text.

2. See Charles Taylor, *A Secular Age* (Cambridge, MA: Harvard University Press, 2007), esp. 1–24.

3. Walt Whitman, "Preface" (1855), in *Walt Whitman: Poetry and Prose*, ed. Justin Kaplan (New York: Library of America, 1996), 7. All references to Whitman, except where otherwise noted, refer in the text by page to this edition. Ralph Waldo Emerson, "The Divinity School Address," in *Emerson: Essays and Lectures*, ed. Joel Porte (New York: Library of America, 1985), 89. All references to Emerson, except where otherwise noted, refer in the text by page to this edition.

4. Taylor, *A Secular Age*, 21. Other critics and philosophers, most notably, perhaps, Jacques Derrida, Stathis Gourgouris, and Judith Butler, have explored the ways in which the end of transcendence can enrich rather than impoverish the potentialities and promises of human life, or at least of literature. Tragedy itself, the experience of human limitation, as Gourgouris argues, can be a positive and necessary prelude to truly ethical engagement with the world. See Derrida, "This Strange Institution Called Literature: an Interview with Jacques Derrida," in *Acts of Literature*, ed. Derek Attridge (New York: Routledge, 1992), 44–47; Stathis Gourgouris, *Lessons in Secular Criticism: Thinking Out Loud* (New York: Fordham University Press, 2013), esp. 36–45; see as well Judith Butler "The Sensibility of Critique: Response to Asad and Mahmood," in Talal Asad, Wendy Brown, Judith Butler, and Saba Mahbood, *Is Critique Secular? Blasphemy, Injury, and Free Speech* (Berkeley: University of California Press, 2009). But this requires an embrace of things as they are in the material present rather than a divination of some metaphysical promise that might save meaning in this world by deferring to an

imaginary world elsewhere or to come. It is this this-worldly project, I think, that Poe, Whitman, and Dickinson explore in their poetry. These secular lyricists of the nineteenth century find the absence of transcendental belief to be exhilarating, the motive force of their poetic engagements with the materiality of human existence and its protean limitations.

5. I am contradicting, or at least complicating, Bakhtin's assertion that poetry, unlike the novel, is the expression of a single illuminating conscious-ness. That consciousness, I would say, for modern poetry, is always engaged and often in conflict with the heterogeneous discourses around it. See Mikhail Bakhtin, "Discourse in the Novel," in *The Dialogic Imagination*, ed. Michael Holquist, trans. Caryl Emerson and Michael Holquist (Austin: University of Texas Press, 1981), 259–422.

6. Matthew Rowlinson, "Lyric," in *A Companion to Victorian Poetry*, ed. Richard Cronin, Alison Chapman, and Antony H. Harrison (Oxford: Blackwell, 2002), 59–79, at 78–79.

7. Benedict Anderson, *Imagined Communities* (New York: Verso, 1983).

8. Rowlinson, "Lyric," 59.

9. Virginia Jackson, *Dickinson's Misery: A Theory of Lyric Reading* (Princeton: Princeton University Press, 2005).

10. Ibid., 126.

11. Michael Warner, *Publics and Counter Publics* (New York: Zone Books, 2002), 81; quoted in ibid., 21.

12. Jackson, *Dickinson's Misery*, 6.

13. Virginia Jackson and Yopie Prins, "Lyrical Studies," *Victorian Literature and Culture* 27, no. 2 (1999): 521–530, at 510.

14. Jonathan Culler, "Lyric, History, and Genre," *New Literary History* 40 (Autumn 2009): 879–899, reprinted in *The Lyric Theory Reader: A Critical Anthology*, ed. Virginia Jackson and Yopie Prins (Baltimore: Johns Hopkins University Press, 2014), 67.

15. Jackson and Prins, "Lyrical Studies," 529.

16. Culler, "Lyric, History, and Genre," in Jackson and Prins, *The Lyric Theory Reader*, 75.

17. See "The Philosophy of Composition," in *Poe: Poetry, Tales, and Selected Essays*, ed. Patrick F. Quinn and G. R. Thompson (New York: Library of America, 1984), 1375.

18. "To T. W. Higginson," July 1862, in *The Letters of Emily Dickinson*, ed. Thomas H. Johnson and Theodora Ward, 3 vols. (Cambridge, MA: Harvard University Press, 1958), 2:411–412.

19. Walter Benjamin, *Illuminations: Essays and Reflections*, trans. Harry Zohn, ed. Hannah Arendt (New York: Schocken Books, 1969), 155–156, 166.

20. See Walter Benjamin, "The Work of Art in the Age of Mechanical Reproduction," in ibid., 217–251.

21. Georg Wilhelm Friedrich Hegel, *Introductory Lectures on Aesthetics* (New York: Penguin Books, 1993), 12–13.

22. See Arthur C. Danto, "The End of Art," in *The Philosophical Disenfranchisement of Art* (New York: Columbia University Press, 1986), 81–115, at 83.

23. For a fascinating account of the afterlife of art and of the thesis about art's end, see Eva Geulen, *The End of Art: Readings in a Rumor After Hegel*, trans. James McFarland (Palo Alto, CA: Stanford University Press, 2006), esp. 1–40 and 65–89. Geulen aptly discusses Hegel's "thesis" of the end of art less as a theoretical statement and more as rumor, one that his own work— indeed the very introduction to his lectures on aesthetics (transcribed by a member of the audience) belies (10–13). Yet the sense that art was at an end or in crisis is notable in the nineteenth century and closely linked to ideas about modernity and secularization and therefore of great use to us here, for our epoch—like the nineteenth century—unfolds itself under the sign of art's end even if that sign has no very precise referent.

24. Baudelaire idolized Poe as a figure of the modern writer, and through Baudelaire Poe became a major influence on generations of French poets from Mallarmé through Verlaine and Valéry. Nonetheless, Baudelaire was more clearly influenced by Poe's fiction, which he translated, than he was by his poetry.

25. Though Charles Taylor cites the secession of elite art forms from popular culture as one of the harbingers of secularization and dates it from the late Renaissance (*A Secular Age*, 87–88), the historical collapse of art into commodity and the interpenetration of high and low forms unfolds in the shadow of art's aftermath (in the Hegelian sense) occurring in the nineteenth century. The politics of the avant-garde, for example, depends upon the availability of art not to fulfill but to oppose the dominant expression of the age in the bourgeois state—a project requiring a differentiation between high and low art, as Andreas Huyssen has investigated in detail in *After the Great Divide: Modernism, Mass Culture, Postmodernism* (Bloomington: Indiana University Press, 1986). As Huyssen says, "The irony of course is that art's aspirations to autonomy, its uncoupling from church and state, became possible only when literature, painting and music were first organized according to the principles of a market economy. From its beginnings the autonomy of art has been related dialectically to the commodity form" (17).

26. Emerson, *Essays and Lectures*, 165.

27. On the altered relationship of art to the marketplace in nineteenth-century America, see, for example, Jonathan Hartmann, *The Marketing of*

Edgar Allan Poe (New York: Routledge, 2008); Michael T. Gilmore, *American Romanticism and the Marketplace* (Chicago: University of Chicago Press, 2005); Meredith L. McGill, *American Literature and the Culture of Reprinting, 1834–1853* (Philadelphia: University of Pennsylvania Press, 2003).

28. On Whitman's pose in "The Song of the Answerer" and his "second person poetry more generally," see Kerry C. Larson, *Whitman's Drama of Consensus* (Chicago: University of Chicago Press, 1988), esp. 7–74.

29. M. H. Abrams, *The Mirror and the Lamp: Romantic Theory and the Critical Tradition* (New York: Oxford University Press, 1953), 84. Abrams notes that the rise of the lyric begins much earlier, in 1651, "the year that Cowley's Pindaric 'imitations' burst over the literary horizon and inaugurated the immense vogue of the 'greater Ode' in England" (85), but that date, while informative, may be somewhat arbitrary. See Virginia Jackson's article "Lyric" in *The Princeton Encyclopedia of Poetry and Poetics* (Princeton: Princeton University Press, 2012).

30. Abrams, *The Mirror and the Lamp*, 88.

31. Of course, this literary fact of the figured speaking subject must not be confused with the empirical fact of the poem's author—a point Paul de Man borrowed from New Criticism and made into a theoretical position in "Anthropomorphism and Trope in the Lyric," *The Rhetoric of Romanticism* (New York: Columbia University Press, 1984), 239–262.

32. Jackson, *Dickinson's Misery*; Jerome McGann, *The Textual Condition* (Princeton: Princeton University Press, 1991), especially his pages on Dickinson; Cristanne Miller, *Reading in Time: Emily Dickinson in the Nineteenth Century* (Amherst: University of Massachusetts Press, 2012); Dana Luciano, *Arranging Grief: Sacred Time and the Body in Nineteenth-Century America* (New York: New York University Press, 2007); Yopie Prins, *Victorian Sappho* (Princeton: Princeton University Press, 1999).

33. Terence Whalen, *Edgar Allan Poe and the Masses* (Princeton: Princeton University Press, 1999); Eliza Richards, *Gender and the Poetics of Reception in Poe's Circle* (Cambridge: Cambridge University Press, 2004).

34. Jackson, *Dickinson's Misery*, 68–117.

35. "Introduction," *The Cambridge Companion to Nineteenth-Century American Poetry*, ed. Kerry Larson (Cambridge: Cambridge University Press, 2011), 6.

36. In the Middle East, in Eastern Europe, and elsewhere, artful poetry other than lyric—public, political, and religious poetry, for example—continues to thrive alongside passionately personal love poetry and other sorts of lyrical laments in ways that it no longer does in the West.

37. Julia Kristeva, *Revolution in Poetic Language*, trans. Margaret Waller (New York: Columbia University Press, 1984), 49.

38. Ibid., 50.

39. Stéphane Mallarmé, "Le tombeau d'Edgar Poe," *Poésie* (Paris: Gallimard, 1992), 60.

40. My translation.

41. Dickinson, like Whitman, does sometimes undermine the common associations with gender and sex in her poetry, and critics as diverse as Shira Wolosky and Susan Howe have read a vital engagement with the Civil War in her poems, but the very obscurity of those poems argues against effective engagement with politics. See Howe, *My Emily Dickinson* (Berkeley: North Atlantic Books, 1985), and Wolosky, *Emily Dickinson: A Voice of War* (New Haven: Yale University Press, 1984).

42. As Roman Jakobson wrote, poetry involves "the projection of the principle of equivalence from the axis of selection to the axis of combination." See "Closing Statement: Linguistics and Poetics," in *Style and Language*, 2nd ed., ed. Thomas A. Sebeok (Cambridge, MA: MIT Press, 1964), 350–377. Or, as he put it in "What is Poetry," "Poeticity is present when the word is felt as a word and not a mere representation of the object being named or an outburst of emotion, when words and their composition, their meaning, their external and inner form, acquire a weight and value of their own instead of referring indifferently to reality." *Language in Literature*, ed. Krystyna Pomorska and Stephen Rudy (Cambridge, MA: Harvard University Press, 1987), 378.

43. R. P. Blackmur noted that "One exaggerates, but it sometimes seems as if . . . a cat came at us speaking English." "Emily Dickinson's Notation," in *Emily Dickinson: A Collection of Critical Essays*, ed. Richard B. Sewall (Englewood Cliffs, NJ: Prentice-Hall, 1963), 80, quoted by Sharon Cameron in *Lyric Time: Dickinson and the Limits of Genre* (Baltimore: Johns Hopkins University Press, 1979), 13.

44. Charles Feidelson's *Symbolism in American Literature* (Chicago: University of Chicago Press, 1953) made the precocious modernity of nineteenth-century American writers an article of faith for two generations of critics. Resisting the definition of the emergent canon as, in Matthiessen's well-known formulation, united by its author's "devotion to the possibilities of democracy," Feidelson observes, "It is more likely that the really vital common denominator is precisely their attitude toward their medium—that their distinctive quality is a devotion to the possibilities of symbolism . . . that produced modern literature" (4).

45. This has usually baffled American critics, most of whom agree with Patrick Quinn's assessment that "the extravagant esteem in which Poe is held in France, and in Europe generally, will remain something of a mystery to me; and I feel sure that Perry Miller was speaking for most of us when he

described his astonishment at witnessing the lengths to which an enthusiasm for Poe can be carried in even so sensible a country as Holland." Patrick F. Quinn, *The French Face of Edgar Poe* (Carbondale: University of Southern Illinois Press, 1957), 4. An exception would be Betsy Erkkila, who in her indispensable study *Walt Whitman Among the French: Poet and Myth* (Princeton: Princeton University Press, 1980) uncovers "a different and more cosmopolitan image of the American poet" to replace the idea of "eccentric national genius" (4–5).

1. POE'S POSTHUMANISM: MELANCHOLY
AND THE MUSIC OF MODERNITY

1. Edgar Allan Poe, *Poetry, Tales, and Selected Essays*, ed. Patrick F. Quinn and G. R. Thompson (New York: Library of America, 1984), 1375.

2. Eliza Richards, who has written the most probing analysis of Poe's market calculations in his verses, writes that "Poe captivates his audience . . . by acting out his self-victimization." Eliza Richards, *Gender and the Poetics of Reception in Poe's Circle* (New York: Cambridge University Press, 2004), 34.

3. Edgar Allan Poe, *Essays and Reviews*, ed. G.R. Thompson (New York: Library of America, 1984), 1331. For literature and its relationship to indefiniteness in a secular age, see Stathis Gourgouris, *Lessons in Secular Criticism* (New York: Fordham University Press, 2013): "It is therefore no surprise that in the long procession of Western thought, whereby the quarrel between poetry and philosophy is relentlessly conducted, the advocates of *poiesis* as material (trans)formation are those who resist the seductions of Platonism and its derivatives" (9).

4. For the association of modernism and antihumanism, see Kate Soper, *Humanism and Anti-Humanism* (La Salle, IL: Open Court Press, 1986), and Tony Davies, *Humanism* (New York: Routledge, 1997).

5. Meredith L. McGill notes that Poe in his early poems like "Al Aaraaf" shows considerable anxiety that his readers will miss the "full range of his allusions" and borrowings from the British and other traditions. "For Poe," she writes, "awareness of his indebtedness . . . is a selling point, an index of authorial self-consciousness and poetic ambition." Meredith L. McGill, *American Literature and the Culture of Reprinting* (Philadelphia: University of Pennsylvania Press, 2003), 152. Joan Dayan argues that Poe's poetry moves from an early indebtedness to romance conventions to a later position that exhibits a "labored elimination of the burden of meaning" and an "excessive attention to things, to the corporeality of words" as well as "attention to the sensible world" and an "exaggerated attachment to form and structure." This, as she points is out, is what made poems like "Ulalume" and "To Helen" important to Mallarmé and Valéry as they developed

their own ideas of pure poetry. See Dayan, "From Romance to Modernity: Poe and the Work of Poetry," *Studies in Romanticism* 29, no. 3 (Fall 1990): 413–437.

6. Yopie Prins places Poe in the Sapphic tradition of suffering poets that comes to prominence in the nineteenth century. See her *Victorian Sappho* (Princeton: Princeton University Press, 1999), 48–49. Eliza Richards demonstrates how Poe's Sapphic poetry participates in a print-based community of largely female poets whose work often inspires his own; see *Gender and the Poetics of Reception in Poe's Circle*, esp. 1–59.

7. See, for example, J. Gerald Kennedy, *Poe, Death, and the Life of Writing* (New Haven: Yale University Press, 1987); Jonathan Elmer, *Reading at the Social Limit: Affect, Mass Culture, and Edgar Allan Poe* (Stanford: Stanford University Press, 1995); Terence Whalen, *Edgar Allan Poe and the Masses: The Political Economy of Literature in Antebellum America* (Princeton: Princeton University Press, 1999); and Richards, *Gender and the Poetics of Reception in Poe's Circle. Poe and the Remapping of Antebellum Print Culture*, ed. J. Gerald Kennedy and Jerome McGann (Baton Rouge: Louisiana State University Press, 2012). See especially McGann's "Poe, Decentered Culture, and Critical Method," 245–260; and his book *A New Republic of Letters: Memory and Scholarship in the Age of Digital Reproduction* (Cambridge, MA: Harvard University Press, 2014), esp. 147–167.

8. McGann, "Poe, Decentered Culture, and Critical Method," 255.

9. In exploring his own ambivalent fascination with Poe, Daniel Hoffman offers suggestive insights into the artist's conflicted relationship to himself and his audience. See *Poe, Poe, Poe, Poe, Poe, Poe, Poe* (Garden City, NY: Doubleday, 1974).

10. McGann, "Poe, Decentered Culture, and Critical Method," 255. McGann expands his reading of *Marginalia* in *The Poet Edgar Allan Poe: Alien Angel* (Cambridge, MA: Harvard University Press, 2014) 14–16.

11. "Poe's Lyrical Media," in McGann, *Poe and the Remapping of Antebellum Print Culture*, 206. See also McGann, *The Poet Edgar Allan Poe*, 114–145.

12. See, for example, Whalen's reading of "The Cask of Amontillado" and "The Purloined Letter" in *Edgar Allan Poe and the Masses* (98–100, 243–248); and John Irwin's analysis of a division of the self at the origin of writing in his extended reading of *The Narrative of Arthur Gordon Pym* in *American Hieroglyphics: The Symbol of the Egyptian Hieroglyphics in the American Renaissance* (New Haven: Yale University Press, 1980), 43–235.

13. John Keats, "Ode to a Nightingale," 6, l. 56, in The *Complete Poems of John Keats*, ed. Jack Stillinger (Cambridge, MA: Harvard University Press, 1982), 281.

14. Yopie Prins speculates that Sappho's poetry may have inspired this idea. See *Victorian Sappho*, 49.

15. Giuseppe Mazzotta, *The Worlds of Petrarch* (Durham, NC: Duke University Press, 1993), 58.

16. Canzon, qui sono ed ò 'l cor via più freddo
de la paura che gelata neve,
sentendomi perir senz' alcun dubbio,
ché pur deliberando ò vòlto al subbio
gran parte omai de la mia tela breve;
né mai peso fu greve
quanto quell ch'i' sostengo in tale stato
che co la Morte a lato
cerco del viver mio novo consiglio,
et veggio 'l meglio et al peggior m'appiglio.

Petrarch, *The Canzoniere*, trans. Mark Musa (Bloomington: Indiana University Press, 1996), poem 264, 374–375.

17. Poe wrote, "originality . . . is by no means a matter, as some suppose, of impulse or intuition. In general, to be found, it must be elaborately sought, and although a positive merit of the highest class, demands in its attainment less of invention than negation." "The Philosophy of Composition," 1380–1381.

18. Gur Zak, *Petrarch's Humanism and the Care of the Self* (New York: Cambridge University Press, 2010). Zak is careful to establish that Petrarch's self-care occurs not primarily in his poetry or in the fashioning of his life into narrative—as for Dante—but through those modes of writing that serve as spiritual exercises. Whether or not Petrarch intended "My Secret Book" for circulation beyond a very few familiar readers is unclear. See esp. Zak 1–22 and 79–120. See also Mazzotta, *The Worlds of Petrarch*, 80–101. Even after his imagined dialogue with Augustine forces him to admit that his love for Laura is not quite so pure as he wants to believe it to be and that it stands, along with the love of glory, as a large stumbling block in his way to salvation, it remains unclear whether he can renounce his passion. See Francis Petrarch, *My Secret Book*, trans. J. G. Nichols (London: Hesperus Press, 2002), 55–95, at 63.

19. The subtitle of Whalen's book speaks to political economy. See especially Chapter 2, "The Horrid Laws of Political Economy," 21–57. Whalen takes the phrase from Poe's review of Charles Dickens's *The Old Curiosity Shop, and Other Tales* in *Grahams Magazine* for May 1841, which is reprinted in *Essays and Reviews*. There Poe writes, "It seems that the horrid laws of political economy cannot be evaded even by the inspired." Poe

understood the mass market, and not the life of spirit, to be the formative influence on any artist.

20. Petrarch, as is well known, was fond of punning on Laura's name—associating it with laudation, with the laurel tree, and with the wreath of his poetic vocation or weaving it acrostically into the verbal texture of a sonnet as in Canzionere 5: When I summon sighs to call for you,/with the name the Love inscribed upon my heart,/ In LAUdable the sound at the beginning/ of the sweet accents of that word comes forth. (*Quando io movo I sospiri a chiamar voi/e 'l nome che nel cor mi scrisse Amore,/ LAU—dando s'incominicia undir di fore/ Il suon de 'primi dolci accenti suoi*), etc. *The Canzoniere*, 6–7. In Poe's poem, he salutes his benefactor, Mrs. Sarah Anna Lewis, whose name is encrypted into successive letters of each of the poem's fourteen lines. See *Poetry, Tales, and Selected Essays*, 91–92, and the note on 1482.

21. William Shakespeare, *The Riverside Shakespeare*, ed. G. Blakemore Evans et al. (Boston: Houghton Mifflin, 1974), 1752.

22. Like Baudelaire's painter of modern life, Poe recognizes his poetry as, inevitably, a fleeting expression of fugitive beauty, rooted in mutable feelings and not an appeal to immortality through art or the changelessness of the ideal in spiritual life. "By 'modernity,'" Baudelaire writes, "I mean the ephemeral, the fugitive, the contingent, the half of art whose other half is the eternal and immutable." Charles Baudelaire, *The Painter of Modern Life and Other Essays* (London: Phaedon, 1995), 12. Wherever that other half of art may reside—in the material or the spiritual realm—it is not, so to speak, part of the picture, not within the frame of the present. The modern artist is, as Baudelaire noted, a feverish figure like the narrator of Poe's "The Man of the Crowd." The world and the subject in it remain for him inscrutable. The final line of Poe's tale, *"Es lässt sich nicht lesen"* (it does not permit itself to be read), might be the epigraph of modernity as a secular age.

23. Mazzotta posits that for Petrarch music and metaphor joined to "gather together the separate, heterogeneous entities of experience or to join the past to the future," and sees this as leading Petrarch "to envision poetry . . . [music and rhetoric] . . . as the foundation of political associations . . . and as a theological activity." Mazzotta, *The Worlds of Petrarch*, 10. Poe, for all the profundity of his investment in poetry, has no such positive program. Whitman perhaps does, but we will wait to assess his state in the next chapter.

24. Jahan Ramazani, *Poetry of Mourning: The Modern Elegy from Hardy to Heaney* (Chicago: University of Chicago Press, 1994), ix.

25. For an extremely useful and concise consideration of humanism and antihumanism, see Tony Davies, *Humanism* (New York: Routledge, 1997), esp. 35–104.

26. Sappho, of course, was more identified with the suffering poetess longing for a lost lover—usually imagined in this case to be male—than with the manifestation of same-sex desire. See Prins, *Victorian Sappho*, and Richards, *Gender and the Poetics of Reception in Poe's Circle*.

27. See Walter Benjamin, *The Arcades Project*, trans. Howard Eiland and Kevin McLaughlin (Cambridge, MA: Harvard University Press, 1999), 333–334.

28. My translation of the editor's summary of Vigny: *"le poète est toujours victim de la société, quel que soit le régime politique,"* "Edgar Allan Poe, Sa vie et ses ouvrages," in *Baudelaire: Oeuvres complètes*, ed. Marcel A Ruff (Paris: Editions de Seuil, 1968), 320 n. 9.

29. *"si M. Poe avait voulu régulariser son genie et appliquer ses facultés créatrices d'une manière plus appropriée au sol américain, il aurait pu être un auteur à argent,* a money making author," *Oeuvres complètes*, 320.

30. My translation. The French reads: *"Si vous causez avec un Américain, et si vous lui parler de M. Poe, il vous avouera son génie; volontiers même, peut-être en sera-t-il fier, mail il finira par vous dire avec un ton supérieur: 'Mais moi, je suis un homme positif'"* (320).

31. Baudelaire allows himself a sardonic aside on an American writer (unnamed) who once lamented Poe's refusal to turn his talent to the production of books suitable for the fireside and the family. *"Demander un livre de famille a Edgar Poe! Il est donc vrai que la sottise humaine sera la même sous tous les climats"* (328). "Asking Poe to write a domestic fiction! It is manifestly true that human stupidity is the same in all climates."

32. Charles Baudelaire, "L'albatros," *The Flowers of Evil*, trans. James McGowan (New York: Oxford World Classics, 1993), with my amendments to the translation. The French reads: *"Le Poëte est semblable au prince des nuées / Qui hante la tempête et se rit de l'archer; / Exilé sur le sol au milieu des huées, / Ses ailes de géant l'empêchent de marcher."*

33. Whalen, *Edgar Allan Poe and the Masses*, 76. See as well Leon Jackson, "'The Rage for Lions': Edgar Allan Poe and the Culture of Celebrity," in Kennedy and McGann, *Poe and the Remapping of Antebellum Print Culture*, 37–61, finds Poe caught between "cynical criticisms of celebrity" and "sincere attempts to achieve it for himself" (50). This ambivalence often motivated his hoaxes and aggressions toward his readers. See Hoffman, who wrote in *Poe, Poe, Poe, Poe, Poe, Poe, Poe*, "Poe's sense of his own uniqueness, his own genius, his own knowledge of what was true but not recognized by the mass of mankind who scorned his gift of that knowledge, made his lot both more bitter and more exalted than that of other Disinherited Aristocrats" (200).

34. Benjamin, *The Arcades Project*, 333.

35. My translation. The original reads,

Il y'a, depuis longtemps déjà aux Etats-Unis, un mouvement utilitaire qui
veut entraîner la poésie comme le reste. Il y'a là des poètes humanitaires,
des poètes du suffrage universel, des poètes abolitionnistes des lois sur les
céréales, et des poètes qui veulent faire bâtir des work-houses . . . . Dans
ses lectures, Poe leur déclara la guerre. Il ne soutient pas, comme certains
sectaires fanatiques insensés de Goethe et autres poètes marmoréens . . .
que toute chose belle est essentiellement inutile; mais il se proposait surtout
pour objet la réfutation de ce qu'il appelait spirituellement *la grande hérésie
poétique des temps modernes.* Cette hérésie, c'est l'idée d'utilité directe. . . .
Nous avons une faculté élémentaire pour percevoir le beau; elle a son but à
elle et ses moyens à elle. La poésie est le produit de cette faculté; elle
s'adresse au sens du beau et non à un autre. *C'est lui faire injure que de la
soumettre au critérium des autres facultés,* . . . Que la poésie soit subséquem-
ment et conséquemment utile, cela est hors de doute, mais ce n'est pas son
but; cela vient par-dessus le marché! (224)

36. By way of contrast, Emerson, in his own poetry, sometimes seems to
want to purify language to make it more practically efficient. In *Nature*, he
adopted an already familiar metaphor that compares language to currency
and modern, conventional language to badly inflated "paper currency" that
is "employed, when there is no money in the vault." Ralph Waldo Emerson,
Nature, in *Essays and Lectures*, ed. Joel Porte (New York: Library of America,
1983), 22. For Emerson, the wise men and poets "pierce this rotten diction
and fasten words again to visible things" restoring the metaphorical and
referential force of "picturesque language" to make both truth and God
present (23). Poe's divorce of literature from truth and from presence, his
embrace in art of beauty and loss, holds no hope for such a restoration of
original force and value commodity to language.

37. My translation. *"Les échos désespères de la mélancolie qui traversent les
ouvrages de Poe ont un accent pénétrant, il est vrai, mais il faut dire aussi que c'est
une mélancolie bien solitaire et peu sympathique au commun des hommes"* (327).

38. *"Il a beacoup suffert pour nous"* (336).

39. James Lowell, "A Fable for Critics," in *American Poetry: The Nineteenth Century, Volume One: Freneau to Whitman*, ed. John Hollander (New
York: Library of America, 1993), 688.

40. Perhaps the most challenging considerations of the independent
importance of sound in poetry may be found in Susan Stewart in her chapter
on sound in *Poetry and the Fate of the Senses* (Chicago: University of Chicago
Press, 2002). Though Stewart mentions Shelly, Keats, Verlaine, Nietzsche,
Coleridge, and even Whitman, she does not mention Poe, though the

chapter seems in some ways to be about him. It draws from and adds to insights from Allan Grossman's sense of maternal presence in poetic language that is "specialized toward sound" and Julia Kristeva's sense of the deeply regressive nature of the "chora" or sound element in verse as an evocation of that which "precedes and underlies figuration." For Stewart, "producing and receiving sounds in order to form intelligible meanings involves mastery over relations of proximity and distance and presence and absence" (62). Thus, an element of mastery over the trauma of loss and the memorialization of absence is present in the music of poetry. This, as Stewart puts it, suggests both "evidence of intended care" and "evidence of human countenance," the longing for and the sometimes disruptive presence of alterity and temporality within the poem (63–64). See also her analysis of rhythm as the inception of poetry, capable of reporting and conveying a mood; see "Freedom from Mood" in *The Poet's Freedom: a Notebook on Making* (Chicago: University of Chicago Press, 2011), 53–84. See as well Allan Grossman, "Summa Lyrica: A Primer of the Commonplaces in Speculative Poetics," in Allan Grossman and Mark Halliday, *The Sighted Singer: Two Works on Poetry for Readers and Writers* (Baltimore: Johns Hopkins University Press, 1992), 205–283; and Julia Kristeva, *Revolution in Poetic Language*, trans. Margaret Waller (New York: Columbia University Press, 1984), 46–51.

41. In general, Poe's poems most intensely evoke mourning when they most closely approximate music in ways that force the reader to register time's passage by the repetition of sounds or beats. Everyone remembers the incessant trochaic thrumming of the long lines of "The Raven" and the insistent recursions of the internal rhyming those long lines allow ("Once upon a midnight dreary while I pondered weak and weary," etc.). In this rhythm, one can almost hear the tick-tock of a case clock.

42. As Elisabeth Bronfen describes Poe's poetics, they "seem to endorse a spectatorship that ignores the referent, the non-semiotic body and focuses its reading exclusively on the image as a self-reflexive, materialized sign." *Over Her Dead Body: Death, Femininity and the Aesthetic* (New York: Routledge, 1992), 71. In Bronfen's brilliant reading, the ambivalence in Poe's treatment of the dead woman as the most poetical topic manifests a fundamental ambivalence between the "desire for the dead other" and "the desire for the death of the other" (62–63) and a melancholy concerning the revelation and the unrepresentability of death, except in the person of the beautiful woman who hides and reveals its presence in life (63–66).

43. Beth Ann Bassein has perhaps taken the most extreme position with regard to Poe's misogyny by advocating expunging Poe and his imagery

from contemporary culture. See *Women and Death: Linkages in Western Thought and Literature* (Westport, CT: Greenwood Press, 1984), quoted in Bronfen, *Over Her Dead Body*, 59.

44. "Nevermore," as Barbara Johnson once observed, becomes "in Poe . . . the figure for poetic language itself." This observation possesses implications beyond the interpretive crux, the focalization on interpretation as rereading and misreading, on which she centers her brilliant analysis. It entails as well a meditation not only on poetic language's relation to common signification but also on its relationship to pure form. Barbara Johnson, "Strange Fits: Poe and Wordsworth and the Nature of Poetic Language," in *The American Face of Edgar Allan Poe*, ed. Shawn Rosenheim and Stephen Rachman (Baltimore: Johns Hopkins University Press, 1995), 46.

45. On sound repetition and regression, see Allan Grossman, "Summa Lyrica: A Primer of the Commonplaces in Speculative Poetics," in Allan Grossman and Mark Halliday, *The Sighted Singer: Two Works on Poetry for Readers and Writers* (Baltimore: Johns Hopkins University Press, 1992), 205–283; and Kristeva, *Revolution in Poetic Language*, 46–51.

46. T. S. Eliot, "From Poe to Valéry," in *To Criticize the Critic* (Lincoln: University of Nebraska Press, 1992), 31–32.

2. POE AND THE ORIGINS OF MODERN POETRY: TROPES OF COMPARISON AND THE KNOWLEDGE OF LOSS

1. Edgar Allan Poe, *Essays and Reviews*, ed. G. R. Thompson (New York: Library of America, 1984), 582. Hereafter cited in text as *ER*.

2. G. R. Thompson, "Literary Politics and the 'Legitimate Sphere': Poe, Hawthorne, and the 'Tale Proper.'" *Nineteenth-Century Literature* 49, no. 2 (September 1994): 167–195.

3. See Erich Auerbach, who in "Figura" notes that for the Church Fathers, allegory "generally refers to any deeper meaning." Auerbach, *Studies in the Drama of European Literature* (New York: Meridian Books, 1959), 47. As Paul Ricoeur argues, for Aristotle and since, metaphor is not simply a deviation from literal usage but "the privileged instrument in that upward motion of meaning promoted by *mimesis*." Ricoeur, *The Rule of Metaphor: Multidisciplinary Studies in the Creation of Meaning in Language* (Toronto: University of Toronto Press, 1977), 41. For Quintilian, who influences all thinking about figurative language that comes after him, "Basically all discourse is a forming, a figure" though the word is especially developed in analyses of poetic or rhetorical forms. Auerbach, "Figura," 26.

4. See Tony Davies, *Humanism* (New York: Routledge, 1997), esp. 1–34.

5. As Denis Donoghue remarks, sometimes Aristotle seems suspicious of metaphor almost in the vein of his mentor Plato, who cast the poets out of

the Republic because they muddled thought. Donoghue, *Metaphor* (Cambridge, MA: Harvard University Press, 2014), 65.

6. Edgar Allan Poe, *Poetry, Tales, and Selected Essays*, ed. Patrick F. Quinn and G. R. Thompson (New York: Library of America, 1996), 1385.

7. *Rhetoric*, trans. W. Rhys Roberts, in *The Complete Works of Aristotle*, 2 vols., ed. Jonathan Barnes (Princeton: Princeton University Press, 1984), 2:2240. Poe's ambivalences about tropes of comparison, like metaphor, must thus be related to his belief, expressed in *Marginalia*, that indefiniteness, not clarity, is the true poem's proper note (*ER* 1331).

8. *Poetics* 1457:25, in *Works* 2:2333.

9. Ricoeur, *The Rule of Metaphor*, 33.

10. The quotations in this paragraph are from Terence Whalen, *Poe and the Masses: The Political Economy of Literature* (Princeton: Princeton University Press, 1999), 77–82 and 189.

11. Susan Stewart remarks that Wordsworth also "makes the brutal absence of absent things present"; see *Poetry and the Fate of the Senses* (Chicago: University of Chicago Press, 2002), 220. Stewart refers to Wordsworth's "Surprised by Joy" which, in many ways, is a thematic precursor to Poe's "Ulalume," which I discussed in the previous chapter. Poe's dwelling with melancholy absence is part of what Terence Whalen identifies as the emergence of a "culture of surfaces" in his work (*Poe and the Masses*, 100). No significant depths are plumed and no losses are redeemed in Poe's poetry. Absence itself fixes on the surface of things.

12. "Now strange words simply puzzle us; ordinary words convey only what we know already; it is from metaphor that we can best get hold of something fresh. When the poet calls old age 'a withered stalk,' he conveys a new idea, a new fact, to us by means of the general notion of 'lost blossom,' which is common to both things. The similes of the poets do the same." Aristotle, *Rhetoric* III 1410 10:11–15, in *The Complete Works of Aristotle*, 2:2250–2251.

13. In "Mourning and Melancholia," Freud writes that the work of mourning is accomplished as the ego, confronted with the loss of its object, withdraws libido from the world and fixes it on "the existence of the lost object [which is] continued in the mind." The image in the mind substitutes for and represents, the lost object and receives the displaced libidinal energy. In successful mourning, this is a transitional moment on the way to a successful recathexis of life; in melancholia, it becomes a fixation that expresses the ambivalences of the original relationship. Freud, *General Psychology Theory: Papers on Metapsychology* (New York: Simon & Schuster, 1991), 163. Since Peter Sacks's work on *The English Elegy*, Freud's view of the mourning work has shaped our sense of the elegiac tradition. I want to add

that the work of metaphor—the creation of verbal and mental images that take the place of the lost lover—is akin to the work of mourning.

14. Ralph Waldo Emerson, "Experience," in *Emerson: Essays and Lectures*, ed. Joel Porte (New York: Library of America, 1983), 473.

15. *The Riverside Shakespeare*, ed. G. Blakemore Evans et al. (Boston: Houghton Mifflin, 1974), 1773.

16. In Paul Ricoeur's terms, Poe collapses the lexical (word for word) and discursive (word referring to entire syntagms or complex concepts) substitutions upon which comparison depends; see *The Rule of Metaphor*, 13–43.

17. *Petrarch: Canzoniere*, poem 292, trans. Mark Musa (Bloomington: Indiana University Press, 1996), 413.

18. Theresa Rizzo, "The Cult of Mourning," in *Edgar Allan Poe in Context*, ed. Kevin J. Hayes (Cambridge: Cambridge University Press, 2013), 148–156, at 150–151.

19. Edward J. Piacentino argues that "Ligeia" is an example of Poe's anti-Petrarchism, though it is important to remember that Poe continues even as he transforms the traditions from which he creates his own originality. See "Petrarchan Echoes and Petrarchanism in Poe's 'Ligeia,'" in *Masques, Mysteries, and Mastodons: A Poe Miscellany*, ed. Benjamin F. Fisher (Baltimore: Edgar Allan Poe Society, 2006), 102–114.

20. Baudelaire imagines that the modern artist is, like the tale's narrator, "always, spiritually, in the condition of that convalescent," observing without being able finally to understand. See Charles Baudelaire, "The Painter of Modern Life," in *The Painter of Modern Life and Other Essays*, trans. Jonathan Mayne (New York: Phaidon Press, 1995), 7.

21. Wordsworth, in "Tintern Abbey," writes of "the mighty world / Of eye and ear,—both what they half create, / And what perceive."

22. As Peter Sacks notes, at least since Spenser "one finds an increasing absence of consolation, coupled with a yet darker distrust of language," in English elegies. Peter Sacks, *The English Elegy: Studies in the Genre from Spenser to Yeats* (Baltimore: Johns Hopkins University Press, 1985). Poe may be seen as troping this distrust of language from a negative moment in the elegy to the positive force of his lyrics, not an impediment to their purpose but a description of it. The Lady Rowena's unhappy fate is to be sacrificed to this impulse.

23. See Aristotle, *Metaphysics*, Book 4; and Bertrand Russell, *The Problems of Philosophy* (New York: Oxford University Press, 1997), 72.

24. Colin Dayan, *Fables of Mind: An Inquiry into Poe's Fiction* (New York: Oxford University Press, 1987), 181. Poe relates metaphor to consistency as the "great thoroughfare" to truth by intuitive leaps in *Eureka* (1269), as we will see.

25. See the sections on linguistic value in Ferdinand de Saussure, *A Course in General Linguistics*, trans. Roy Harris (New York: Bloomsbury, 2013), 131–144.

26. On the story's "repeated variations on the theme of *dis*" and its emphasis on revolution, inversion, returning, and overturning, see Dayan, *Fables of Mind*, 139.

27. Dayan traces the figuration of teeth in the Song of Songs and in Augustine's "De Doctrina Christiana," by contrast, she argues, Berenice's teeth are "keys to the operations of mind and memory . . . a call to unremitting translation" (ibid., 136–137), which is not a bad definition of the movement inscribed within metaphor itself. However, I think Poe works more to disrupt and fixate this movement toward translation and meaning than he does to perpetuate it.

28. As Dayan points out, "although Poe theorizes about an absolute ideal of beauty and purity in 'The Poetic Principle,' in practice his tales never remain ethereal. As searing examinations of mind, they are never freed from a highly sensuous though disturbing material contamination and decay" (ibid., 136). They always end, I would add, within the enclosure of pure materiality.

29. "Clarity," as Paul Ricoeur says, "is obviously a touchstone for the use of metaphor," though he, like Aristotle, grants more leeway to poetic metaphor (as opposed to metaphor in prose discourse) in terms of the apparent appropriateness of the comparison. See *The Rule of Metaphor*, 32–33.

30. Dayan has noted that this last apocalyptic observation places the reader along with the narrator within the sort of projective madness from which Poe constructed "The Tell-Tale Heart" and also noted the inadequacy of a Christian framework for understanding it (*Fables of Mind*, 202). I would add that any transcendental framework (and Poe at times here seems to parody Emerson's nature with its myths of shrinkage and fables of the fall) will fail to capture the determined materialism of Poe's poetic vision.

31. Emerson, *Essays and Lectures*, 46, 48.

32. Terence Whalen reads this tale as a key moment where Poe dreams of a purely material language, an illustration of "unfettered material signification" that expresses Poe's longing "to escape the mediation of capital." Whalen, *Poe and the Masses*, 268. I take Whalen's point, though Poe's secularization of poetry may well be a strategy engaged with capitalism's mediations rather than an attempt to escape them. For a more flexible account of Poe's relationship to the marketplace, see Eliza Richards, *Gender and the Poetics of Representation in Poe* (Cambridge: Cambridge University Press, 2004), 1–59.

3. WHITMAN'S POETICS AND DEATH: THE POET, METONYMY, AND THE CROWD

1. Walt Whitman, *Poetry and Prose*, ed. Justin Kaplan (New York: Library of America, 1996), 87. References to Whitman's poetry are to this edition and appear parenthetically in the text.

2. Roland Greene, *Post-Petrarchism: Origins and Innovations of the Western Lyric Sequence* (Princeton: Princeton University Press, 1991), 133–152. See also Mark Maslan, *Whitman Possessed: Poetry, Sexuality, and Popular Authority* (Baltimore: Johns Hopkins University Press, 2001), 62–77.

3. Compare Whitman's poem to these lines from Baudelaire's sonnet: "Around me roared the nearly deafening street./Tall, slim, in mourning, in majestic grief,/A woman passed me, with a splendid hand/Lifting and swinging her festoons and hem;/.... One lightening flash ... then night! Sweet fugitive/Whose glance has made me suddenly reborn,/Will we not meet again this side of death?/Far from this place! too late! *never* perhaps!/Neither one knowing where the other goes,/O you I might have loved, as well you know!" "To a Woman Passing By" ("A une passante"). Charles Baudelaire, *The Flowers of Evil*, trans. James McGowan (Oxford: Oxford University Press, 1993), 189. On Baudelaire and Whitman, see Laura Katsaros, *New York-Paris: Whitman, Baudelaire and the Hybrid City* (Ann Arbor: University of Michigan Press, 2012).

4. Katsaros argues that realism is what links Whitman and Baudelaire, despite their obvious differences (8–9). Whitman's later interest in Lucretius—whose noble but still too negative attempt to absorb science to poetry Whitman identifies in 1871 as the future project of the poet of "these States" (see "Democratic Vistas," 1012–1013)—is already prepared by his earliest poetic embrace of materialism. The atoms that begin "Song of Myself" in 1855, "I celebrate myself,/And what I assume you shall assume,/For every atom belonging to me as good belongs to you." already place the American poet in the great materialist's orbit of influence. See Martin Priestman, "Lucretius in Romantic and Victorian Britain," in *The Cambridge Companion to Lucretius*, ed. Stuart Gillespie and Philip Hardie (Cambridge: Cambridge University Press, 2007), 289–335, esp. 303–304.

5. Max Cavitch, *American Elegy: The Poetry of Mourning from the Puritans to Whitman* (Minneapolis: University of Minnesota Press, 2006), 243–244.

6. Harold Aspiz, *So Long! Walt Whitman's Poetry of Death* (Tuscaloosa: University of Alabama Press, 2004), 37.

7. This, as Paul Ricoeur points out, is a view of metaphor that dates to Aristotle's *Rhetoric*; see Ricoeur, *The Rule of Metaphor* (Toronto: University of Toronto Press, 1975), esp. 17–43; and Aristotle's *Rhetoric* and *Poetics*.

Among the voluminous literature on metaphor and metonymy, I have found especially useful Mark Turner, *Death Is the Mother of Beauty* (Chicago: University of Chicago Press, 1987); George Lakoff and Mark Turner, *More Than Cool Reason: A Field Guide to Poetic Metaphor* (Chicago: University of Chicago Press, 1989); and Zoltan Kövecses, *Metaphor: A Practical Introduction* (Oxford: Oxford University Press, 2002).

8. Ralph Waldo Emerson, "The Poet," in *Emerson: Essays and Lectures*, ed. Joel Porte (New York: Library of America, 1983), 456.

9. John Irwin, *American Hieroglyphics: The Symbol of the Egyptian Hieroglyphics in the American Renaissance* (New Haven: Yale University Press, 1980); C. Carol Hollis, *Language and Style in Leaves of Grass* (Baton Rouge: Louisiana State University Press, 1983); Kerry Larson, *Whitman's Drama of Consensus* (Chicago: University of Chicago Press, 1988); Michael Moon, *Disseminating Whitman: Revision and Corporeality in Leaves of Grass* (Cambridge, MA: Harvard University Press, 1991); and Mark Bauerlein, *Whitman and the American Idiom* (Baton Rouge: Louisiana State University Press, 1990) link Whitman's use of metonymy to his desire for self-evidence or presence. But the cost of self-evidence or presence is, paradoxically, the absence of significance or the impossibility of reading in any traditional sense. Like the Man of the Crowd, Whitman will not allow himself to be read.

10. I am thinking of course of "Out of the Cradle Endlessly Rocking" and many other scattered instances as well. It is not too large a claim to say that Whitman attempts to revalue the Western horror of the corpse that has, according to Philippe Ariès, been a central figure in European culture since the fifteenth century (though one also remembers the maggots that drop from Gilgamesh's friend's nose). See *Western Attitudes Toward Death* (Baltimore: Johns Hopkins University Press, 1973), esp. 41, where Ariès quotes the following verses from de Nesson (1383–1442): "O carrion, who art no longer a man, / Who will hence keep thee company? / Whatever issues from thy liquors, / Worms engendered by the stench / Of thy vile carrion flesh." See, as well, the fuller account of the "Les thèmes macabre" in Ariès's *L'homme devant la mort* (Paris: Seuil, 1977), 113–125. Poe, of course, had exploited this early modern and modern horror of putrefaction many times in his tales and poems to undermine the sentimental tradition's attempts to whitewash death (see *Western Attitudes Toward Death*, 58–63). Ariès evokes Mark Twain's satires of sentimental elegies and mourning poems as evidence of the alteration in Western sensibilities (see *Western Attitudes Toward Death*, 61, 67).

11. Cognitive linguistics attempts to capture this feature of metaphor by abandoning the terminology of vehicle and tenor to speak instead of

mapping one discursive field over another. The maps in such a view of metaphor meld their terms in interesting ways. See Lakoff and Turner, *More Than Cool Reason.*

12. The violence translation does to the original has been, of course, the worry of translators and of translation studies at least since Schleiermacher's "On the Different Modes of Translating" (1813) brought the issue into modern focus. See *The Translation Studies Reader,* 2nd ed., ed. Lawrence Venuti (New York: Routledge, 2004), 43–63. As Emily Apter describes this aspect of translation, it entails "the traumatic loss of native language," but in that trauma she sees, as did Walter Benjamin, the perpetuation of literature. See *The Translation Zone: A New Comparative Literature* (Princeton: Princeton University Press, 2006), xi and 88–93; Walter Benjamin, "The Task of the Translator," in *Illuminations,* trans. Harry Zohn, ed. Hannah Arendt (New York: Schocken Books, 1968), 69–82.

13. There is here something of the logic of the dangerous supplementarity attending any form of representation or signification, as Derrida demonstrated in *Of Grammatology,* rev. ed., trans. Gayatri Spivak (Baltimore: Johns Hopkins University Press, 1997), 141–163.

14. Adam C. Bradford finds the link between Poe and Whitman definitive for both and suggestive of their links to a pervasive culture of mourning, *Communities of Death: Whitman, Poe, and the American Culture of Mourning* (Columbia: University of Missouri Press, 2015). I think he underestimates the degree to which both poets deviated from the culture surrounding him, even as they undeniably engaged it. On the pervasiveness of mourning ritual in nineteenth-century U.S. culture, see Dana Luciano, *Arranging Grief: Sacred Time and the Body in Nineteenth-Century America* (New York: New York University Press, 2007), 1–24. For Poe and the Sapphic poetesses, see Eliza Richards, *Gender and the Poetics of Reception in Poe's Circle* (New York: Cambridge University Press, 2004).

15. *American Elegy,* 271. Cavitch refers here to Betsy Erkkila's *Whitman: The Political Poet* (Oxford: Oxford University Press, 1989), 234.

16. Cavitch, *American Elegy,* 271.

17. Larson, *Whitman's Drama of Consensus,* 240, 291.

18. Cavitch, *American Elegy,* 258–285.

19. Ibid., 276.

20. Irwin, *American Hieroglyphics,* 40.

21. Here I part from Mark Bauerlein's attempt to identify Whitman's poetics with a nativist American "anti-intellectualism" and especially with a resistance to theory and to language both in the interests of immediacy, sensation, and simple self-presence. See *Whitman and the American Idiom* (Baton Rouge: University of Louisiana Press, 1990), esp. 1–52.

22. The importance of the jeremiad and of Orpheus should be evident as well, though the pressure of enlightenment traditions seems more germane to the present discussion.

23. Betsy Erkkila, *Walt Whitman Among the French: Poet and Myth* (Princeton: Princeton University Press, 1980), 14–15. Esther Shephard, years ago, accused Whitman of plagiarizing from Sand's romance. See Esther Shephard, *Walt Whitman's Pose* (New York: Harcourt, Brace, and Co., 1936). For a more balanced account of Whitman's borrowings, see, in addition to Erkkila, David Goodale, "Some of Walt Whitman's Borrow-ings," *American Literature* 10, no. 2 (May 1938): 202–213, esp. 208–213.

24. C. F. Volney, *The Ruins or, Meditation on the Revolutions of Empires: and the Law of Nature* (NP: Bibliobazaar, 2006), 52. Section 41 of "Song of Myself" in which the poet undertakes, somewhat satirically, to estimate the values of the world's religions seems most indebted to Volney's thought:

> Magnifying and applying come I,
> Outbidding at the start the old cautious hucksters,
> Taking myself the exact dimensions of Jehovah,
> Lithographing Kronos, Zeus and his son, and Hercules his grandson,
> Buying drafts of Osiris, Isis, Belus, Brahma, Buddha,
> In my portfolio placing Manito loose, Allah on a leaf, the crucifix engraved,
> With Odin and the hideous-faced Mexitli and every idol and image,
> Taking them all for what they are worth and not a cent more . . . (233)

25. Erkkila, *Whitman Among the French*, 41.

26. Ibid., 16–17. David Goodale demonstrates that "Salut au Monde" also borrows directly from the moment in Volney's *Ruins* when the narrator takes the prophet's hand and feels himself "wafted to the regions above." Volney continues: "Thence, from the aerial heights, looking down on the earth, I beheld a scene entirely new. Under my feet, floating in the void, a globe . . . variegated with large spots, some white and nebulous, others brown, green, or gray. . . . I cast my eye over the whole of our hemi-sphere. . . . All Asia lies buried in profound darkness" (52). And in fact Whitman seems to learn something about enchaining moments of transcen-dent vision into long metonymic strings from Volney's narrator's catalogs of the peoples and places he sees while suspended in the air. But of course, once cited, the passages in Whitman's poetry that most recall Volney also mark what is most distinctively Whitman's. This has to do with the invention and the interposition of that particular democratic self and poetic "I" with which Whitman replaces Volney's more prosaic and authoritarian legislator. It involves the insistently rhythmic enchainment of what that I sees and utters. Larzer Ziff analyzes the ways in which Whitman's poetic "I," his democratic

self, moves from moments of elevation to identification and transformation in his poetry, become the point of contact between the one and the many, the cosmic order of the self and the possible anarchy of the many. See "Whitman and the Crowd," *Critical Inquiry* 10 (June 1984): 579–591.

27. Here, as explained in the introduction, I refer to Charles Taylor's sense that a secular age denotes not the end of belief but a proliferation of possible beliefs, including a belief in science or progress, that make untroubled adherence or naïve subscription to any one belief untenable. See Taylor, *A Secular Age* (Cambridge, MA: Harvard University Press, 2007), esp. 1–22.

28. On repetition, parallelism, and anaphora as structuring devices in Whitman's poetry, see Gay Wilson Allen, "Biblical Analogies for Walt Whitman's Prosody," *Revue anglo-americaine* 10 (1933): 490–507; *American Prosody* (New York: American Book, 1935), 217–243; *The New Walt Whitman Handbook*, 207–248; and James Perrin Warren, *Walt Whitman's Language Experiment* (University Park: Pennsylvania State University Press, 1990), 70–106; Allan Grossman, "The Poetics of Union in Whitman and Lincoln: An Inquiry toward the Relationship of Art and Policy," in *The American Renaissance Reconsidered: Selected Papers from the English Institute, 1982–83*, ed. Walter Benn Michaels and Donald E. Pease (Baltimore: Johns Hopkins University Press, 1985), 183–208. Others have noted a political ambition in Whitman's metonymies. C. Carroll Hollis argues that Whitman's desire to touch the lives and the feelings of his reader lead him to write a metonymic poetry that emphasizes oratorical performance and physical sensation; see *Language and Style in Leaves of Grass*, esp. 154–203; and Bauerlein, *Whitman and the American Idiom*, esp. 17–52.

29. Betsy Erkkila notes the determinately detranscendental aspect of Whitman's verse. See *Whitman the Political Poet*, 68–91.

30. Michael Moon analyzes the evolving tensions between identity, difference, and indifference in the various editions of *Leaves of Grass* between 1855 and 1860. See *Disseminating Whitman: Revision and Corporeality in Leaves of Grass* (Cambridge, MA: Harvard University Press, 1991), 133–134.

31. Among the most telling of these is Philip Fisher's "Democratic Social Space: Whitman, Melville, and the Promise of American Transparency," in *The New American Studies: Essays from Representations*, ed. Philip Fisher (Berkeley: University of California Press, 1991), 70–111. For a contrasting reading, see Allan Grossman, "The Poetics of Union in Whitman and Lincoln: An Inquiry toward the Relationship of Art and Policy," in Michaels and Pease, *The American Renaissance Reconsidered*, 183–208.

32. I am at odds here with Philip Fisher's influential reading of Whitman as an exemplar of an "American aesthetics [that] is intrinsically an aesthetics

of abstraction, or even more radically, an aesthetics of the subtraction of differences." See "Democratic Social Space: Whitman, Melville, and the Promise of American Transparency," 81. Whitman's indifference bespeaks not the distance of abstraction but an impossible ethos of contact and even obligation that registers difference in its most profound form—though necessarily superficial, since difference nearly by definition suggests impenetrability. As Michael Moon puts it, "Rather than simply meaning 'no difference,' 'indifference' functions in this text as a power of transgressing the predominant boundaries of the culture while preserving those boundaries as a (negative) value for critique." *Disseminating Whitman*, 134. Somewhat in this vein is also Donald Pease's analysis of Whitman's disavowal, revelation, and exploitation of the nation's expansionist violence in "Colonial Violence and Poetic Transcendence in 'Song of Myself,'" in *The Cambridge Companion to Nineteenth-Century American Poetry*, ed. Kerry Larson (Cambridge: Cambridge University Press, 2011), 225–247.

33. Warren, *Walt Whitman's Language Experiment*, 80. Warren is writing specifically about "The Sleepers," but this is a familiar succession in Whitman's poetry.

34. Recently Hans Ulrech Gumbrecht has argued for a critical focus on intensities of experience created by the presence of the world or of art rather than our traditional obsession with meaning. Whitman's poetry depends for its best effects on something similar. See Hans Ulrich Gumbrecht, *Production of Presence: What Meaning Cannot Convey* (Stanford: Stanford University Press, 2004).

35. Volney, *The Ruins*, 168–169. Critics have long noted Whitman's self-declared affinity for Volney. See Horace L. Traubel, *With Walt Whitman in Camden* (New York, 1908); Goodale, "Some of Walt Whitman's Borrowings," 208–213; Erkkila, *Walt Whitman Among the French*, 12–20.

36. In this materialist rejection of higher significances one senses the nearly ubiquitous presence of Lucretius and through him of Epicurus in modernity. See Stephen Greenblatt, *The Swerve: How the World Became Modern* (New York: Norton, 2012).

37. Warren, in *Walt Whitman's Language Experiment*, finds a similar inspiration in Whitman's interest in Von Humboldt's evolutionary linguistics. Warren cites a passage from Whitman's notebooks (19) that summarizes an account of Von Humboldt in Christian C. J. Bunsen's *Outlines of the Philosophy of Universal History*. Whitman's notebook entry reads: "Language expresses originally objects only, and leaves the understanding to supply the connecting form—afterwards facilitating and improving the connections and relations by degrees." Walt Whitman, *Daybooks and Notebooks* 3, ed. William White (New York: New York University Press, 1978),

721. Here I am more interested in Whitman's sense that the original and poetic power of language resides in metonymic description rather than (as commonly asserted in eighteenth-century theories of language) in metaphoric comparison than I am in his subscription to the evolutionary theories of language or culture that Warren so thoroughly documents. See Warren, esp. 7–31 and 109–138.

38. Near the end of his life, Whitman famously described his poetry to Horace Traubel as a language experiment. See *With Walt Whitman in Camden*; see as well Warren, *Walt Whitman's Language Experiment*, and Erik Ingvar Thurin, *Whitman between Expressionism and Impressionism* (Lewisburg, PA: Bucknell University Press, 2008).

39. *"La plus part des occasions des troubles du monde sont Grammeriennes . . . Combien des querelles et combine importantes a produit au monde le doute du sens de cette syllable:* hoc!*"* (my translation, emphasis in the original). Michel de Montaigne, *Essais* 2:12, in *Oeuvres complètes*, ed. Maurice Rat (Paris: Gallimard, 1962), 508. Ralph Waldo Emerson, a devotee of Montaigne's, had strong feelings about the pernicious effects of founding a sacrament upon a likely misunderstanding of this metaphor. See "The Lord's Supper," in *Emerson: Essays and Lectures*, 1129–1140.

40. Whitman's insistence on the materiality of his own body reminds the reader frequently of Montaigne's celebrated earthiness, and Whitman's tropes equating his body and his book also find a precursor in Montaigne's identification of himself as consubstantial with his *Essais*, as he says in "Du Repentir," *"Icy, nous allons conformément et tout d'un trein, mon livre et moy. Ailleurs, on peut recommander et accuser l'ouvrage à part de l'ouvrier; icy, non; qui touche l'un, touche autre."* *Essais* 3:2, 783. "Here we go along together, my book and I; Elsewhere one can praise or blame a work apart from the worker; here, no, who ever touches one touches the other" (my translation). The echoes in Whitman are obvious at many points, for example, in "So Long" where he writes: "this is no book,/Who touches this touches a man."

41. Moon, *Disseminating Whitman*, 82. As Moon says, "The text can serve to empower others—genuine others, that is, women and nonwhite men, not just homotypes of the (male) poet—to assert their own respective difference or 'untranslatability'" (83).

42. Jonathan Culler, in *Theory of the Lyric* (Cambridge, MA: Harvard University Press, 2015), frequently makes the point that epideictic or descriptive rhetoric is essential to lyric performance—in essence, the lyric always makes statements about the world or the poet's place in the world. See, for example, 307–314.

43. Roman Jakobson, "The Metaphoric and Metonymic Poles," in *Metaphor and Metonymy in Comparison and Contrast* (New York: Mouton de

Gruyter, 2002), 47. By contrast, Ricoeur comments that (following Fontanier's typology of tropes) whereas a metonymy brings together "two objects," metaphor presents *"one idea under the sign of another"* and "does not even [in its definition] refer to objects" (emphasis in the original). See Ricoeur, *The Rule of Metaphor*, 56–57.

44. For this reason, Clare figures largely in Fletcher's argument. See Angus Fletcher, *A New Theory for American Poetry: Democracy, the Environment, and the Future of Imagination* (Cambridge, MA: Harvard University Press, 2004), esp. 17–22. In the background of Fletcher's remarkable synthetic work are, of course, many works dealing with the relationships of form and description over the history of Western literature. See, especially, Eric Auerbach, *Mimesis: The Representation of Reality in Western Literature* tr. Willard R. Trask (Princeton: Princeton University Press, 1953); Stephen Halliwell, *The Aesthetics of Mimesis: Ancient Texts and Modern Problems* (Princeton: Princeton University Press, 2002); Gérard Genette, *Figures of Literary Discourse*, trans. Alan Sheridan, (New York, 1982); Jonathan Bate, *Romantic Ecology: Wordsworth and the Environmental Tradition* (New York: Routledge, 1991); Roy Porter, *The Creation of the Modern World: The Untold Story of the Enlightenment* (New York: Norton, 2000); Laurence Buell, *The Environmental Imagination: Thoreau, Nature Writing, and the Formulation of American Culture* (Cambridge, MA: Harvard University Press, 1995), and *Writing for an Endangered World: Literature, Culture, and Environment in the U.S. and Beyond* (Cambridge, MA: Harvard University Press, 2001).

45. Jonathan Culler makes the intriguing observation that Plato's famous quarrel between philosophy and poetry may originate in the fact that both are forms of epideictic discourse—not representations of actions (as in Aristotle's description of dramatic poetry) but statements about the world. Culler, *Theory of the Lyric*, 308–312.

46. Fletcher, *A New Theory for American Poetry*, 30.

47. *The Republic*, trans. Paul Shorey, in *The Collected Dialogues of Plato*, ed. Edith Hamilton and Huntington Cairns (Princeton: Princeton University Press, 1989).

48. In this sense, Whitman continues and transforms Wordsworth's project to, as Thomas Pfau describes it, "counter the dissolution of the 'public' into regionally, demographically, and spiritually incompatible smaller communities" by, as Jonathan Culler says, "reconfiguring a heterogeneous middle-class public into a more cohesive aesthetic community that would be moved in common ways." See Pfau, *Wordsworth's Profession* (Stanford: Stanford University Press, 1997), 249–250; See Culler's discussion of Pfau's point, *Theory of the Lyric*, 325–326. On Whitman's aspiration to

discover a commonality for the rapidly dissolving United States, see Larson, *Whitman's Drama of Consensus*.

49. Fletcher, *A New Theory for American Poetry*, 156.

50. James Perrin Warren remarks that in Whitman's catalog poems like "The Sleepers," "Song of Myself," and "Crossing Brooklyn Ferry," "our attempts to find a thematic progression to tally with the progressive formal surface are repeatedly frustrated." *Whitman's Language Experiment*, 96. I think this is less an interpretive problem (Warren's point) than the very thrust of Whitman's poetic invention. Mark Bauerlein argues that Whitman attempted to imagine a language of pure energy or sound. Whitman, he writes, "almost holds the intelligible, conceptual side of language in contempt," and emphasizes "vocalization" (the "valved voice) and energy or eloquence as "sound divorced from meaning." *Whitman and the American Idiom*, 42–43. At its most extreme, pure metonymy would be mere syntagms of signifiers or sounds. Yet, of course, the semantic in Whitman continues to assert its force. For instance, Bauerlein quotes a passage from *Walt Whitman in Camden* in which the poet quotes a Quaker woman who tells him "Walt—I feel thee is right—I could not tell why but I feel thee is right!" and about whom Whitman says, "and that seemed to me more significant than much that passes for reason in the world," thereby echoing the sacramental echoes of his own lines from "Song of Myself" surpassing "all the argument of the world" in the passage I've just quoted above. See Bauerlein, *Whitman and the American Idiom*, 39.

51. In *Whitman the Political Poet*, Betsy Erkkila notes that "In Pursuit of a new measure and a new way of measuring expressive of the modern democratic world, Whitman tried to avoid simile, metaphor, and the highly allusive structure of traditional verse. Rather his catalogs work by juxtaposition, image association, and metonymy to suggest the interrelationship and identity of all things" (88). Erkkila's book is still, I think, the most suggestive and comprehensive treatment of its topic. See especially the chapters "Leaves of Grass and the Body Politic" and "Democracy and (Homo)sexual Desire," 92–128 and 155–189.

52. Erotic union is, of course, a predominant topic in Whitman's antebellum poetry, whether he be speaking of amativeness—homosocial love—or sex. He expresses amativeness directly, for example, in lines that eventually become part of "Over the Carnage Rose Prophetic a Voice," the end of which first appeared in "Calamus" but became part of "Drum Taps" after the war: "Be not dishearten'd, affection shall solve the problems of freedom yet,/Those who love each other shall become invincible,/They shall make Columbia victorious." Whitman's investment in a manly eroticism that makes states cohere as embodiments of manly love follows in a

long queer tradition of political male friendship literature that includes
Aristotle, Cicero, Seneca, and Montaigne.

53. See, for example, Bloom on Whitman in *Agon: Towards a Theory of
Revisionism* (New York: Oxford University Press, 1982), 184–186.

54. *Whitman's Drama of Consensus*, 10.

55. This good cheer in the face of death's materiality was not easily won
for Whitman nor casually sustained. In 1856 he wrote the nearly gothic
"This Compost" and in his final arrangement of the poems placed it near
the book's conclusion. There he finds the ubiquity of death, corruption, and
fecundity so repulsive he withdraws from the world in terror. He wrote:

> Something startles me where I thought I was safest . . .
> I will not strip the clothes from my body to meet my lover the sea,
> I will not touch my flesh to the earth as to other flesh to renew me . . .

And he addresses the charnel house he imagines the Earth to be:

> Where have you disposed of their carcasses?
> Those drunkards and gluttons of so many generations?
> Where have you drawn off all the foul liquid and meat? . . .
> I will run a furrow with my plough, I will press my spade through the sod
> and turn it up underneath,
> I am sure I shall expose some of the foul meat . . . (495)

As Emory Holloway notes in *Aspects of Immortality in Whitman*, while it is
true that Whitman sometimes rebels against personal mortality—as he does
in "To Think of Time," first written in 1855 and included near the end the
final arrangement of poems, "If all came but to ashes and dung, / If maggots
and rats ended us, then Alarum for we are betrayed" (556)—it is also true
that it is "difficult to discover in his verse any clear indication that he
expected or desired anything else" (but that death meant "material transformations which do to man's body exactly what they do to the animals, the
trees and the sea grasses") (Westwood, NJ: Kindle Press, 1969), 19–20. I
would add that to conclude, as Whitman does in "To Think of Time," with
"I swear I think there is nothing but immortality!" carries vastly less poetic
conviction and force than the images of dissolution that precede it. Besides
to discover immortality everywhere—in trees, sea-weed, and animals (close
to a reversal of Wordsworth's despair in his mourning poem that Lucy now
rolls "round in earth's diurnal course / With rocks and stones and trees")
seems actually to dilute its personality and to discover it nowhere, just as
pantheism and materialism become, for theologians, indifferently heretical
in their denial of a personal deity, Whitman's fervor about immortality,
early and late, finds itself constrained to forgo personal survival, at least in
the usual sense.

4. WHITMAN AND DEMOCRACY: THE "WITHNESS OF THE WORLD"
AND THE FAKES OF DEATH

1. Jason Frank, "Aesthetic Democracy: Walt Whitman and the Poetry of the People," *The Review of Politics* 69 (2007): 402–430, at 404. In recent years it seems that political theorists have been more sympathetic to Whitman's sense of democracy than have literary critics. Frank follows and elaborates George Kateb's work in "Walt Whitman and the Culture of Democracy," *Political Theory* 18, no. 4 (1990): 545–571, and *The Inner Ocean: Individualism and Democratic Culture* (Ithaca, NY: Cornell University Press, 1994).

2. Mohammed A. Bamyeh, *Of Death and Dominion: The Existential Foundations of Governance* (Evanston, IL: Northwestern University Press, 2007). Bamyeh's fundamental claim, that "the orientation toward death has had an unbroken grip on the foundational character of the philosophy of governance" (3) resonates with Whitman's meditations on democracy and death. Bamyeh's views also recall, in an important sense, Agamben's specification of "bare life," the life of the sacred man set outside the limits of common law or religious practice. Outside the life of sovereignty or governance, is no life at all but a sort of death in life, a life that can be killed but not murdered or sacrificed, and is thus still understood in its orientation toward death. See Giorgio Agamben, *Homo Sacer: Sovereign Power and Bare Life*, trans. Daniel Heller-Roazen (Stanford: Stanford University Press, 1998). I am indebted to Donald Pease, who, developing a different line concerning Whitman's poet's point of enunciation and the questions of sovereignty, first associated the poet and Agamben for me. Donald Pease, "Whitman and the Unclaimed Scene of Writing," talk delivered at the University of Rochester, November 6, 2008.

3. Jacques Derrida, *The Gift of Death*, trans. David Wills (Chicago: University of Chicago Press, 1995).

4. Russ Castronovo, *Necro Citizenship: Death, Eroticism, and the Public Sphere in the Nineteenth-Century United States* (Durham, NC: Duke University Press, 2001), 6.

5. Ibid., 5.

6. Michael Moon, *Disseminating Whitman: Revision and Corporeality in Leaves of Grass* (Cambridge, MA: Harvard University Press, 1991), 71.

7. Angus Fletcher, *A New Theory for American Poetry: Democracy, the Environment, and the Future of Imagination* (Cambridge, MA: Harvard University Press, 2004), 186.

8. R. W. B. Lewis, "Walt Whitman: Always Going Out and Coming In," in *Trials of the Word: Essays in American Literature and the Humanistic Tradition* (New Haven: Yale University Press, 1965), and in *Walt Whitman: Modern Critical Views*, ed. Harold Bloom (New York: Chelsea House, 2006),

61–90, at 66. Lewis also divides Whitman's career into an early authentic part and a later, post–Civil War, part marked by willful self-concealment, self-misrepresentation, and the creation, through editorial emendation and arrangement, of a "persona radically other than the being that lay at the heart of his best poetry."

9. I have argued this point in *Identity and the Failure of America from Thomas Jefferson to the War on Terror* (Minneapolis: University of Minnesota Press, 2008), 12–21.

10. Kerry C. Larson, *Whitman's Drama of Consensus* (Chicago: University of Chicago Press, 1988), xv.

11. Ibid., 115. Larson makes reference to Pease's observation that Whitman "literally meant that his singing brought a self into being," see Donald Pease, "Blake, Crane, and Whitman: A Poetics of Pure Possibility," *PMLA* 96 (1981): 77.

12. Larson, *Whitman's Drama of Consensus*, 115, 127. On the catalogs, see Basil de Selincourt, *Walt Whitman: A Critical Study* (New York: Russell and Russell, 1965); John F. Lynen, *The Design of the Present: Essays on Time and Structure in American Literature* (New Haven: Yale, 1969); Larzer Ziff, *Literary Democracy: The Declaration of Cultural Independence* (New York: Viking, 1981); and Allan Grossman, "The Poetics of Union in Whitman and Lincoln: An Inquiry toward the Relationship of Art and Policy," in *The American Renaissance Reconsidered: Selected Papers from the English Institute, 1982–83*, ed. Walter Benn Michaels and Donald E. Pease (Baltimore: Johns Hopkins University Press, 1985), 183–208.

13. Larson, *Whitman's Drama of Consensus*, 131.

14. William James, *Pragmatism*, in *William James: Writings 1902–1910* (New York: Library of America, 1987), 554–555.

15. Fletcher describes this aspect of Whitman's poetry as a form of the middle voice in *A New Theory for American Poetry*, 165–174. James Perrin Warren analyzes Whitman's catalogs and their dependence on anaphoras constructed through repetitions of nouns, participles, stative clauses, and noun phrases for their "grammar of syntactic parallelism." See Warren, *Walt Whitman's Language Experiment* (University Park: Pennsylvania State University Press, 1990), 70–106.

16. This is closely linked to what Ronald Schleifer has argued is a controlling trope of modernism as a paradox of death linked in turn to the "accidental metonymic phenomenal data of experience" distanced from any meaning that might sum that experience up. *Rhetoric and Death: The Language of Modernism and Postmodern Discourse Theory* (Urbana: University of Illinois Press, 1990), 9–11. Whitman, I am suggesting, stands as an early and extremely radical example of this modernist rhetoric.

17. William Wordsworth, *The Major Works including The Prelude*, ed. Stephen Gill (New York: Oxford University Press, 2008), 147.

18. David Bromwich, *A Choice of Inheritance from Edmund Burke to Robert Frost* (Cambridge, MA: Harvard University Press, 1989), 164.

19. Just before this passage, Dimock has demonstrated in a tour de force linking Rawls and Chomsky that liberal theories of justice depend upon the patterns of recursion and formal equivalence that form syntax and are less capable of recognizing the differences and distinctions of the semantic. *Residues of Justice: Literature, Law, Philosophy* (Berkeley: University of California Press, 1996), 113. Other critics who have considered the relationship between Whitman's "language experiment" in his poetry and democracy include Peter Bellis, "Against Representation: The 1855 Edition of *Leaves of Grass*," *Centennial Review* 1 (Winter 1999): 71–94; Mark Bauerlein, *Whitman and the American Idiom* (Baton Rouge: Louisiana State University Press, 1991); and Stephen John Mack, *The Pragmatic Whitman: Reimagining American Democracy* (Iowa City: University of Iowa Press, 2002). On the generative syntax of Whitman's poetry, see Warren, *Walt Whitman's Language Experiment*; Warren also notes that "attempts to find a thematic progression to tally with the progressive formal surface are repeatedly frustrated" (96). Order in Whitman's world is not a matter of content but of form.

20. See, again, Castronovo's account of the complexities this entails in *Necro Citizenship*.

21. In addition to Dimock's *Residues of Justice*, see Philip Fisher, "Democratic Social Space: Whitman, Melville, and the Promise of American Transparency," in *The New American Studies: Essays from Representations*, ed. Philip Fisher (Berkeley: University of California Press, 1991), 70–111. As Castronovo notes, liberal democracies tend to imagine their citizens as already dead and therefore decorporealized; see *Necro Citizenship*. Michael Sandel is the contemporary philosopher who has most effectively criticized the abstract individualism and deontologized being at the core of John Rawls's (and by implication anyone's) theory of liberal justice. See Sandel, *Liberalism and the Limits of Justice* (New York: Cambridge University Press, 1982). I have written on the topic of liberal justice as a practical matter elsewhere, see "Liberal Justice and Particular Identity: Cavell, Emerson, Rawls," *Arizona Quarterly* 64, no. 1 (Spring 2008): 27–47, and *Identity and The Failure of America from Thomas Jefferson to the War on Terror*.

22. Edgar Allen Poe, "The Man of the Crowd," in *Poetry, Tales, and Selected Essays*, ed. Patrick F. Quinn and G. R. Thompson (New York: Library of America, 1984), 388–396.

23. Walter Benjamin, "On Some Motifs in Baudelaire," in *Illuminations*, ed. Hannah Arendt (New York: Schocken Books, 1969), 155ff.

24. Kateb, "Walt Whitman and the Culture of Democracy," 568.

25. Ibid., 552.

26. Michael Moon observes, as I have noted, that Whitman's opening of options for resistance, despite his repetition of some of his era's obnoxious "political commitments," is not only because he enfolds various abolitionist and women's rights discourses into his poetry but also because the poet's stance toward the fluid interpermeability of identities and identifications opens a space in which difference can register. See Moon, *Disseminating Whitman*, 80–83.

27. Whitman's primary allegiances were, no doubt, with white working men, but he came to identify slavery not only with a threat to their prerogatives but also as an evil in its own right. See "The Eighteenth Presidency!" Walt Whitman, *Poetry and Prose*, ed. Justin Kaplan (New York: Library of America, 1996), 1331–1349.

28. Larson, *Whitman's Drama of Consensus*, 8.

29. Remember, "1. Words are signs of natural facts. 2. Particular natural facts are symbols of particular spiritual facts. 3. Nature is the symbol of spirit." Ralph Waldo Emerson, *Nature*, in *Emerson: Essays and Lectures* (New York: Library of America, 1983), 20. John Irwin has found "Song of the Rolling Earth" an "effort to recapture the language of physical objects in his role as poet of the Edenic New World." John T. Irwin, *American Hieroglyphics: The Symbol of the Egyptian Hieroglyphics in the American Renaissance* (New Haven: Yale University Press, 1980), 29. That effort, however, seems doomed to fail in the crowded secularity of the United States and Whitman seems as likely to render the material world verbal as he is to make the verbal matter. Rather, Whitman's poetry, like his democratic vision, seems to depend on the metonymic power of language to "combine and recombine in endless permutations of meaning, indifferent, as it were, to the constraints of human experience." Mack, *The Pragmatic Whitman*, 8. Unlike Mack, I find Whitman, at his strongest, not overly concerned with the "infinite human experience of self and things to which language can only imperfectly refer" (ibid.) because the strongest moments in Whitman conjure the contents— the selves and experiences—to which his metonymies seem to refer.

30. If there is an ethics in Whitman's poetry, it seems more akin to Levinas's impossible demands to respect an otherness that remains opaque than it does to liberalism's putative inability to imagine difference.

31. This repetition of death comes close to depriving the word of any significance whatsoever and rendering it a merely repeated sound, a pure metonymic enchainment of a sound, an example of what Mark Bauerlein calls Whitman's fascination with "vocalization" and with "phonetic poetics" and natural language or "calls" like "Kush! Kush! Kush!" (children calling to

cows) or "Ku-juk! Ku-juk! Ku-juk" (the same to horses). Bauerlein, *Whitman and the American Idiom*, 45.

32. Peter M. Sacks, *The English Elegy: Studies in the Genre from Spenser to Yeats* (Baltimore: Johns Hopkins University Press, 1985), 30.

33. Susan Stewart, *Poetry and the Fate of the Senses* (Chicago: University of Chicago Press, 2002), 256.

34. Ibid.

35. As Jacques Derrida indicates in "Literature in Secret," one crucial facet of literature in the Euro-American tradition of the last several hundred years is that it stands as a non-sacred text that demands pardon or forgiveness for not meaning to mean and moreover derives its function from the way in which it does not mean—which is far different from saying that it is meaningless. See Derrida, *The Gift of Death and Literature in Secret*, 2nd ed., trans. David Wills (Chicago: University of Chicago Press, 2008), esp. 130–142. Whitman, for example, is full of portent and promise, but though he delivers his teeming and self-contradictory self to his readers through his poetry, dying and living only in those who visit his pages, he does not communicate meaning to them. He itches at their ears, as he says at the end of "Song of Myself," he filters and fibers their blood and is good health to those who will have him, but he does not convey meaning to them.

5. THE POET AS LYRIC READER

1. Emily Dickinson, *The Poems of Emily Dickinson*, ed. R. W. Franklin (Cambridge, MA: Harvard University Press, 1998). All references to Dickinson's poetry follow this edition and appear in the text using the number Franklin has assigned.

2. As I note in the Introduction, critics like Virginia Jackson and Jerome McGann have made Dickinson the central example in their arguments against any transhistorical idea of lyric as the genre defined by the self-contained reflection of a solitary voice. Jonathan Culler has recently argued that this polemic mistakes an overly restrictive, New Critical strategy of reading—one based on an expressive theory of lyric that associates the genre with the voice of a fictive or formal poet in the poem—for a universal definition of the genre. See, for example, Virginia Jackson, *Dickinson's Misery: A Theory of Lyric Reading* (Princeton: Princeton University Press, 2005), and her entry on "Lyric" in the *Princeton Encyclopedia of Poetry and Poetics*, ed. R. Greene, S. Cushman, C. Cavanagh, J. Ramazani, and P. Rouzer (Princeton: Princeton University Press, 2012). Jerome McGann, *The Textual Condition* (Princeton: Princeton University Press, 1991), is an early call for material studies of textuality. Culler's fullest critique of the expressive theory of lyric in the new lyrical studies may be

found in *Theory of the Lyric* (Cambridge, MA: Harvard University Press, 2015), esp. 39–90.

3. The phrase comes from "The New Lyrical Studies," *PMLA* 123 (2008): 181–234.

4. Virginia Jackson's critique of lyric reading in *Dickinson's Misery* has been most immediately influential, but Paula Bernat Bennett paved the way with *Emily Dickinson: Woman Poet* (Iowa City: University of Iowa Press, 1990). Jackson's work in turn has influenced more recent studies like Alexandra Socarides, *Dickinson Unbound: Paper, Process, Poetics* (New York: Oxford University Press, 2014), and polemical response like Cristanne Miller's *Reading in Time: Emily Dickinson in the Nineteenth Century* (Amherst: University of Massachusetts Press, 2012), which argues that emphasis on the text's materiality ignores its relationship to song.

Biographers have always sought to explain Dickinson with reference to her family. Most recently, see Lyndall Gordon, *Lives Like Loaded Guns: Emily Dickinson and Her Family's Feuds* (New York: Viking, 2010). The indispensable classic linking Dickinson to the events of her day remains Jay Leyda, *The Years and Hours of Emily Dickinson*, 2 vols. (New York: Anchor Books, 1970). More idiosyncratic is Susan Howe's *My Emily Dickinson* (New York: New Directions, 2007).

5. Socarides, *Dickinson Unbound*, 5.

6. Socarides believes that taking Dickinson's materiality seriously requires the dismissal of the "protocols of reading" deployed by those who consider her a lyric poet. She notes that twenty years after Jerome McGann appealed to students of literature to take up the mode of historical/materialist scholarship he helped pioneer, "we have yet to pay this kind of attention to Dickinson's textual materials." For her, "The reason for this is obvious: Since the protocols of reading that twentieth-century readers of Dickinson had been taught depend on poems in print isolated from each other and from the paper on which they were written, this paper simply didn't—or couldn't—matter. . . . It was practically impossible to revise our reading habits" (4–5). She is referring to McGann's *The Textual Condition*. Her polemic is similar to the critique of lyric reading in Jackson's *Dickinson's Misery*. I am arguing, by contrast, that Dickinson's text demands and helps shape these modernist protocols of reading.

7. Socarides, *Dickinson Unbound*, 13.

8. Jackson, *Dickinson's Misery*, 7. History is at the center of many of these debates surrounding the lyric and Dickinson in particular. In Virginia Jackson's influential view, "the lyric has been misunderstood as the genre most isolated from history—indeed, as the exemplary model of literary genre as a category separable from history"; ibid., 55. Jackson's critique of

lyric reading most urgently evokes historicism as a way to recover the immediacy of Dickinson's embeddedness in a particular social situation and a specific practice of poetry as a form of epistolary and personal communication. Jackson contrasts immediate acts of personal communication with the anonymity or distance from any particular person in the lyric's printed form. The immediacy of the communicative situation here often seems essential to those who have attempted to identify Dickinson's engagements with the great events of her day. See, for example, Shira Wolosky, *Emily Dickinson: A Voice of War* (New Haven: Yale University Press, 1964); Susan Howe, *My Emily Dickinson* (Berkeley, CA: North Atlantic Books, 1985); Paula Bernat Bennett, *Emily Dickinson*. For criticism of earlier attempts to contextualize Dickinson within an immediate social circle for removing her from the larger arenas of political and artistic engagement and returning her to the domestic sphere, see Margaret Dickie, "Dickinson in Context" *American Literary History* 7, no. 2 (Summer 1995): 320–333.

9. The main thrust of such work on Dickinson has been to revise the idea of lyric isolation to which Sharon Cameron's widely influential work, to take a notable example, seemed to consign her. In *Lyric Time*, Cameron claims that "all of Dickinson's poems fight temporality," and that such a distancing of the lyric speaker in the poem from time and from context is, whatever Dickinson's personal peculiarities are, in fact, "really only exaggerations of those features that distinguish the lyric as a genre." Sharon Cameron, *Lyric Time: Dickinson and the Limits of Genre* (Baltimore: Johns Hopkins University Press, 1979), 203, 201.

10. Jackson, *Dickinson's Misery*, 117.

11. Ibid., 132–133.

12. "To T. W. Higginson," July 1862, in *The Letters of Emily Dickinson*, ed. Thomas H. Johnson and Theodora Ward, 3 vols. (Cambridge, MA: Harvard University Press, 1958), 2:411–412.

13. Charles Anderson remarks, "Her essential kinship lies not with literary realism but with the development of poetry *From Baudelaire to Surrealism* so persuasively set forth by Marcel Raymond. Although she had no knowledge of the French symbolists and their successors, nor they of her, the literary historian will enrich our understanding of this great modern tradition by finding her proper place in it." *Emily Dickinson's Poetry: Stairway of Surprise* (New York: Holt, Rinehart and Winston, 1960), 92. See also Marcel Raymond, *From Baudelaire to Surrealism* (London: P. Owen, 1957). To situate Dickinson in this "great modern tradition" is also to situate her in a tradition that originates with Edgar Allan Poe, despite her assertion to Higginson "Of Poe, I know too little to think," December 1879, *Letters* 2:649.

14. As Socarides notes, it "is only in the last twenty-five years that critics have begun to treat her letters as a mode of writing that offers something other than an explanation for her poems"; *Dickinson Unbound*, 52. She also remarks that in most recent studies the hierarchy between prose and poetry—frequently supported with citations from Dickinson's poems—allows critics to maintain a distinction between public and private that she sees Dickinson frequently working to subvert in both genres: "It was precisely in this state of physical distance [characteristic of her relationship to Higgenson, whom she met only twice in twenty-four years] that she was able to play with the tension between public and private communication that is activated in both poetry and epistolary correspondence" (53). Dickinson carefully subverts the protocols of letter writing, as Socarides shows, especially—though not exclusively—in her correspondence with Higginson (54–77). See also *Reading Emily Dickinson's Letters: Critical Essays*, ed. Jane Donahue Eberwein and Cindy MacKenzie (Amherst: University of Massachusetts Press, 2009); Marietta Messmer, *A Vice for Voices: Reading Emily Dickinson's Correspondence* (Amherst: University of Massachusetts Press, 2001).

15. Michael Moon, *Disseminating Whitman: Revision and Corporeality in Leaves of Grass* (Cambridge, MA: Harvard University Press, 1991), 4–5.

16. Socarides, *Dickinson Unbound*, 70.

17. Ibid., 19.

18. This is not a criticism of what Socarides is doing as a historian but a tribute to her acumen as a critic. That acumen as a critic, as a lyric reader, is evident in much of what follows in her book. Far from abandoning lyric reading, she applies what she has learned about practices like poem groupings on pages in the fascicles to readings of the juxtaposed lyrics in ways that investigate and invigorate their meanings for the "I" who speaks them and the reader who reads them; *Dickinson Unbound*, 35–44. And her sense of Dickinson—as when she writes that she "recognized this potential for transgression and boundary crossing when she saw it" (70) seems to me precisely right and, in precisely the modern sense I have been using it here, wonderfully lyric.

19. Jackson's own reading of the letters tends to support this point. See *Dickinson's Misery*, 68–92. Cristanne Miller takes a different tack in her study of the many ways Dickinson borrows from and transforms the sounds and rhythms of contemporary popular poetry and songs—especially hymns and ballads; Miller, *Reading in Time*, 24.

20. See Giorgio Agamben, *The End of the Poem*, trans. Daniel Heller-Roazen (Stanford: Stanford University Press, 1999), 17–21; Paul de Man, "Anthropomorphism and Trope in the Lyric," in *The Rhetoric of Romanticism* (New York: Columbia University Press, 1984), 239–262. W. K. Wimsatt Jr.

reminds readers "to impute the thoughts and attitudes of the poem" to the dramatic or fictive speaker and not to the author. "The Intentional Fallacy," in *The Verbal Icon: Studies in the Meaning of Poetry* (Lexington: University Press of Kentucky, 1954), 5.

21. Quoted in Gordon, *Lives Like Loaded Guns*, 276. Gordon is citing an article that appeared in *Smith Alumnae Quarterly* (February 1954).

22. Paul de Man, "Anthropomorphism and Trope in the Lyric," 239–262.

23. As Jackson remarks, following Yopie Prins, Dickinson as a personality may be as much a product of poetic reading as Sappho was of Victorian poetics. Such literary anthropomorphism may not just be an imposition on Dickinson's text, but something she, as a modern Sapphic poet, calculated on pushing to a limit. See *Dickinson's Misery*, 118–120, and Yopie Prins, *Victorian Sappho* (Princeton: Princeton University Press, 1999), esp. 23–73.

24. Paula Bernat Bennett, "Review of Alexandra Socarides, *Dickinson Unbound: Paper, Process, Poetics*," *Emily Dickinson Journal* 21, no. 2: 111–113, at 113; Gordon, *Lives Like Loaded Guns*.

25. There are notable exceptions. Aliki Barnstone, in her remarkable *Changing Rapture: Emily Dickinson's Poetic Development* (Hanover, NH: University Press of New England, 2007), 1–29, argues against both those that would link the poetry too closely to the life and those, often the same critics, who have usually argued that Dickinson does not develop across the long span of her poetic career. In contrast, Barnstone argues that she produced works that dealt profoundly with questions of faith and of the self and that the work divided into four distinct stages—an early stage of wrestling with the dogmas of her father's Calvinism; a second period centered on 1863 when she struggled with issues of faith and love; a third phase in which she struggled with Emersonian ideas of self and nature; and a final phase where she interrogates the very limits of poetry as a form linking self and others. I do not think, as Barnstone does, that a poet's seriousness requires a belief in the poet's development, though her scheme for reading Dickinson's trajectory is interesting. Here I emphasize the ways in which Dickinson's poetry from first to last revolves around questions that are essential to poetry itself whatever developments in thematic or formal aspects may occur. Which is to say, I am focusing on the ways in which Dickinson's poetry from the first relates to problems of signification that relate to poetic making in the modern era whatever one believes the meaning of a specific act or utterance may be.

26. Gordon, *Lives Like Loaded Guns*, 8.

27. Ibid., 9.

28. Gordon herself addresses some of these issues in her book, especially in the chapter dedicated to that crux of biographical speculation in the

Dickinson corpus, the so-called Master letters (see 93–114). Yet she cannot resist the biographer's love of explanation. Dickinson's poems, her reclusiveness, and her other eccentricities, she offers, might be explained by epilepsy. This might in turn give Dickinson's poetry a meaning for cognitive science that our positivistic colleagues have yet to appreciate: "If the twenty-first century is to explore unknown pathways of the brain, Dickinson's poetry is replete with information about dysfunction and recovery. Here's what she has to tell: 'I felt a funeral, in my Brain.' A plank in reason broke, she says, and 'I dropped down, and down—.' She feels a 'Cleaving' in her brain, as though the lid of the brain gets 'off my head' and can't re-attach. Logic and its sequential language are disrupted." *Lives Like Loaded Guns*, 116. By this logic, however, any example of disjunction in poetry—and modern poetry is unimaginable without disjunction, indeed troping itself is a form of disjunction that disrupts language's common logic and often in eccentric ways—then poetry becomes a symptom of dysfunctional neurons and poetic genius, as the Neoplatonists and Romantics believed, must close to madness lie. Playing off one of Dickinson's most difficult lyrics, "My Life had stood—a Loaded Gun" (764), Gordon concludes: "What's clear, on the evidence of Dickinson's writing and the sheer volume of her output, is that she coped inventively with gunshots from the brain into her body" (136). What is clear to a reader less inventive than Gordon is that Gordon's thesis is driving her reading here and constructing the malleable mysteries of her text into evidence to support her founding assumptions. I mention this not to criticize Gordon but to deploy her as an especially vivid example of the sorts of desires and frustrations reading Dickinson tends to entail.

29. Dickie, "Dickinson in Context," 320.

30. Barnstone, *Changing Rapture*, 31.

31. "So We'll Go No More a Roving," in *The Poetical Works of Byron: Cambridge Edition*, ed. Robert F. Gleckner (Boston: Houghton Mifflin, 1975), 229–230. For the midcentury Byron craze in the United States, see Christopher Benfey, *A Summer of Hummingbirds: Love, Art, and Scandal in the Intersecting Worlds of Emily Dickinson, Mark Twain, Harriet Beecher Stowe, & Martin Johnson Heade* (New York: Penguin Press, 2008), 107–132.

32. Jackson, *Dickinson's Misery*, 139.

33. Ibid.

34. Ibid., 141–142.

35. Stéphane Mallarmé, "Le mystère dans les lettres," in *Igitur, Divagations, Un coup de dés* (Paris: Gallimard, 1976), 273; my translation. *"Tout écrit, extérieurement à son trésor, doit, par égard envers ceux dont il emprunte, après tout, pour un objet autre, le langage, s'il traîne présenter, avec les mots, un sens*

même indifférent: on gagne de détourner l'oisif, charmé que rien ne l'y concerne, à première vue."

36. Ibid., 279; my translation. *"Les mots, d'eux-mêmes, s'exaltent à mainte facette reconnue la plus rare ou valant pour l'esprit, centre de suspense vibratoire; qui les perçoit indépendamment de la suite ordinaire, projetés, en parois de grotte, tant que dure leur mobilité ou principe, étant ce qui ne se dit pas du discours."*

37. Giorgio Agamben, "The Dream of Language," in *The End of the Poem*, 46. Agamben is meditating on the difficulty of sense in *Hypnerotomachia Poliphili* (Polyphilus's Strife of Love in a Dream, 1499) and the emergence, after Dante, of vernacular poetry and the status of a "dead" language like Latin. He is especially interested in the anonymous authors use of obscure Latinate and Greek-rooted words and grammar in the Italian text. One thinks, of course, of Dickinson in this context, and of Mallarmé as well.

38. Culler, *Theory of the Lyric*, 304.

39. Agamben, *The End of the Poem*, 60–61.

40. Agamben also explores the continuation of this traditional struggle with language in poetry as it becomes modern. In his commentary on the late nineteenth-century Italian poet Pascoli, Agamben writes, "Such is this people's difficult and enigmatic relation to their mother tongue, by which it can only find itself in it if it succeeds in hearing it as dead and by which it can only love it and make it its own in breaking it into fragments and anatomical segments." Agamben, *The End of the Poem*, 74.

6. DICKINSON'S DOG AND THE CONCLUSION

1. This unveiling of the earth is close to what Heidegger saw as the origin of art itself, for example, when he says "The work lets the earth be an earth." See "The Origin of the Work of Art," in *Poetry, Language, Thought*, trans. Albert Hofstadter (New York: HarperCollins, 1971), 17–86, at 45.

2. Jackson is noting that the poem "Sic transit gloria mundi" (F2) does not sound like Dickinson. I have argued in the previous chapter that in important ways it does.

3. As Charles Anderson put it, at the beginning of a great chapter on Dickinson's "wit," "Emily Dickinson approached language like an explorer of new lands. . . . She used words as if she were the first to do so, with a joy and an awe largely lost to English poetry since the Renaissance." *Emily Dickinson's Poetry: Stairway of Surprise* (New York: Holt, Rinehart, and Winston, 1960), 3. Anderson gives an excellent account of the various techniques by which Dickinson borrowed from and distorted received forms to fulfill her "compulsion to make it new" (23). Anderson acknowledges Dickinson's modernity and the power in her wit; see 3–29.

4. See Sigmund Freud, *Jokes and Their Relation to the Unconscious: The Standard Edition*, trans. James Strachey (New York: Norton, 1960, 1989); Sigmund Freud, *The Uncanny*, trans. David McLintock, ed. Adam Phillips (New York: Penguin Books, 2003), 123–162. While the uncanny is not purely a linguistic concept, the *"Witz"* for Freud is nearly exclusively a verbal *"jeu d'esprit."*

5. "The frightening [or uncanny] element is something that has been repressed and now returns . . . 'something that should have remained hidden and has come into the open [according to Schilling],'" Freud writes, adding, "this uncanny element is actually nothing new or strange, but something that was long familiar to the psyche and was estranged from it only through being repressed" (147–148). Sigmund Freud, "The Uncanny," in *The Uncanny*, trans. David McLintock (New York: Penguin Books, 2003), 123–162, 147–148.

6. Freud, *Jokes and Their Relation to the Unconscious*, 168.

7. For T. S. Eliot, such an effect was essential to "genuine" poetry of any era. It was with regard to Dante that he suggested that a test for "Genuine poetry" was its capacity "to communicate before it is understood," "Dante" (1929), in *Selected Essays* (New York: Harcourt, Brace and Co., 1932), 199–239, at 200. Of course, this is not communication in a cognitive sense.

8. See Eleanor Elson Heginbotham, *Reading the Fascicles of Emily Dickinson: Dwelling in Possibilities* (Columbus: Ohio State University Press, 2003), 7.

9. It is worth quoting Elizabeth Barrett Browning's entire poem, since fragments of it figure throughout Dickinson's response:

> How do I love thee? Let me count the ways.
> I love thee to the depth and breadth and height
> My soul can reach, when feeling out of sight
> For the ends of Being and ideal Grace.
> I love thee to the level of everyday's
> Most quiet need, by sun and candle-light.
> I love thee freely, as men strive for Right;
> I love thee purely, as they turn from Praise.
> I love thee with a passion put to use
> In my old griefs, and with my childhood's faith.
> I love thee with a love I seemed to lose
> With my lost saints,—I love thee with the breath,
> Smiles, tears, of all my life!—and, if God choose,
> I shall but love thee better after death.

10. Heginbotham, *Reading the Fascicles of Emily Dickinson*, 13.

11. Other examples familiar to readers of Dickinson of course include her rewriting of the last lines of Keats's "Ode on a Grecian Urn," "I died for

beauty but was scarce" (F448), and of Emerson's essay, "The Poet," into the elliptical lines of "This was a poet" (F446).

12. Friedrich Schlegel, Fragment 9, *Critical Fragments* in *Philosophical Fragments*, trans. Peter Firchow (Minneapolis: University of Minnesota Press, 1991), 2.

13. See Freud, *Jokes and Their Relation to the Unconscious*, esp. 106–111. Samuel Weber both suggests this and performs it by ending his chapter on the shaggy dog story by retelling a long conceptual joke that is, in fact, a shaggy dog story. See *The Legend of Freud*, expanded edition (Stanford: Stanford University Press, 1982), 138–157. Sharon Cameron in *Choosing Not Choosing: Dickinson's Fascicles* (Chicago: University of Chicago Press, 1992), and especially in her reading of fascicles 15 and 20, constructs Dickinson's mounting of a narrative about mourning and desire, repetition and obsession, sex and death, and also focuses our attention on the ways in which these poems depend upon repetitive performance (115–135). I would add that this emphasis on repetitive performance creates a role that can only be furnished by the reader, even if that reader is an alternative projection of the self. In that sense, these poems that seem so intensely personal as to be almost illegible seem, at the same time, to require a public and to be intensely theatrical, staged in a way that foregrounds the reader's role in their rehearsal. In this specific way, they are as rhetorical as Whitman or Poe, and similarly involved with the dynamics of desire and death intimately related to reading as well.

14. Friedrich Schlegel, Critical Fragment 14, in *Philosophical Fragments* 2.

15. Rodolphe Gasché, "Foreword: Ideality in Fragmentation," in Schlegel, *Philosophical Fragments*, vii–xxxi.

16. Cameron, *Choosing Not Choosing*, 178.

17. The quotations from Cameron in this paragraph are in ibid., 183–188.

18. See Jay Leyda, *The Years and Hours of Emily Dickinson*, 2 vols. (New Haven: Yale University Press, 1960), 1:59. On alterations in grieving and the presence of death in the nineteenth century, see Dana Luciano, *Arranging Grief: Sacred Time and the Body in Nineteenth-Century America* (New York: New York University Press, 2007), esp. 1–68.

19. Diana Fuss offers a brief survey of "the story," as she calls it, of death's retreat from modern consciousness in *Dying Modern: A Meditation on Elegy* (Durham, NC: Duke University Press, 2013), 1–43.

20. Ralph Waldo Emerson, "Experience," in *Emerson: Essays and Lectures*, ed. Joel Porte (New York: Library of America, 1983), 473.

21. Wallace Stevens, "The Emperor of Ice-Cream," in *The Palm at the End of the Mind: Selected Poems and a Play*, ed. Holly Stevens (New York: Vintage Books, 1990), 79.

22. D. H. Lawrence, *Studies in Classic American Literature*, ed. Ezra Greenspan, Lindeth Vasey, and John Worthen (Cambridge: Cambridge University Press, 2003), 148.

23. "Ode on a Grecian Urn," in John Keats, *Complete Poems*, ed. Jack Stillinger (Cambridge, MA: Harvard University Press, 1982), 283.

24. Helen Vendler, *Dickinson: Selected Poems and Commentaries* (Cambridge, MA: Belknap Press of Harvard University Press, 2010), 16, 17, 23.

25. Ibid., 18.

26. Anderson, *Emily Dickinson's Poetry*, 144.

27. Ibid., 232, 227.

28. Ibid., 162.

29. Ibid., ix–xiv.

30. Cameron, *Choosing Not Choosing*, 29.

31. Emerson, "Circles," in *Essays and Lectures*, 406.

32. Ibid., 407.

33. Emerson, "Self-Reliance" in *Essays and Lectures*, 265.

34. Charles Anderson writes of Dickinson's relationship to Royce's pragmatic view of science as tentative modeling rather than absolute truth. Her attitude toward nature seems more to bespeak the limitation of perception and estrangement from certainty rather than transparency or transcendence. Anderson, *Emily Dickinson's Poetry*, 88.

35. Walter Benjamin, *Illuminations: Essays and Reflections*, trans. Harry Zohn, ed. Hannah Arendt (New York: Schocken Books, 1969), 155–156, 166.

36. Often those struggles involved her gendered place in a family and a society where gender was very much an issue and very much embedded in the language of the time. In her verse, she both rebels against and sometimes relishes this domesticity, and often makes it part of what Paula Bennett has called the "risks" she took with "her language and risks with her audience's willingness to play along." The best analysis of this as aspect of Dickinson's negotiation with the language of her tribe is still Paula Bennett, *Emily Dickinson: Woman Poet* (Iowa City: University of Iowa Press, 1990), 28. See also *Emily Dickinson: Personae and Performance* (University Park: Pennsylvania State University Press, 1988).

37. Betsy Erkkila, "Dickinson and the Art of Politics," in *A Historical Guide to Emily Dickinson*, ed. Vivian R. Pollak (New York: Oxford University Press, 2004), 133–174, at 144.

38. In my sense of the secular welter of meanings, I am recalling Charles Taylor's *A Secular Age* (Cambridge, MA: Harvard University Press, 2007), which I discussed in the introduction.

39. See Louis Hartz, *The Liberal Tradition in America* (New York: Harcourt Brace, 1955). Recent work on the persistence of this tradition in

American literature and life include Christopher Newfield, in *The Emerson Effect: Individualism and Submission in America* (Chicago: University of Chicago Press, 1996), and John Carlos Rowe, in *Emerson's Tomb: The Politics of Classic American Literature* (New York: Columbia University Press, 1997), who both trenchantly criticize Emerson's transcendental individualism on these grounds. Phillip Fisher criticizes Whitman for creating an abstract individuality, empty of interiority and consonant with the demands of liberal democratic abstraction. Philip Fisher, "Democratic Social Space: Whitman, Melville, and the Promise of American Transparency," in *The New American Studies: Essays from Representations*, ed. Philip Fisher (Berkeley: University of California Press, 1991).

40. Colleen Glenney Boggs, *Animalia Americana: Animal Representations and Biopolitical Subjectivity* (New York: Columbia University Press, 2013), 25. Less poetically, Russell Sibriglia's dissertation, "*Dissensus Communis*: Skepticism, Sympathy, and Conservatism in the American Renaissance" (University of Michigan, 2012), skillfully reconstructs an alternative ideological tradition in the American renaissance.

41. Jacques Derrida, *The Animal That Therefore I Am*, ed. Marie-Louise Mallet, trans. David Wills (Stanford: Stanford University Press, 2008), 7.

42. Ibid., 52.

43. R. P. Blackmur, "Emily Dickinson's Notation," in *Emily Dickinson: A Collection of Critical Essays*, ed. Richard B. Sewall (Englewood Cliffs, NJ: Prentice-Hall, 1963), 80.

44. Jennifer Ratner-Rosenhagen's phrase to describe the American readoption of Nietzsche at the end of the nineteenth century as the "the European Axis of American Cosmopolitanism." See Ratner-Rosenhagen, *American Nietzsche: A History of an Icon and His Ideas* (Chicago: University of Chicago Press, 2012), 1–28, 35–44.